Women of Ancient Greece

Women of Ancient Greece

Pierre Brulé

Translated by Antonia Nevill

Edinburgh University Press

English edition with illustrations first published and © 2003 by Edinburgh University Press
Translation © Antonia Nevill, 2003

First published in France as
Les Femmes grecques à l'époque classique
© Hachette Littératures, Paris, 2001
Hachette Littératures,
43, Quai de Grenelle
75015 Paris

Edinburgh University Press Ltd
22 George Square, Edinburgh

Typeset in Sabon
by J&L Composition, Filey, North Yorkshire, and
printed and bound in Great Britain by
The University Press, Cambridge

A CIP record for this book is available from the British Library

ISBN 0 7486 1643 8 (hardback)

Frontispiece: **Departure of the wedding cortege**. The bridegroom, wearing a laurel crown, lifts the nymphe, who has a crown and is wrapped in a cloak, onto the chariot. The driver holding the reins also has a crown. Antikensammlung, Staatliche Museen zu Berlin – preussischer Kulturbesitz.

English edition published
with the aid of a translation
subvention kindly given by the
French Ministry of Culture

Contents

Publisher's Acknowledgement   vi

Prologue: Which paths will lead us to them?   1

1   The feminine and the sacred   6

2   Women of the epics   43

3   On the body and sexuality   74

4   Joys and miseries of married life   114

5   The woman in the 'house'   151

6   The women on the outside   186

Epilogue: How shall we take our leave of them?   221

Bibliography   225

Index of Classical Authors   229

General Index   233

Publisher's Acknowledgement

The publishers wish to thank the following for their contributions to this book. Mrs Antonia Nevill has, as always, provided a fluent and readable translation. Professor Brian Sparkes gave advice on technical matters, adapted the Bibliography and guide to further reading for English-speaking readers, and ensured the accuracy of, and in many cases provided new, translations of ancient Greek sources. Professor Pierre Brulé, having in the first place written such an excellent French text, then devoted much time to helping in the preparation of the English version. He also chose and wrote the captions for its illustrations for which Mrs Karen Morgan then obtained copies from museums in Greece, Belgium, France, Germany, Italy, Russia, Switzerland, the United Kingdom and the United States. Our thanks go to all these, and also to the museums and their curators for having provided prints for the illustrations and allowed their reproduction.

Now I am nothing on my own. But I have often observed the nature of women in this way, that we are nothing. When we are young, the life we live in our father's home is the sweetest, I think; for folly always raises children in happiness. But when we come of age and have understanding, we are pushed outside and sold, far from our household gods and from our parents, some to foreign husbands, some to barbarians, some to homes with no joy, others to ones full of abuse. And this, when a single night has joined us, we must commend and consider to be happiness.

Procne, speaking in Sophocles, *Tereus*, fr. 583
(original translation by Brian Sparkes)

'Myself, I do not believe that a man can differ from other men to the point of having totally incomprehensible reasons. There are no such things as strangers. There are *no* strangers; do you understand that, old chap?'

Jean Giono, *A King without Amusements*, 1948

Poseidon's abduction of Amymone. Kinetic transference of divine lust into hunting scenes: Poseidon (a specialist) is about to carry off Amymone. This is a mythological transposition of urban dangers for the *parthenos*; the hydria carried by Amymone indicates that she is there only because she is going to the fountain. The State Hermitage Museum, St Petersburg

Which paths will lead us to them?

When setting out to meet Greek women we need to adjust our sights to the memory of a period, and to consider two preliminary questions: where are they spoken about and who is speaking about them? To be born a woman vastly diminishes the likelihood of an individual leaving any traces in history; and the handicap is cumulative, so much so that if the problems of poverty, political exclusion and inferior status are added, women are likely to be consigned to oblivion. This is true everywhere and at all times, even quite recently, but there were many in ancient Greece who suffered from two handicaps: they were – being women *and* slaves, women *and* foreigners, women *and* excluded from the social system. Only chance, therefore, can explain such traces of them that have survived: their contemporaries had no interest in them. One of the few irrefutable facts is this: there must be thousands, millions, of shadowy figures behind a few faintly illuminated foregrounds. As a historian, I can only adhere to the principle of the reality of the sources of information; because it is impossible to do otherwise, this book will generally deal with those whose feminine gender is their one and only hindrance, women who are socially favoured, who form a tiny proportion of the whole gender. As for the question of who is speaking about these women, the answer is simple: it is Greek men who speak. On the one hand, we have fragments of the lines of Sappho, and on the other an entire library written by men. I might as well say it once and for all: nearly everything about women comes from men, and nearly everything returns to men, for one cannot see how they could not profit from their dominance. It is a well-known and well-defined trap, always under my feet: when these men speak of women they are speaking above all of themselves; therefore so do I. My search for Greek women is thus presented with a challenge: to disengage them from this masculine screen that falls between them and my gaze and to catch a glimpse of that 'everyday world' of theirs, tucked away in the heart of the discourse of a culture which took so little notice of them. But since only the words of men are audible, there is no other way than to listen to them carefully. And although it would be an illusion to think we had gained access this way to women's intimate thoughts, or even their view of the world, let us at least try to get some idea of the life men made them lead. Women will not be alone on stage, however, as our enquiry into the feminine obviously teaches us in return a great deal about men, about the 'association' of the sexes (as one of the characters in this book says), about the societies in which they lived, and the culture in which they were steeped.

It would surely be impossible to write a book that simultaneously reconstructed the everyday life of Greek women and their history. Not that I doubt the legitimacy of the search for the 'everyday': the habitual is life in its greatest density; it is what makes it bearable. Nor am I complaining of the paucity of the sources, but how are the two opposites of history and the repetitive daily fabric of life to be united? In the matter of the 'daily round', how is one to answer the legitimate, innocent and 'unheard of' request to give an account of one of their days? Which woman would we write about, and when? Of course, there are texts and images (though skimpy and rare); and if one started from those, one could attempt to say, for example, what they did with their hands; but such a reconstruction offers only a utopian day, which is never revealed anywhere. The everyday kills history, whereas history swamps the everyday. And how is one to reply – if possible, at the same time – to that other request to recount how and whither this human maelstrom slipped away, composed as it was of their thousands of days, filled with words, gestures, thoughts; a gradual evolution that could have been called history, if we had preserved more than an ounce of it? Despite being a daily occurrence, the 'everyday' changes, but how can we pinpoint its movement? It would be far easier with men. We know about the development of their ways of building and fighting, their political, philosophical and religious ideas, even their dreams; but their total lack of interest in the actions of their female contemporaries – cooking, washing, spinning, weaving, pregnancy, childbirth, caring for children, to say nothing of their feelings and emotions – deprives us of that history. History gets its own back on the everyday by concealing it. Greek women were in the shade, and stayed there. Bad luck should not be blamed for this 'cover-up'; the absence of a historical 'Greek woman' is explained by the life that their society made them lead, a life whose main characteristic was their inferior status to men.

Faced with these two models, at such depressing extremes, the choice must be made: the fixed image, based on a kaleidoscopic accumulation of the objects of 'everyday life' – spindles, distaffs, grindstones and so on – gleaned here and there, mixing facts from the day before yesterday and the day after tomorrow to paint the richest picture possible; or the film, with only a few continuous sequences and with many blanks which are the black holes in our documentation. Of the two solutions, I plump for history: history as the route and the means of visualizing a world.

Greek women in everyday life, like your sisters in other times, lands and cultures – you are absent, anonymous and silent. What a paradox. For how active and full of sound are those other women who inhabit the 'ideological palaces' of masculine discourse. When it comes to those fictional heroines, whose names are known even outside specialist circles, everything is turned upside down, and what a great deal is said about them. How much more numerous (and endlessly reworked by playwrights, musicians and philosophers) in the whole of Greek, and then western, culture are Ariadne, Iphigenia, Phaedra, Helen, Nausicaa, Andromache, Electra, Antigone and Penelope than the rare Odysseus and Agamemnon. The long and brilliant line of Greek heroines illustrates the incomparable richness of their sex, fixed in accounts which impressed their readers so greatly that for a long time they defined the archetypes on which succeeding imaginations were able to build or reconstruct.

A paradox lies in the enduring quality of these feminine models: their dazzling images were born in a culture where masculine domination stifled women's voices to an extent rarely found elsewhere.[1] Was it because of the discreet silence of one group that the voice of the others rang so loudly? Their fame did not prevent their sisters in everyday life from being placed totally beyond the concern of historians – thus doubly mute and anonymous and having to wait until the second half of the twentieth century to slip into their field of vision? They are at opposite poles: the unknown women, concealed 'in the depths of their obscure homes' and absorbed in their habitual tasks, and the heroines whom the Greek poets set before us, whom Offenbach makes sing, Giraudoux makes quiver, Goethe makes weep and Racine makes proclaim.

Daily life and private life? The association is automatic, and thus symptomatic: when it comes to women, we look at once towards the private, even the intimate, side because now, as then, it is 'within' that we 'naturally' look for them. But obviously nothing, in these matters, is 'natural'. Open a book about women; we find *them* less often than the home, the family, their sexuality. As if men had neither home, nor family nor sex.

1. Of course, the status and role of women were not uniform in ancient Greece, and were sometimes more favourable than in Athens; but it is here that they are best known, and at the same time it was here that the situation was one of the most difficult.

Here the chiasmus is obvious: in contrast to the collective masculine, the feminine is shattered into a thousand individual interiors. The wives of men, for whom the most important part of life is elsewhere, are not heard. And they make a virtue out of this misfortune, unless it is the men who attach more worth to their modesty, their way of effacing themselves. Let women achieve this, they say, and their whole being will be greatly enhanced. 'In a woman, silence is an element of beauty.' In a famous speech, Pericles, after devoting all his time to evoking the richness and diversity of a citizen's virtues (of male adults), contents himself with one sentence regarding women: 'If you do not fall short of your nature [*physis*], it will be a great glory to you; and similarly for those women whose merits or failings cause them to be least spoken of among men (Thucydides, *History of the Peloponnesian War* ii. 45.2).

Stifle their voice – women suffer also from a real identity problem. Although they receive from their father an 'official' name of their own, their male contemporaries use all manner of expressions, pronouns, demonstratives and grammatical processes to deny them a personal identity when talking about them among themselves. If they do name them, it is in a relative manner – relative to the man, father or husband, as 'daughter-of' or 'wife-of'. Since, at the same time, men were extremely careful about the way in which they named themselves, and the symbolic interpretation of their names, this concealment of the identity of women discloses a certain social nonentity. True, the problem goes beyond Greek women, and a glance elsewhere shows that from this point of view they were not the worst off: for example, the Romans did not even give a woman a name, as she was normally called by the feminine version of her father's family name.

The main object of this book is to breathe fresh life into accounts of Greek women which have come down to us through more than two millennia. To fulfil this aim, I have chosen to arrange this discovery of the feminine from the starting point of a few 'lives', because taking this option meant choosing texts as well. The successive stories of several women, from Penelope to Neaera, from the early eighth to the late fourth century BC, will certainly bear witness to some singular destinies, but by their interweavings will also contribute to the reconstruction of the image of a gender. We shall leave the soldiers' barracks of the *Iliad* to go and visit the 'houses' of Athens, and also its courts of law.[2] Some of our guides will be illustrious,

2.   The Greek house – the *oikos* – presents the translator with problems; the term simultaneously designates an ensemble of real estate, such as land and possessions (including livestock), even intangible assets, and an ensemble of people: the citizen's family and slaves, a legal entity and a symbolic and religious unit. Written as 'house', in this book the word will describe this rich whole. Written as "house", in Chapter 6, it will refer to houses of another kind, the "houses" of prostitution.

like Homer, while others are anonymous. From such a perspective, the ideal would be total self-effacement, leaving the bare Greek words; but that is impossible, overlaid as they are by a thick layer of scholia, glosses, foot-notes, philological commentaries, historical and anthropological interpre-tations by generations of the learned. Nevertheless, I shall remain careful to preserve the 'freshness' of these texts; respecting not only the content but also the spirit. I shall therefore fairly frequently, like the Greeks, call a spade a spade; this should not be mistaken for gratuitous licence, so-called improper terms are no longer translated into Latin footnotes.

From the special nature of the documents on which the historian of Greek women works, specific ways emerge of getting to them; so among these chapters whose content borrows both from women and a privileged source (Homer and the maidens of the epics, Plutarch and the 'house' of Pericles, Xenophon and that of Ischomachus, Apollodorus and prostitu-tion), two other viewpoints will be interposed, embracing a longer period: the body and religion. The body, and bodies, of females and women, but also of males and men: I shall try to reconstruct the view of them through doctors (the Hippocratics) and Aristotle's biological writings. But the inquiry will begin with what compartmentalized history always places last – religion, an examination of the relations which the women of Greece maintained (or were compelled to maintain) with the sacred. I place reli-gion first (although everyone says that it is what matters most in this world and then promptly forgets this priority), because it is the source of enlight-enment least likely to be affected by short-term fluctuations and because it makes a powerful contribution to defining the feminine.

CHAPTER 1

The feminine and the sacred

In the quest for the Greek concept of the feminine, it would be unthinkable to neglect the religious trail, which encompasses the broadest framework of thinking and the longest period of time. In that world, it would be impossible to omit this dimension. There and at that time, the major part of what we term religion was completely integrated into social, and even political, life and often formed an essential part of it, with religious practices and beliefs conveying and expressing an entire conception of the world and man's relations with it. The reason for that primacy is deep-seated and simple: if religion in Greek lands provides such propitious ground for investigation of society, it is because, far from forming a somewhat exogenous truth, it is imbued with the colours of that period and world. Distinctions that are so familiar, so 'normal' to us, such as those between the profane and the sacred, the natural and the supernatural, existed but did not follow the same dividing lines. Another difficulty arises from our modern ideas about belief. The list of all that the Greek equivalent does *not* contain would be endless: no prophets, no Messiah, no revelation, no *book*, no dogma, no clergy in the modern sense, no Church, no belief detached from ritual, no omnipotent, creator god who decides everything.[1] Not *one* god, but *gods*, each in the comparative and none in the superlative, in great numbers unknown to the Greeks themselves, as well as other divine beings who were not all gods. No *soul* (in the Christian sense), no 'eternal life', no Manichaeism of good and evil with a celestial accountability . . . What *did* they have, then? The popularizer's problem is that it is far harder for him to say what *is* than what is *not*.

---

1. I am speaking here of religion, not metaphysical speculation. There is every reason to believe that the philosophers' ideas on these matters – of someone like Plato, for instance – had little or no influence on society.

They did have a cosmos inhabited simultaneously by men, gods, heroes and the dead, together with – luckily for men – rules of communication between men and these various manifestations of the supernatural. We commonly lump those rules together under the useful term 'ritual'. Here again, Greek ideas differ from our own: far from being secondary in their 'religion', ritual is, at least, on an equal footing with belief. Here, the social aspect takes precedence. Apart from a few details, it could be said that ritual was more for the collective – there was no strong or significant act in social life without ritual sanction – and that belief was more for the individual. In that human and superhuman were not thought of as radically separate, or even contrasting, the dichotomy of the world in its two parts, male and female – a polarity whose nature and effects I shall examine in the following chapter – obviously cuts across the worlds of both men and gods. It is curious, therefore, that it falls to Greek culture, whose distressing misogyny is so often to be observed, to include in its pantheon some of the most beautiful images of the feminine. A daunting element for reflection on the feminine in Greek lands: there, the gods are also goddesses.

The Feminine in the Divine

In the distribution of genders (and sexes) among the Greek immortals, the feminine position is by no means subordinate. Goddesses such as Demeter, Athena or Hera are not concerned with under-secretaryships of state for the affairs of Olympus. Of course, the long history of those gods and the populations who passed on their images helped to shift the divine sex ratio in favour of the masculine; in other words, from the time that gods were recorded in Greece (the middle of the second millennium BC) up to the period that interests us, representation of the feminine in this pantheon showed a decline. Nevertheless, it still holds a record 'feminization rate' among religions. This femininity is far from evanescent, its image is socialized.

The first classification is obvious: goddesses are classed as women in a status whose definition is derived from the sexual, the biological and the social at the same time. This triple conjunction of conditions defines three of the greatest – Athena, Artemis and Hestia – as *parthenoi*, 'virgins'. Other qualities are associated with them: they are pure, indomitable, fierce. They are proud of their virginity, and proclaim it: 'Grant me, O father, eternal virginity', says Artemis to her father (Callimachus, *Hymn to Artemis* 6). They are daughters-of-their-father, Artemis and Athena of Zeus and Hestia of Cronus, with Athena, especially so. 'For to Athena alone among his daughters . . . Zeus granted the same powers as her father; no mother

The judgement of Paris. The shepherd-prince Paris has to choose the most beautiful: in the wake of Hermes, who leads them, each goddess shows herself: first, the *parthenos* Athena, then the wife Hera, but the young man will choose Aphrodite, veiled like a *nymphe* at her wedding. Antikensammlung, Staatliche Museen zu Berlin – preussischer Kulturbesitz

gave birth to the goddess, but the head of Zeus himself' (*Homeric Hymn to Athena* xxviii. 4).[2] If this father arranges no matrimonial strategy with a son-in-law for any of them, it is because the virginity of these fortunate ones is eternal, essential, even spiteful, and may tend towards cruelty. Witness to the dreadful fate awaiting those who violate their privacy are the myths describing how mortals lost their sight or perished for having seen one of them bathing. Another testimony to this implacable defence of their virginity is the foreknowledge of death which the dreamer must obtain from dreaming of intercourse with them. In fact, whereas making love with a god or goddess, 'if they enjoy it, predicts (to the dreamers) help from superiors', that is only so with certain goddesses, while with

> Artemis, Athena or Hestia, it is harmful to lie, *even if it brings pleasure*: this dream indeed predicts imminent death for the one who has experienced it; for these are noble goddesses, and tradition has taught us that those who have laid hands on them have suffered terrible punishments. (Artemidorus, *Interpretation of Dreams* i. 80)

2. On this myth and what we learn from it of the father's relationship with his *kore*, see p. 53.

Athena making a libation. Covered from head to foot, the virgin (*parthenos*), absolutely pure, unassailable and invincible, proffers a libation to Heracles (not visible). Antikenmuseum Basel und Sammlung Ludwig, Inv., 418

In this 'perfect' family, each of the three has her own attributes. Athena is probably the most complex; within her field of action she includes technical know-how, as well as the protection of children and young people, effectiveness in war and, in many city-states, the outstanding position of a deity – that is to say, political.

Artemis shares with Athena her characteristics of protectress of childhood and youth, her part being specifically birth, pregnant women and those in childbirth. She also has pre-eminence over the natural world, especially animals, and therefore the hunt. 'She enjoys archery and killing wild beasts in the mountains; she also likes the *phorminx* lyre, dancing, the high-pitched songs of women and shady woods and the city of just men' (*Homeric Hymn to Aphrodite* (v) 18–20). In contrast, Artemis features less in the political domain than her sister (by the same father, but not mother) Athena.

The third daughter, Hestia, Zeus' sister, specializes far more. She is the goddess of the interior – of the 'house' – and even of the inside of the interior: the home's focal point, the hearth, known as *hestia*. Taking the city-state as a metaphor for the 'house', we find her as the divine protectress of institutions, buildings and also of the men who are at the centre, the heart and head of the political community.

There could be said to be three types of virgin: the first of the world of men, the second of that of wild animals, but also of women in labour, and the third, the real *parthenos* of the heart of the 'house'. Why are these goddesses virgins, holding these powers and fulfilling these functions? What explanation is there for the virginity of those important goddesses of Greek welfare, Athena and Artemis, whom no fighting community could ever forget at the moment of battle, or beforehand or afterwards? Is it because of the equation virgin = fierce = stubbornly courageous? Could that kind of virginal femininity attain the impossible *andreia* (virility) (see p. 76)? There is an evident transition from the virginity of the maiden to the inviolability of the place, and a concern for the protection of the community.

Other goddesses who inhabit Olympus have a sexual life; These include the Muses, Nymphs and the Mother of the Gods, but those who matter most are Aphrodite, Hera and Demeter.

'Though Aphrodite cannot persuade them, Athena, Artemis and Hestia, or seduce them, no one else – blessed god or mortal – can ever escape her' (*Homeric Hymn to Aphrodite* (v) 33–4). For Aphrodite's main preoccupation is love:

> Cypris [Aphrodite's nickname] awakens sweet desire in the heart of the gods and subdues the tribes that fly in the air of mortal men, the birds, all the animals that both land and sea raises in great numbers: they all have a care for the works of crowned Cytherea.[3] (*Homeric Hymn to Aphrodite* (v) 2–6)

---

3.   Aphrodite's origin is variously attributed: she comes from Cyprus, from the waves or, as here, Cythera.

There is no doubt at all that Aphrodite is the force that brings beings together and unites their sexes. True, there is another god, in competition or addition, whose power is feared and vaunted, a more masculine god who also possesses an inordinate ability to arouse desire: 'Eros, the most beautiful of the immortal gods, who shakes limbs and, in the breast of every god and man alike, overcomes the mind and wise counsels' (Hesiod, *Theogony* 120–2). But unlike Eros, Aphrodite goes beyond these feminine/masculine categories. With her, the whole of life is embraced, above and beyond pleasure; her law applies to all – men, gods and the cosmos – and sweet is the path for anyone who adheres to her first principles (obviously in contradiction to those professed by the virgin goddesses, above all the untamed ones):

> The holy Uranus[4] loves to penetrate Gaia (the earth) and love lays hold of earth to join in marriage; and desire moves Gaia to enjoy coitus; the rain falls from the streaming Uranus and impregnates Gaia; and she brings forth for mortals the pasturage of sheep and Demeter's sustenance;[5] and from their moist union the season of foliage is perfected. Of this I, Aphrodite, am the cause. (Aeschylus, *Danaïdes* fr. 44N, quoted by Athenaeus xiii. 600B)

Aphrodite has at her disposal all the effective means of attaining her end, most of all beauty. Her body is a dazzling sight, as are her garments, perfumes, adorments, flowers, smiles, to the extent that upon her arrival the 'Immortals stretched out their hands towards her; each desired to make her his wife and carry her off to his 'house'' (*Homeric Hymn to Aphrodite* (vi) 15–16). Is this goddess of love a wife? Yes, certainly. But how can it be said of the goddess of love that she is 'married'? Whoever is ascribed to her as 'husband and lord', she has a terrible tendency to love others. The *Odyssey* contains the most famous episode of her unseemly love affairs, when she dares to sully her husband Hephaestus' very own bed in the company of Ares, god of war. Does her lovemaking make her a mother? Yes, if only of Eros, in certain stories. Yes, because she is clearly in favour of creating children, but she is not the kind of mother one would propose as a role model.

If we keep only to Hera's fundamental quality, she is a wife. A great goddess, assuredly, the 'Lady' is, however, merely relative. Without Zeus, there is no Hera. Like Hestia, she is his sister, but above all his wife. Of course,

---

4. The name of the god of the sky, Uranus, means 'he who urinates'; the rain falling from the sky is the sperm of Uranus.
5. This is the cornseed, characteristic attribute of the goddess Demeter.

Zeus and Hera at the wedding of Thetis and Peleus. Among other deities invited to the wedding, the divine couple take part in the procession as if it were their own: Zeus drives the chariot and, at his side, Hera draws her cloak over her face with one hand, as mortal maidens did at their own wedding. © British Museum

she takes only third place in the 'chronological' list of his official unions, after Metis (Athena's 'mother') and Themis ('Justice'). It is said, or whispered, that when Zeus and Hera were very young, and Cronus still ruled the cosmos, they had been in love and that their youthful lovemaking produced four divine children: Hephaestus, Ares, Eileithyia and Hebe. But poets most enjoy recounting their fabulous nuptials. Whether on the summit of Mount Ida or in the Garden of the Hesperides, the divine copulation formed the model for the *hieros gamos*, the 'divine coitus', or 'sacred marriage', a mythical motif of which the Greeks were extremely fond: husband and wife take their pleasure and are fruitful. In many places in Greece, people delighted in commemorating the event. Hera was represented by a statue dressed as a bride, drawn along in a procession similar to that of a human wedding, to the sanctuary, where she came to a nuptial bed. Zeus' sexual partner Hera was also his 'legal' spouse, and if there was a Greek wife who suffered more than any other from sexual competition, because of her husband's insatiability, it was surely she. Later, on the downhill slope of her marriage, she plays to perfection the role of cantankerous and jealous wife. On Olympus she ceaselessly rails against all his mistresses and bastards. Heracles has no other reason for carrying out his Twelve

Labours than to expiate Hera's wrath towards him. Her portion is the protection of women and marriage, as an institution, and like Athena in Athens, she sometimes also assumes the much more important place of an omnipotent and sovereign city-goddess (Argos, Samos).

There remains Demeter, who is by no means the least of the goddesses. She comes second among the siblings of the principal generation of Greek gods, children of the Cronus/Rhea couple.

> Rhea yielded to the demand of Cronus and bore him glorious children, Hestia, Demeter, Hera of the golden sandals; and the mighty Hades, pitiless god, who established his dwelling beneath the earth; and the resounding shaker of the ground (Poseidon); and the wise Zeus, father of gods and men . . . (Hesiod, *Theogony* 453–7)

This group of siblings is not without interest. On the one hand, although split into three persons – Zeus (sky), Hades (subterranean world) and Poseidon (sea) – the masculine evidently adopts only one form: that of the mature adult (we have only to think of the very similar statues of Poseidon and his brother Zeus). On the other, the feminine appears in many forms, in a perspective in which sexual of social roles are defined straightaway: Hestia is the virgin of the interior; Hera, with her 'golden sandals', is the wife, and Demeter the mother. Demeter is so in her very name. Of course, the indispensable fertility of the fields and vital fruitfulness of animals and men come under the aegis of other immortals, other gods and heroes whom humans propitiate in order propagate and prolong life and increase wealth. The goddesses named above, and others, and even (a Greek speciality) certain gods make their contribution in one way or another. In Greek imagination, however, no divine entity other than Demeter represents the image of *the* fertile and fertilizing mother.

Two other deities may perhaps introduce some confusion: Earth and the Mother of the Gods. Gaia, or Ge, 'broad-hipped Earth', who, as we have just seen, was seized by desire for intercourse and received the fertilizing 'rain' from Uranus or Zeus, forms a gigantic womb producing a large quantity of offspring (she sometimes does so on her own). Strictly speaking, she is genealogically among the ancestors of Demeter. Moreover, although these goddesses who are so akin to Demeter have a formidable rate of conception and childbearing, they are not as attached to their children, or their children to them, as Demeter: the bond between Demeter and her offspring is indestructible. Demeter's maternal qualities are truly and continually at work. Indeed, the goddess is inseparable from her daughter, the beautiful Kore, the divine 'Young Maiden'. Their bond and unity are so powerful that the Greeks call them the 'Two Goddesses'. Zeus is certainly his niece's (Kore) father (nothing especially extraordinary about this), but is insignificant. Of course, in the same way that the Greek pantheon includes other mothers than Demeter, there are other daughters – the famous trio of *parthenoi*, Athena-Artemis-Hestia – but if Kore is also a *parthenos*, she is more than just that. Like the Homeric *kourai*, like Briseis and Chryseis and Nausicaa (see below), she shifts, she moves on.

Kore's story illustrates these 'oscillations' (a word I borrow from Stérenn Quéméner), which are typical of the Greek females in the next chapter. First, she is a child, in the company of her childhood friends (including Athena and Artemis), gathering flowers in a meadow and brutally carried off by her paternal uncle,[6] a gloomy adult male god, Hades, lord of the Underworld, who wants to possess her and conceal her below ground. From the moment of that violent assault, Demeter ceaselessly searches for her daughter. Her wrath against gods and men is inextinguishable, and her search stubborn. By her will, the earth becomes sterile. Things are going wrong with the cosmos and Zeus, who had been aware but had let it slide, has to take matters in hand and order his abductor/rapist brother to hand the girl back. But Kore has eaten a pomegranate seed, an almost magical act which binds her to the lord of the Underworld. No one can return 'intact' from the 'house' of Hades. It was a real marriage, so the break is accompanied by a change of name: Demeter's daughter will henceforward be known as Persephone. Like a *nymphe*, from the *kore* she was before, lo and behold, she is now an adult. There is a necessary compromise for the return of fruitfulness, the revival of the world, related to the Kore-Persephone division: in winter, Persephone will be sovereign of the infernal world, wife of Hades, then, each spring, returning to her mother, Kore will rise from the furrows as the crops germinate. The Kore/Persephone myth incorporates the virginity/fertility contrast into a perspective that is certainly divine, but also fully human; it illustrates what Greek femininity will initiate us into: alternative roles, ambivalence and ambiguity.

This portrait gallery is inevitably short but is enough to illustrate how, through the divine entities that were born, developed and transformed by it, Greek imagination conceived the feminine supernatural as diverse, varying in type, 'instrumental' and social. Looking at the list again, we find the young girl, Kore, daughter-of-her-father; *kore* and *thygater* (daughter as direct descendant), like Athena; the virgin *parthenoi* Athena, Artemis, Hestia; and *nymphai* (young brides) (Nymphs); and the legitimate spouse, Hera; and the mother, Demeter. In short, the feminine was defined as usual in several ways: biologically – daughter, virgin, mother; socially –

---

6. The close kinship would not have shocked the Greeks.

wife; sexually – virgin, young bride, mother. These are the many categories by which men refer to the feminine. It is true that, among the goddesses, only wives and mothers are likely to have lovers. It is no surprise that the Greek supernatural shows such readiness to 'mould' itself on completely human categories, because that is peculiar to polytheism. There remains one blind spot, however, in their series of divine types based on the ages of life – that of widowhood and the menopause; there is apparently nothing akin to an *old* goddess. Nor does age among mortals confer the same qualities on men and women. From the Nestor of the *Iliad*, Greek culture interminably praises the attributes of old men. 'To the young, actions; to adults, carefully weighed intentions; to the old, prayers' (Hesiod, fr. 321, H–W). Old age brings wisdom, valuable counsel, the superiority of experience and a life unencumbered by the empty search for pleasures. That is why cities chose fairly elderly citizens for magistrates. Perhaps less expectedly, the Greek taste for the immature body does not prevent an appreciation of the beauty of old men: for instance, in the procession of the Panathenaea in Athens a group of *thallophoroi*, the handsomest old men in the town, parades bearing olive branches. In contrast with this esteem for masculine old age, the feminine often forms a negative pole of disgust. Thus the most menial, the most drunken, the most dissolute of women (in comedy and paintings) are old. It comes as no surprise, therefore, that female old age is not represented in the family of the immortals. Polytheism, however, has its resources. At Stymphalus (a city-state in the Peloponnese), a Hera exists with three nicknames: she is called, both separately and at the same time, *Pais*, 'Child', *Teleia*, 'Fulfilled' Wife, and *Chera*, 'Empty', that is, empty of man, hence 'Widow' (Pausanias, viii. 22. 2). Here, Hera expresses the complete woman in her three ages or conditions, virgin child, wife and old woman. It is the relationship with man which marks out the rhythm of a woman's life: that of marriage more than that of puberty, widowhood, abandonment, and even of menopause.

Humans seeking the Divine

So far, so good with the Greek gods in their polytheism, those beings who are so hard to define, to pin down. But a religion worthy of the name – a sufficiently complex system – does not merely offer the image of a certain deity endowed with a certain form and certain qualities; it establishes and regulates the relationships that men have with one or with many divine figures. Rites are bound up with belief, and vice versa. Either extreme may exaggerate the other's weaknesses, but the one does not exist without the other, lest the whole thing can no longer be called 'religion'. But, fundamentally, what are rites if not a complex instrumental communication system between men-who-eat-bread and the immortals? The problem of ritual arises in an unusual way in polytheisms. In this context, any catechism is unimaginable for want of a rule that can be applied in every instance. In fact, each of the gods, goddesses and immortals who compose the divine is defined according to two main themes: his/her function – in which area has he/she the most influence, or the highest level of skill – *and* his/her own particular way of intervening in the cosmos – using this quality or that. When Ares, a rather brutish lout, uncovers adultery, he kills his rival; in the same situation, Hephaestus, discovering his wife Aphrodite in her lover's arms, fashions a marvellous net which imprisons the lovers in their bed of debauchery, sheepish and unable to move. I hunt, fish, sow corn, desire good harvests, am a general, want to conquer the enemy, so I propitiate a deity[7] who includes hunting, fishing, cereal growing, or fighting among his attributes; at the same time as choosing from those who have the necessary power, in a given context, I set great store by the *way* he acts.

It is, however, far from being enough to pinpoint with certainty the most efficient deity, because much also depends on the request and from whom it originates. For the warrior or magistrate, the most effective deity for armed violence could be Ares, or it could be Athena: brute force on the other hand, and intrepidity, but also tactics and finesse, on the other. But there are other variables, such as knowing from where and in what circumstances the request for the divine emanates, a question that brings in variables of age and sex. Still on the subject of war, in certain circumstances the young men – the *epheboi* – would turn to a particular group of deities, some of whom were almost theirs alone, whereas the adults, officers or other categories would address those and others besides.

This question of the nature of men's requests for benefits from the gods is of course eminently social. For surely men's powerful dominance over women must influence a negative reply to the nonetheless burning question: if there were goddesses, and priestesses in Greece, did a 'feminine religion' exist there and, if so, what forms did it take? Although the pantheon includes a number of goddesses and heroines, and many priesthoods were undertaken by girls and women, that does not imply the existence of a 'feminine religion', enjoying a kind of autonomy, versus another 'religion' which would then be described as 'masculine'. In the Greek scale of values, it is difficult to imagine feminine access to the divine without the ultimate control of men. On the other hand, the fact that such a 'feminine religion' did not exist does not imply an absence of paths, specific to women,

---

7. Initially a simplification, this singular is justified also by the fact that experience most often results in the definition of a single god.

allowing access to the gods. At all events, if a 'religion' of this kind could be identified, the evidence cited above definitely limits its scope: it could not go against or, above all, harm this masculine domination. One might even wager that it would contribute to it.

It may be safely suggested that the political community used women (all or some) as actresses, even as privileged actresses, in the rituals, *for its greater gain*. It has been possible to show that feminine rituals for Demeter, spread throughout the year, corresponded exactly to the various phases of the growth of cereal crops and the human (masculine) labours involved. Note that I said that *women*, not the feminine, were used. Men, indeed, used all categories of the feminine, from virgins to old women. We shall see how and why.

WHOSE VOICES MAY SPEAK TO THE GODS?

The gods hear (each god hears) some messages and some interpreters better than others. Consequently, the community entrusts certain of its members with the task of ensuring the best kind of communication with the divine, and this is the characteristic of priestly functions. As the divine had many forms, priesthoods were distributed throughout all categories of society: the young, adults, the old, men and women. Even if there were numerous exceptions, there were general rules in this area, such as the one expressed by Hesiod, according to which the old are better prayers, and another that caused heroes and gods to have priests, while heroines and goddesses had priestesses. The Greeks were very concerned with liturgy and, city by city and god by god, laid down the rules devolving upon the corresponding priesthoods. For goddesses, matters were quite clear: virgins for the virgins, adults for the adults. Regarding the former, the texts specify what is meant – the priestess must be in the state of *parthenos* – but was more precision needed? Then her state is defined in respect of the man: the maiden will be a priestess 'until she reaches the moment of marriage', 'until she arrives at her nuptials', 'until the time comes for her to be sent to a man' . . .

For a better understanding of what is at issue, here are three choice stories of priestesses, as recounted in cities, to explain the reasons that impelled the ancestors to choose a certain type of woman for a certain type of priesthood. These aetiological myths illustrate the fact that feminine priesthoods presented men with quite a few specific problems.[8] Women, as we shall see, were deemed to heed only their impulses and would always be in danger of sullying their surroundings; hence divine wrath. First, a

8. Real or imaginary problems, it matters little because what we are seeking is the Greeks' way of conceiving the relationship of the feminine with the divine.

tear-jerking love story which Pausanias, a traveller in the second AD, picked up in Patras.

> Over there lie a sanctuary and a temple of Artemis, known as Triklaria
> . . . The goddess's priesthood was held by a *parthenos*, until such time as
> she was sent to a man. Formerly, the priestess was named Komaitho
> ['The Redhead'], one of the most beautiful *parthenoi*, who was loved by
> one Melanippus ['The Black Horse'], the best and handsomest of the
> young men of his age. When he managed to get the *parthenos* to share
> his love, he asked her father for the girl. Older people are often opposed
> to youth in all kinds of matters, and are particularly insensitive to the
> desires of those in love. Like many others, the story of Melanippus
> proves that love is capable of breaking human laws and profaning the
> worship rendered to the gods; indeed, their erotic ardour culminated in
> the very sanctuary of Artemis, which they used as a bridal chamber.
>
> Then Artemis' wrath began to destroy the inhabitants.[9] The land no
> longer produced crops, and strange illnesses appeared, of an unknown
> nature. When they appealed to the Delphic oracle, the Pythia (propet-
> priestess of Apollo at Delphi) blamed Melanippus and Komaitho. The
> oracle ordered them to be sacrificed to Artemis, and that every year the
> most beautiful *parthenos* and the handsomest *pais* ['youngster'] were to
> be sacrificed to the goddess. (Pausanias, vii. 19. 1–4)

Thus the fairest young couple were sacrificed to the irascible goddess, the one who does not take purity lightly. Happily, this stain arising from amorous sacrilege was washed away thanks to the arrival of one Eurypylus, who instituted a new youth ritual which appeased the goddess. Once again, as before these annoying events, Artemis' priestess was chosen from the *parthenoi*. She – probably the most beautiful – held the office 'until the moment came for her to be sent to a man' (Diodorus, xvi. 16. 2).

Second story: the Arcadians had always chosen a 'virgin maid' (*kore parthenos*) as the priestess of Artemis Hymnia. But it is the common fate of *parthenoi*, at least in myths, to be pursed by lustful boys, and a certain Aristocrates fell in love with one of them. The girl resisted him, but the inevitable happened:

9.   The sexual act performed in such a place sullies it and also sullies the deity. In all myths
     the consequences are the same: divine wrath expressed by visiting a scourge on men,
     consultation of the oracle by men to understand the reason and/or know the god's will,
     execution of this in the form of a new ritual. It is precisely this ritual which is known
     to the men recounting the myth.

he subjected her to the final outrage near the statue of Artemis. When the assault became known to all, the Arcadians stoned the guilty party and took care to alter the law. Henceforward, they would no longer choose a *parthenos*, but a woman (*gyne*) who had had enough relations with men. (Pausanias, viii. 5. 12)

What else can this mean but that Artemis Hymnia 'hears' an 'old woman' just as she hears a *parthenos*, doubtless because, vis-à-vis the divine, the new priestess of Artemis Hymnia offers qualities similar to those of a virgin. This crosscheck seems to prove that in the final analysis virginity counts for less than chastity.

The last story is about antiquity's most famous priestess, the Pythia, who in Apollo's sanctuary at Delphi explained the god's wishes and answered requests for clarification brought by mortals. According to several testimonies, the Pythia is an 'old woman'. It is said that she is fifty years old, too old to remarry, or that she abstains from marrying a man. It is all the same. The inhabitants of Delphi tell that formerly a *parthenos* had officiated, but that a young Thessalian named Echecrates had fallen in love with the maiden . . . Faced with the danger of such a taint, the people of Delphi changed the rules of the game, and henceforward the priestess would be a 'woman aged fifty' who would have to dress like a virgin (the detail is symbolic).

Of course, in all these stories, the 'old woman' is not as good as the virgin; she is a virgin in a minor key. Nevertheless, there is the same outcome. When the virgin is lacking, neither a man nor an adult woman is chosen, but a woman 'who-has-had-enough-relations-with-a-man'. In the liturgy, the life of a Greek woman, like that of Hera, is clearly divided into three parts: before the man, during the man and after the man.

So much for the important priesthoods. If divine service was extended to the people who spent a fairly long period of seclusion in the sanctuaries, or even to those who took part in religious processions, the fundamental teachings did not alter. In the many processions for this or that god or goddess, the (men) placed neither men nor women at the head, but virgins. These leading maidens are often called '*kanephoroi*', for like the Caryatids of the Erechtheion on the Acropolis in Athens, they carry on their heads baskets containing the cult's sacred objects – ribbons and sacrificial knives – which only pure hands may touch. They are chosen from the most beautiful, they are pubescent, the daughters of citizens (and not the least among them). Purity – therefore strict sexual abstinence – is their golden rule. They are *parthenoi* of pre-marriageable age. The place? The town, outside the 'house'. The public? The community, men of all ages, citizens. They are jubilant, the god is being fêted, and soon there will be feasting. This pomp-filled march of the maidens – with as many *thygatres*[10] as *parthenoi* – filing past under the masculine gaze, resembles a parade of marriageable girls.

All these priesthoods and religious services of virgins in the pre-marital days could not be embraced in a 'feminine religion' or even in specifically feminine ways of gaining access to the divine. The purpose of the processions was to lead men and beasts to the place of sacrifice, and if one looks at the raison d'être of the entire display and of the actions and of the participants, there is nothing feminine and not a trace of 'femininity' about them. The language used by men in those circumstances, confident as they were of being understood by the gods, comprised nothing peculiarly feminine. On the contrary, what could be more masculine than the bloody sacrifice, with the ritualized slaughter of the domestic animal, its butchery, cooking and communal consumption, which were the aims of these processions? The presence of virgins – or old women – in these ceremonies can therefore be explained only by this reason: their purity. If adult women are kept apart from such divine service, if virgin (or old) priestesses are chosen, if pre-pubescent virgins are placed at the head of processions, it is not so that the latter can take part as women, it is to avoid taint: menstrual blood, contact with men, and having being touched by the wings of death.

We return to the axiom of masculine dominance. How can any form of worship be imagined that could challenge it or even, on a minor scale, be content to occupy itself with anything other than the well-being of the political community and its members? Even if feminine ways could find any echo in the divine as conceived in Greek heads, their effectiveness could be exerted only to the profit of men. Nevertheless, even understood as a depraved version of the masculine, the feminine exists in Greek culture, and we shall meet it in misogyny and anatomy, physiology, eroticism, demography, society . . . If polytheism really reflects the world here below, 'femininity' must be hiding in there somewhere. If this is so, its ways of access to the divine must have a different resonance, the idiom used must comprise something that contrasts it with, or at least differentiates it from, the language of the majority, that of men.

WOMEN SPEAK THE FEMININE RITUAL LANGUAGE

Every year in the autumn, in most Greek cities, citizens' wives emerged from their homes to assemble for three days in a sanctuary, often outside the walls, with the intention of celebrating Demeter and Kore. Men were

10.   Plural of *thygater*: daughters in the sense of lineage.

excluded; they were not to know anything about it (including the symbolic 'message' conveyed by the ritual) or, *a fortiori*, to be present physically. This secrecy explains why not everything is clear when it comes to describing the content of these rites. It is known that, after remaining chaste for three days, some of the participants raised from the depths of natural or man-made pits the putrid remains of piglets which had been thrown into them some months before, accompanied by dough facsimiles of *phalloi* and snakes. This animal 'humus' possessed powerful fertilizing virtues, and was afterwards mixed with seeds to ensure good germination and growth – Demeter's customary and normal fields of activity. The second day, which was inauspicious, was a Fast. In Athens, the women ascended the hill of the Pnyx in a body, and stayed sitting on strewn branches of the wild pepper shrub, an anaphrodisiac plant. In this way they commemorated the mourning of Demeter as she went is search of her Kore. This day was as inseparable from its morrow as a crotchet from its quaver in the heart of a syncopation; their way of putting their body to sleep on that day, and starving it (food and sexual appetite was one and the same to the female belly), made them ready for the coming day, which was the third, that of the Beautiful Birth. From the minor key, as they waited, they passed to the major, in the actualization. The time had come to procreate; the atmosphere was one of gaiety, the women exchanged obscenities, sacrificed pigs, feasted with one another. And all that was for the greater good of the living world: human fruitfulness and the fertility of the fields.

Now for a change of scene. These same wives left their 'house' (abandoning it to its fate) for a place that was far from men and even from human beings; they would walk a very long way and meet by night on the mountain. But once there, they became unrecognizable. They had already started on the mimetic process that would bring them closer to their model, their master Dionysus. Barefoot, a garland of ivy on their free-flowing hair, with a typical long, pleated tunic, a girdle of coarse wool, the *nebris* – a tanned fawn- or goat-skin – over their shoulders, knotted by its feet over their breast, holding the *thyrsus* – a long wand made of the stem of a large umbellifer – adorned with ribbons and topped with a pinecone – thus appeared the votary of Dionysus, commonly known as a bacchant or maenad. They might also carry the ritual instruments, tambourines, and torches. This get-up was the ritual costume for women, but also for Dionysus, and for the bacchants as well. How are we to understand it? For the god, the answer is easy; he is androgynous, he is the man-woman god. As for the bacchants, if there were plenty of them, it proves that in order to participate in the Dionysiac ritual – the orgiastic ritual – they had to transform themselves into women. In the ecstatic worship of Dionysus, the feminine dominated outrageously, although it was not exclusive. Is there any need to emphasize that, for the faithful follower, this might mean abandoning his manliness, if only symbolically?

Donning the Dionysiac costume was an important step in the direction of what, *crescendo*, the whole being of the female zealot was striving for: possession. Wives, who the day before had been confined in their 'houses' but were now immersed in the rawness of the wild, acted out the orgies of Dionysus which turned them into 'madwomen' (the first meaning of maenads). For the 'costume' of the maenad was that of Dionysus and the imitation of the god, even identification with him, was one of the mainsprings of this cult. The first act of dispossessing oneself, which was in the strict sense an ecstasy – *ekstasis*, a 'displacement', 'distraction' – putting on the garments, also incorporated the faithful into the Bacchic community, which was at first calm but then gradually led by ritual into trance and 'enthusism' – from *entheos*, 'having the god inside oneself', whence 'possessed' or 'inspired'. Rendered beside herself by ecstasy, the maenad left room within herself for the coming of Dionysus. That could not happen all by itself.

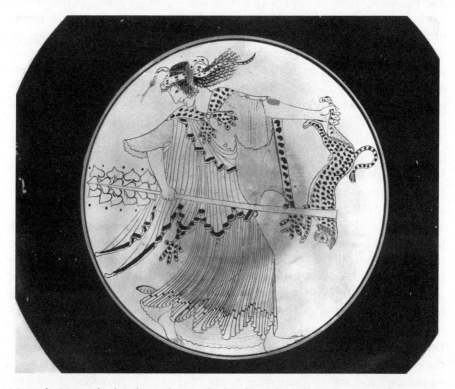

Maenad. Acting the bacchant also involved 'taking the habit'. The maenadic costume expressed freedom and wildness; garments that flowed free like their hair, *thyrsus* in the left hand and a leopard in the other, a *nebris* (fawnskin) slung over their shoulders. Staatliche Antikensammlungen und Glyptothek München

First of all fatigue had to be taken into account: having left her 'house', she had walked a long time to reach the mountain where, away from her own home, she was in the home of the god. The Delphic *thiasos* thus ascended to the summit of Parnassus, at an altitude of some 2,500 metres. What kind of state was she in when the nocturnal celebrations began, preceded by the ecstatic dancing? The latter lasted long enough for her to attain that detachment from reality which she was seeking. Here, everything was strange, with strange music, strange rhythms, haunting insistent cries. Each woman reached her state of 'enthusiasm' in a different way. One might have the gift of getting there quickly, the gift of delirium, and paintings would show such a woman with her head thrown back, vaguely waving her arms, a pronounced bending of the small of her back, her hair flying, eyes rolled upwards, a convulsive attitude. These characteristics were both common and idiosyncratic. Another might show less aptitude for trance and remain outside the whole affair. An adage said that there were many *thyrsi* – many zealous devotees of Dionysus, both male and female – but few of the faithful who reached the state of possession by the god.

> In many Greek towns, *baccheia* of women are held every two years, and it is the rule that the *parthenoi* must carry the *thyrsus* and take part in the manifestations of possession by giving cries of *evoe* and honouring the god; as for the (married) women, they sacrifice to the god in a body, act the bacchants and with various chants celebrate the coming of Dionysus, imitating the Maenads, whom history makes the god's companions. (Diodorus, iv. 3. 3)

Here what matters is the mimetic aspect of the women who 'act the maenads' by imitating the mythological maenads, companions of the god's coming, and the contrast between the behaviour of the adult women who really act the bacchants and that of the young girls who are merely in a preparatory stage, contenting themselves with holding the *thyrsus* and uttering the ritual cry. Observation of similar rites such as voodoo teaches this clearly; one must pass through an apprenticeship with those who already know how to attain ecstasy in order to achieve it oneself.

But what has become of the wife, mother, mistress of the house? Women loved to fête Dionysus, to celebrate him in all sorts of ways, but above all to lose themselves in order to find themselves again in him. In our search for them, much of what we have to go on comes from what men wrote about them so the sincerity and true feelings of the maenads themselves are necessarily and regretfully missing, and it is left to us to try to recreate and imagine their enjoyment. All the same, let me quote Lysistrata, in the play by Aristophanes, noting the late arrival of the women she has called together to start up the 'love strike' which is to keep the peace: 'Ah! if they had been invited to a *baccheion*,[11] or to Pan's or Aphrodite's shrine . . . there wouldn't be room to slip between the tambourines' (Aristophanes, *Lysistrata* 1–3). We can see in which direction Aristophanes is looking when he associates the Bacchic cult with what H. Jeanmaire calls 'devotions of a questionable kind'. He likens cults, which should certainly have a distinction drawn between them, to one another, but the unbridled feminine libido is a mechanism of comedy whose success is assured. However, it cannot be denied that similarities do exist. The idea of pleasure is connected with maenadism, which is why it is contrasted with domestic work. Those who would set such a great store on virtue that, for the sake of the 'house', they would stoically reject the pleasure of going to 'maenadize' with their friends, must be out of their mind: 'Minyas, the son of Orchomenos, had three daughters: Leucippe, Arsippe and Alcathoe, and they became absurdly workaholic. They had nothing but reproach for the other women who deserted the town to act the bacchants in the mountains . . .' (Antoninus Liberalis, *Metamorphoses* x. 1).

We all know that myths simplify, but here are two opposite ends of the scale. There is that of feminine work, with Athena, in which everything focuses inward – chastity, temperance and hard work – and that of Dionysus and Aphrodite, in which everything is extrovert – love, dancing, music. This conflict is witnessed by one Nicarete who, having 'had enough of working on Athena's shuttles', decides to 'throw into the fire, before the temple of Cypris, her basket, her bobbins and all the other tools of her trade' to become a courtesan: 'Farewell, wretched drudgery of women who are not worthy of the name, who know only how to wither their youth, [I choose] to have garlands and a harp and to lead a joyful life in banqueting and celebrating' (*Palatine Anthology* vi. 285, Nicarchos?).

Any of these attitudes carries a risk. On the one hand, to spend one's time acting the frenzied, tousle-haired maniac up in the mountains, losing the very notion of what is illusion and what is real, what is human and what is divine, going as far as challenging one's own position – from every point of view, sexual, social, religious, men would find it all quite unbearable if they were not reassured by its temporary, localized and *ritualized* nature. There is no knowing in what condition the mother of the family returned home after those frantic nights on the mountain, but return she did and she resumed the prosaic daily chores. On the other hand, rejecting those mountain rituals of the sake of housework (or temperance), like

---

11. Like the *thiasos*, the *baccheion* is the material, human and institutional setting of the ecstatic worship of Dionysus.

Minyas' three daughters, constituted at the very least a proud stance. Above all, it was a challenge to the power of a god like Dionysus, and you did not know him well if you defied him like that. To get some idea of the risk they ran, hear the end of the myth:

> Dionysus, in the guise of a young girl, exhorted them not to miss his rites and mysteries. But they paid no heed. Irritated by this attitude, Dionysus changed himself, no longer into a maiden but into a bull, a lion and a leopard, and from the height of the weaving looms nectar and milk flowed in his honour.

> Seeing these prodigies, the girls were seized with terror. Without wasting a moment, all three put dice in a jar which they shook; it was Leucippe's die which fell out; she vowed to offer a victim to the god and, with the help of her sisters, she dismembered Hippasos, her own son. (Antoninus Liberalis, *Metamorphoses* x. 2–3)

When Dionysus showed his power, he made those who resisted him truly *mad*, taking the effects of the maenads' trance to extremes for those conceited girls. If we try to understand this unheard-of cruelty, a murder committed in common, we must look at the maenads of the world. We know how Leucippe's child was killed: he was torn to pieces with their bare hands. In another version, they 'tore him apart as if he were a fawn'. Then off they went, 'acting the bacchants in the mountains, nibbling at ivy, convolvulus and laurel.' The climax of the experience was the feeling of losing the boundaries between oneself and the others, oneself and the god, oneself and the world, which was a transcedence at the same time as an escape. Not much is known about the ways in which the ecstatic dance became transformed into a chase or a hunt. In this setting there lies a feminized, thus untamed, recollection of the customary sacrificial behaviours – masculine and civilized. The *thiasos* pursed a young animal, a fawn or a kid (an acolyte may have released it into the wild), hunting it in what was known as 'Aphrodite's hunt'. It was encircled, one of the women pinned it down with her body, the others came up and began to tear at it with their bare hands and rip it to pieces. This was the 'dismemberment', the ritual form of the Bacchic sacrifice, and that was how Leucippe killed her son. Such is the behaviour of those whom Dionysus punishes with his madness. Cries and shouts punctuated the completion of the dismemberment, when they hurled themselves on what the still quivering animal offered them: its blood and flesh, obviously raw. This gorging filled with the powerful odours of the living animal added a dizzying dimension. It was said that the Thracian bacchants ended by devouring one another.

With the chase (which corresponded to the procession), the killing, the meal of flesh, combined in a wild, ferocious, 'cannibalistic', uncivilized and therefore 'feminine' way, we see a reflection of the stages of political, cultural and masculine sacrifice. There is the same inversion regarding Demeter. Men did not sacrifice pigs by throwing them into pits; if they slaughtered that animal, it was not so that it could rot, but to have it cooked and eaten. Against a common backdrop, feminine 'sacrifices' and the customary masculine sacrifice are poles apart. It goes even further in that, while in 'normal' sacrifices the protagonists are kept at a distance from one another, the man from the beast and the god, the beast from the god and the god from the earth, Dionysiac ritual works towards a confusion of types. The fawn or the kid is Dionysus himself. From the ascent onto the mountains, the rite always had as its aim to do away with the distance between the natural and the supernatural but also, within the *thiasos*, to bind together those who had come to lose themselves collectively. If communities of women, a feminine sociability, existed in Greek cities, it is to be found in these groups of celebrants: among the maenads as among women in their celebrations of Demeter.

The tension wound down, the women descended again from heaven to earth and went back to their 'house'. They retained the power of a memory, of the Dionysiac images. Euripides passed it on in his extraordinary play the *Bacchae*:

> How sweet it is in the mountains, coming from running with the *thiasoi*, to let oneself sink to the ground, wearing the holy *nebris*, to hunt the blood of the goat that is slain, the delight of raw meat, racing to the mountains of Phrygia and Lydia.[12] The Roarer[13] leads the dance. The ground streams with milk and wine, it streams with the nectar of bees . . . (Euripides, *Bacchae* 135–40)

One of the shepherds sent to spy on the bacchants in the mountains by Pentheus, the rather misogynistic and argumentative king of Thebes, who was inimical to Dionysus and his cult, tells us:

> Your mother, sprang to her feet amidst the bacchants, and gave the ritual signal to awaken them . . . Shaking the deep sleep from their eyes, marvels of ordered calm, all arose, all, young and old, and virgins ignorant of the yoke. First, they let down their hair over their shoulders; then I saw them pull up their fawnskins, whose ties had been loosened,

12.   Regions of Asia Minor where the Greeks believed that Dionysus originated.
13.   'Bromios', one of Dionysus' many names.

girdling those dappled hides with snakes which licked their cheeks; and others, picking up little fawns or wolf cubs, offered them the white milk of their new motherhood – young mothers who had deserted their children. All adorned their foreheads with coronets of ivy, oak or flowering bryony. And when one of them rapped the rock with her *thyrsus*, a flow of limpid water immediately sprang forth from it; another having struck the ground with her narthex [the stem of a giant umbellifer], the God made a spring of wine emerge from it. Those who felt thirsty for the white beverage, scratching the soil with their fingertips, collected jets of milk in plenty. Sweet streams of honey dripped from the ivy-garlanded *thyrsi* . . .

When the time was right, they waved their *thyrsi* for the bacchic dances. With one voice, they invoked Iacchos, the son of Zeus, the Roarer. The whole mountain, and its wild animals, took part in their trance; nothing remained still before their running . . . (Euripides, *Bacchae* 723–7)

But the spying shepherds were discovered by the bacchants:

We at least were able to escape the bacchants by fleeing, or they would have torn us to bits. But without so much as a weapon in their hands they fell upon our cattle which were grazing in the meadow. You would have seen a bellowing heifer with distended udder seized by one of them

Dionysus in his world. The god is on his throne, a vine stock in his right hand (or hanging) and a wine flask in his left, in a setting of *enthusiasmos* or Dionysiac frenzy. In the dishevelled procession two dancing maenads frame a *silen*, wild man, playing a double pipe. Staatliche Antikensammlungen und Glyptothek München

with her two arms open wide; others tore full-grown cows to pieces; you would have seen ribs and cloven hooves hurled to and fro and strips of flesh hanging on the fir trees, dripping blood. Raging bulls with anger mounting in their horns stumbled to the ground, countless hands of girls attacking them and tearing all the flesh that covered them . . . (Euripides, *Bacchae* 734–46)

And like a flock of birds taking flight, they launched themselves towards the plains below . . . like an enemy horde . . . they laid waste to everything, snatching children from their homes. Everything they bore on their shoulders remained there, without being attached, without falling to the black soil; no, not even bronze or iron. Even fire, mingling with their hair, failed to burn them. The villagers, infuriated by this pillage by the bacchants, took up weapons. O king! then there was a terrifying spectacle. The spears' metal tips did not so much as draw blood; but they, merely by hurling their *thyrsi*, covered their enemies with wounds. Those women made men turn their backs in flight, proof that a god was helping them! Then they returned to the place where their race had begun, to the very springs that the god had created for them; they washed off the blood, and their snakes licked away all traces of the blood dripping down their cheeks.

Whoever this deity is, my master, welcome him to your city. He is surely great and, from what I hear, they say he is above all the one who gives mortals the vine that drives away sorrows. (Euripides, *Bacchae* 748–72)

There is no doubt that it is a far cry from these bacchants of the theatre to the wives on the mountain. But Euripides' play would have been unacceptable if the public had not recognized in it at least part of the common dimension of the strangeness of the figure of Dionysus and the unique nature of the maenadic experience, individually and collectively. The message was simple: no to the intellectuals, to that 'wisdom' that derives its strength from reason alone and 'superhuman thinking' as practised by 'people who think themselves superior', which 'jibs at the god's call'; it will be dissolved by his will, at the risk of true madness. 'Life is short' and 'what the simple crowd accepts and practises, that is what I would accept,' declares the one who yields to Dionysus. Historically, ecstatic Dionysiac ritual opened its arms to the underprivileged; emanating from the feminine part of society, it is not surprising that it made gains among its neighbours in hopelessness. The *thiasoi* were gradually filled with slaves and foreigners: new followers of this pure and simple message, of 'communion with nature and simplicity of heart'. Besides this earthly happiness that must be 'naturally' enjoyed, Dionysus offered 'extras': promises of gentle deaths, if not bliss in the hereafter.

AN EPISODE IN THE 'BATTLE OF THE SEXES'?

It is a very revealing point that maenadism was essentially feminine, and that when men took part in the orgy they slipped into feminine garments and behaviour. So it is customary to interpret these ritual practices on the basis of what I call the 'safety-valve theory'. Bacchic celebrations are supposed to have formed permissible compensations, tolerated by men, an (inexpensive) counterpart to the confined life of the 'houses', on the lines of 'Go ahead, dance to your heart's content, but then come back calmly, until the next time.' Ecstasy conceived as a periodic behavioural safety-valve? Certainly. How can it be denied that the rites up in the mountains could form an appropriate backdrop to the expression of repressed desires? In that case, on the social level, Dionysism would be no more than the result of a masculine permissiveness, a 'magnanimity' that would engulf the feminine frustrations which were born and developed in that 'androcracy'. This escape-valve theory can moreover be transposed to the more general level of Greek 'religion'. Indeed, it is certainly not erroneous to understand women's liking for maenadism as a result of the derelict condition in which men's 'religion', political 'religion', left them. When they were still virgins, they certainly played uniquely instrumental, and prestigious, roles. Once women, they appeared only as spectators (if that), whereas, like the cult of Demeter, maenadism let them play the major part.

Although the cathartic element of these dances and chases is totally believable, and there is little doubt that they could partly allay the social neurosis caused by the life imposed on women, that does not take account of their *raison d'être*. Such an explanation is in fact somewhat fanciful and does not pay enough attention to the primary principle of masculine domination. It would be difficult to explain away this tolerance by a male 'philogyny', which is unexpected here. How can we understand why this hierarchical and repressive society, which fully intended to bend women's necks beneath the yoke, should accept in its bosom such a subversive cult, even if it found its expression far off in the mountains? The answer must necessarily satisfy that first requirement according to which, in the final analysis, it is men who have to derive benefit from the feminine ritual, as they do from the actions of the wives/mothers in their festivals of Demeter, in order to have fine children and good harvests. Since it is hard to picture them as caring about their wives' nervous indispositions, we must look elsewhere. We must rethink the relationship between the partners in the ritual exchange. There are three partners: man in this plea for protection, the divine as conceived by the human mind, and the language which, by virtue of this conception of the divine, men believe to be effective in expressing that plea. First of all, the divine. Why should we imagine other reasons for the worship of Dionysus than those fundamental ones which prevail for other gods? Like them, he is generous: he distributes growth, youth, vigour, and more specifically, the vine, wine, pleasure and the theatre. There are therefore a 1,000 reasons to propitiate him. But he is also one of the most terrible gods: his speciality is to insinuate himself into the mind of man and to drive him mad. When men witness displays of madness, they think of Dionysiac mania. When Heracles, a prey to monstrous hallucinations, kills his own children, the spectator knows that it is not a matter of the *ritual* madness of the maenads, but that the causes of the hero's dementia are different; he nevertheless clearly recognizes in Heracles' behaviour the behaviour of a bacchant. Now, the same god who punishes by inflicting dementia is a psychotherapist. This is the usual ambivalence of Greek gods: Apollo sends illness and heals, Artemis sends scourges and institutes rites to appease. Whether to obtain good or prevent ill, human communities must above all not forget Dionysus and his august rituals. Look what happened to the daughters of Minyas.

There remains the matter of voice, language and its modulation – in other words, how? How best to propitiate this terrible yet beneficent god; to which form of speech is Dionysus most susceptible? To the voice of women. The linguistic setting in which they used to speak to the god was not radically different from that used by men. It, too, was linked by wandering, chanting (including prayers and dances), sacrifices (peculiar ones) and the eating of meat. Similarly, when it came to organizing the worship of Demeter, the women based their 'institutions' on those of men, gathered in political groupings, held meetings, elected 'presidents' and deliberated like true citizenesses. It is said that they were imitating them, but was there any other way of envisaging social and political life when one lived in a city? Interpreting the Greek feminine as less-than-masculine, one may think that, if there is a feminine pathway leading to a deity, who was himself imagined to be receptive, it expresses less a divergent language – a kind of barbarianism incomprehensible to men – than a different modulation in a common language, less perfect but with a particular colour, scent and tone, and one which the god hears.

To absolve Greek culture of the sin of misogyny by pleading the existence of goddesses and priestesses is to bow to appearances. If we examine the imagery and consider all we know of the unfolding of the rituals, we can see clearly that the priestess is on her own in the midst of a wholly masculine world. Her presence in these circumstances by no means implies that we are dealing with a 'feminine' ritual. The opposite is happening.

Whatever the reason – sometimes given by an aetiological myth – invoked by men for the presence of a female, of a *particular* female, as a major feature of the rite, she is never there on her own account. Rather, she is used by them as an instrument, to serve them on the social as well as on the political plane, and in the end she merely maintains masculine domination.

Religion forms both an accurate and powerful indication of Greek femininity. The means of access to the divine followed by the rituals for Demeter and her daughter and for Dionysus are far more feminine than the rituals for other gods in which girls and women take part; the language is violent, wild and ecstatic, coarse and earthy, sexualized; virgins do not yet know how to express it, only the adult, married woman, mother speaks it well. If for the Greeks there is just one true, single form of the feminine, the feminine with the greatest difference, it is this one.

Intermezzo: Origins of Greek Misogyny

The history of the common opinion about women contains enough invariables to defy time, at least partly. Thus there is little so constant in men's discourse on women as their sad refrain of ill-will towards them. Misoygyny runs throughout Greek history, forming a permanent backdrop although, along the way, it temporarily assumes new colours.

We enter the subject by way of a strange document that goes directly to the heart of the matter. This *Iambic on Women*, the work of Semonides of Amorgos,[14] breaks several records: it is the first text in western literature to have woman as its sole subject, and it is by far the most scathing. From the outset, it is no holds barred: 'In the beginning, the deity created the mind, without taking account of woman.'[15] Ontologically, women are inferior beings; this is fundamental, and will remain so, defining woman as a being *without a mind*, with the immediate result that she is outside humankind. From this metaphysical viewpoint, strictly speaking, we could stop there, if Greek men were concerned with nothing but the human. But they were also interested in their surroundings, in domestic animals for example, and it was from that same perspective that they could take an interest in the women who, like the animals, lived alongside them. The study of women

14. This poem was recopied by a compiler of the fifth century AD, Stobaeus, in his chapter 'On Marriage', 'Women rebuked' section (iv. 22. 193). Almost nothing is known about Semonides, who probably lived in the mid-seventh century BC.

15. M. Trédé has shown that the sense is programmatic: from the outset the woman is thought of as lacking in mind.

could thus be conducted like that of the subjects of systematic zoology, a kind of zootechnics, which at the time was not without interest. It is this type of science, the essence of woman, which Semonides reveals throughout the poem devoted to it: by virtue of her defects, he embodies each 'breed', or rather, each type of woman, in a kind of 'heraldic' animal. To do this he dips deeply into a shared knowledge where nothing needs to be demonstrated, which can be taken as read, a living knowledge which persists simply because men experience a certain relish in hearing this criticism rehashed. Rather like Aesop (to whom he is chronologically close), Semonides brings animals on stage in order to illustrate the particular features of this abject and non-human being, woman.

A BESTIARY TO EXPRESS THE OPPROBRIUM OF WOMEN

We begin with the dirt/disorder group of the foul-smelling woman. This feminine defect is expressed in three animal species. The sow model develops it to extremes, for 'never taking a bath' is indeed almost non-human. The 'haughty mare with the long mane' also belongs to this breed, paradoxically, considering her appearance: lazy and mad about her body, this strumpet does not even take the trouble to throw out her rubbish. Lastly, the wretched weasel-woman can be imagined only enveloped in an indescribable stench.

Laziness can be found in as diametrically opposed behaviours as that of the 'grey she-ass' which has to be beaten and 'does nothing without reluctance', and that of the aristocratic 'long-maned mare', with her tendency to make others do the work. Stupidity is another feminine quality that is much shared. This is the instance of earth-woman, who is so inept that she 'does not realize that it is cold and has not enough sense to move her seat nearer to the fire'. There is also the sea-woman, 'unbearable to look at and be with . . . so wild one cannot approach her', and then the monkey-woman who to her other imperfections adds that of not being aware of her own appearance. And then there is malice, that of the sow-woman, bitch-woman and sea-woman, 'hard and hateful towards everyone, friends or enemies', and also the monkey-woman who 'spends all day wondering how she can do the most ill possible.' The husband, who dreams only of a peaceful life, is at a loss when faced with this aggressive being who '(always) finds something to reproach him with and arms herself for the fray.' Voraciousness, an expected feature of the sow-woman, is also present in others such as the earth-woman and the she-ass-woman who, although beaten, 'eats night and day in the depths of her dwelling, and eats by the hearth', in other words, just as much in the female part of the house as in the part that is open to guests. The champion is the weasel-woman, that 'poor and miserable creature' whose greed drives her to the point of eating raw meat. Eating raw food is feminine (compare p. 25): she is an animal, we keep on being told.

Incontinence in the matter of 'Aphrodite's works' is the trait most shared by the women of the various tribes. Moreover, if the bee-woman is the only species that merits attention, it is 'because she does not like to remain seated in the company of women when they are talking about love.' The horrors that are recounted among the battalion of confirmed nymphomaniacs. They include the she-ass who 'accepts any partner whatever' when making love, and the weasel, whose lustfulness ends by making her partner ill. As for the 'long-maned mare', she excels in using her body as a trap into which the husband falls and remains prisoner (like Hesiod's Pandora, see p. 36). In any case, in the everyday Greek imagination, many of the poem's animal models, like the sow, the bitch and the mare, evoke images – sometimes rich and accurate – connected with an unbridled sexuality (see pp. 98–9).

Fickleness is included in the models of the vixen-woman and the sea-woman. What can be expected of a being who is unable to distinguish between good and evil (vixen-woman; earth-woman), and is therefore incapable of virtue; what of a thief (ass-woman), of one who is eternally dissatisfied, constantly looking to the outside world, 'who wants to hear and know everything, casting avid glances everywhere', like the bitch-woman, nosey and envious? This extrovert nature, allied with laziness (the second linked to the first) and with piggishness, explains why 'whoever lives with a woman . . . will not drive Famine, that hateful companion, terrible deity, from his home in a hurry'. It would be less dreadful if the husband managed to suffer in silence and the matter was hushed up, but that is impossible. His misfortune becomes public simply because of the one who is its cause. Even if he 'keeps his mouth shut', his neighbours learn of it and 'like to see him up to his ears in it', and he becomes the object of general derision. Furthermore, having this animal in his home, how could he live up to the sacred demands of hospitality when 'wherever there is a woman, one cannot even keep a warm welcome for the guest who turns up'? Bearing in mind that woman is obviously uncivil by nature, and that hospitality is reciprocal, it is equally not a good thing to find oneself in the company of a bitch-woman 'at one's host's, for nothing can be done to stop her barking'. All this can best be summed up in Semonides' conclusion: 'Women – the greatest evil Zeus created . . .'

However, all is not lost: one possible, bearable form of the feminine remains – the bee, the only one to enjoy a flattering portrait:

Lucky is the man who has received her, for she alone escapes reproach, his fortune prospers and grows thanks to her and she grows old beside her husband who loves her and whom she loves, after giving him fine and praiseworthy offspring; she stands out among all women and a divine grace surrounds her . . . This kind of woman is the best and wisest which Zeus has granted to men.

What a joy to possess such a 'house', when it thus imitates the hive. An army of workers with, at their head, a worker-in-chief, industrious herself and inspirational. Through her care and her good management of wealth (and thanks to her lack of appetite), she contributes to the prosperity of her husband's 'house'. Then she has this *charis*, the divine gift which attracts attention and renders her lovable. *Charis* is far from negligible, and some 1,000 years later, Plutarch makes a neat comment on its power:

> The union of a man and a woman . . . can only lead to love, if only by the 'grace' (*charis*) that accompanies it. 'Grace' . . . is the word used in antiquity to describe the woman's consent to the man's amorous desire. So it was that Pindar declared that Hera conceived Hephaestus 'without grace'. (Plutarch, *Eroticus* 751c–d)

If this queen bee, endowed with *charis*, who loves her 'king' and gives him fine children, exists, then there may be some advantage in living with women in this world. But the battle is lost beforehand, in no way does the bee upgrade the value of the gender to which she belongs; if we take a closer look at her, she has only a relative value, she is worth less in herself than for what she contributes to her husband; she *gives* endlessly – children (who will look after him), work (which brings riches, building up the fortune) and solicitude (taking care of him when he is old). However, since this 'extreme' example, the bee, is nonetheless a woman, like the rest of the species, she is basically lacking intellect.

Systematic as it appears at first, the *Iambic on Women* is arranged around a small number of key ideas, the main ones to be found in the work of another poet, Hesiod, one or two generations earlier. The tone and subjects are different, however. Hesiod recounts the origin of the world and the gods and, in doing so, the creation of the Greek Eve like that of the mountains or rivers. If Semonides' theme is partly aimed at being amusing, that of this illustrious predecessor is quite different: a brother in misogyny, he is more serious, more sententious.

HESIOD AND PANDORA, THE GREEK EVE

As we read in Hesiod,[16] Pandora is enough to define the 'race of women', since from her came 'the race of women, those female beings. From her came the accursed breed, the tribes of women' (Hesiod, *Theogony* 590–1). The detail is important: women were born of Pandora. It is clear that, just as Adam was not born of a woman, Greek men were not the issue of their ancestral Eve; only women were descended from her. This comes as no surprise for us, who have just read about Semonides: had not the deity, from the start, 'created mind without taking account of woman', with the result that she belonged to a different species from man?[17]

Pandora thus means woman, and she alone. First, her origins: Zeus uses her as a lure in the plan he has formed to take revenge on the deceptions of Prometheus and, further still, on humankind. He has decided to send an evil upon men: not just any evil but, cunning as he is, a 'beautiful evil', a seductive evil. At his request , the gods will take it in turns to manufacture it. Hephaestus models moistened clay and from it fashions 'a pleasant virgin's body' (Semonides' earth-woman); Athena both adorns her and teaches her *illico*, how to weave cloth (hardly has she been born when she has turned her shuttle to good advantage, and that is part of her power of attraction). The breeds of women never stop working, day and night, summer and winter. Aphrodite endows her with the *charis* that makes Semonides' queen bee so attractive, and arouses 'painful desire, the cares that gnaw limbs' (Hesiod, *Works and Days* 60–6); and then she has garlands, spring flowers and gold necklaces. A bride . . . that's the good part, but the ill is still to come, which in divine terms means that Hermes has yet to intervene. He gives a name to this lovely object – she will be Pandora – he adds speech and pours into her 'a shameless mind, a deceitful heart'. It is exactly that which brings Pandora into Zeus' scheme, the 'deep trap, with no way out, destined for humans'. Then, naively, trusting in divine plans and realizations, Epimetheus, the brother of Prometheus, accepts as his wife the *good* – what is on the surface – 'and, when he suffers his misfortune, he understands.' After Pandora has lifted the cover of the box, leaving nothing but hope inside it, 'innumerable sorrows were released among men: the earth and the sea are full of evils! . . . There is no way of escaping Zeus' schemes' (Hesiod, *Works and Days* 101–4).

16. On two occasions: the myth of Pandora's birth is evoked in expected fashion in the *Theogony* (lines 570–612) and also in *Works and Days* (lines 53–105).
17. Following other lines of thinking, Aristotle would later say the same thing (p. 89).

Epiphany of Pandora. The first woman is depicted *inanodos* (emerging from earth), with a diadem and partly veiled, like a nymph; above, an Eros, then Epimetheus, her 'husband', who welcomes her, hammer in hand. Then comes Hermes, who looks at Zeus but goes towards Pandora to breathe the 'deceiving words' into her. Ashmolean Museum, Oxford

WOMAN-AS-SNARE

Primordial woman was *hollow*, and in that empty space lay the trap. Her seductiveness was blindingly obvious. Aphrodite and the deities in her train: Charites,[18] Persuasion and other wearers of garlands and roguish smiles, all carried *charis* and desire to their apogee. Like that of the 'long-maned mare', this desirable body is the trap into which the husband swoons and is swallowed up. We can easily follow this line of thought but, on the other hand, from the cultural distance at which we find ourselves, we see less clearly how the absence of know-how in the textile field is a handicap to the attractions of primordial woman. Are we to imagine a symbolic and magical construction which likens the fabric woven to the net cast by the woman over the man she covets? Or are we to think that in the archaic

---

18. A group of three feminine divinities, personifying 'grace.'

poets' view of woman the 'economic' element (what she costs, what she brings in) is a determining factor, because having a mediocre weaver for a wife condemns you to wearing only poor-quality garments.

To give an account of how Pandora's snare works, Hesiod too uses the metaphor of the hive but looks on the black side, in a scenario with altered roles. Women are now identified with the drones which, lurking in the depths of the beehive, stuff themselves (compare this with Semonides' sow-woman who 'grows fat') on the wealth produced by others. Who? Those who, 'without respite, bustle around every day until sunset' (Hesiod, *Theogony* 596), those on the outside: men. While they go round about the hive and wear themselves out with toil, the feminine,[19] personified in these drone-parasites, 'stores up in (her) belly the fruit of other people's toil' (Hesiod, *Theogony* 599). The female does not manage to tame the appetite of this disturbing parasitic belly, she lacks the firmness of soul necessary to be able to adjust to 'hateful poverty'. Conversely, that virtue which sits so well on the poor prevades Greek morality, from Bias, one of the mythical Seven Sages, for whom 'the unfortunate is he who cannot endure misfortune' (Diogenes Laertius i. 5), up to the classical era, when it was considered an honour for the wife to 'bear adversity'. For the Hesiodic wife, 'nothing but plenty' will do.

It is from within that the trap shows itself to be most effective. Once in place, the woman 'devours the "house"' (Hesiod, *Works and Days* 704) in the heart of which she is installed. This image of the woman 'always on the look-out for the table' (Hesiod, *Works and Days* 375) (cf. the sow-, she-ass- and earth-woman), the parasite on the 'house', is common in Hesiodic poetry. The creature that the peasant has brought into his home is only after his barn, and the poet adds his maxim: 'He who trusts a woman, trusts thieves' (Hesiod, *Works and Days* 373). Man experiences physically the destructive effect of the insatiable feminine appetite. To live with a woman is to invite in famine, that odious companion, and also to risk one's health in more ways than one. She uses arguments that are impossible to fight against, too easily does he lose the sense of his own interests in the presence of the 'dolled-up rump' of a woman (the mare-woman, Pandora), and moreover she is so eager for intercourse that 'however vigorous he is, he wears himself to a shadow' (Hesiod, *Works and Days* 705). In ancient Greece, as often elsewhere, eating and copulating were all one. Living in the

19. An obviously strange kind of feminine for anyone who knows a little biology: when it comes to the queen, it is hard to find anything more female that she in the hive, whereas the drones are male; only the very interior position of the queen bee perfectly suits the Hesiodic metaphor. The hive will also pose problems for Aristotle (see pp. 78–9).

company of the mouth-woman or vagina-woman, man loses all his peace, then all his substance. For Zeus, the fact of having sent upon men an evil that is *beautiful* completely changes the nature of the punishment, which is not temporary but permanent; the attraction which woman continues to exert in fact guarantees the enduring quality of the trap laid by Zeus. Man will go so far as to love what costs him so much and brings him so many misfortunes.

In order to avoid the 'disastrous anxieties brought by women' and escape the perpetual snare, the solution would be to do without. But that would be quite another story. Of course, he who does not take a wife into his home 'does not go short of bread'. This is a refrain which is taken up by numerous later misogynistic writings: the father says, a daughter eats, a daughter costs; the husband says, a wife eats . . . Daughterless, wifeless, our man is thus better fed and wealthier. But he cannot live by bread alone, he also worries about the future of his possessions. Certainly, 'while he lives', he wants for nothing but 'as soon as he is dead, his assets are shared among the relatives' (Hesiod, *Theogony* 606). And this leads to the disappearance of the capital on which his 'house' is based. The prospect for his lineage is suicidal (with the subsequent concerns: who will take care of his burial?). If he marries, he knows there is little likelihood of winning the bee 'in the lottery of marriage' (Hesiod, *Theogony* 219), 'but even so, all his life he (will see) the bad countering the good'. In the contrary, and most frequent case, he must expect 'to bear in his breast a sorrow that will never leave either his soul or his heart, and his ill (will be) without remedy.' A moral Susarion would later proclaim, 'Fellow-citizens . . . women are an evil; and yet my companions . . . it is impossible to live without that evil; for whether we marry or not, they are still an evil' (Susarion, fr. 1 K–A).[20]

It is but a small step from the Hesiodic Pandora to the animal-women of Semonides. They represent the same overall, common and 'vernacular' idea of the feminine. Regarding women, the case is open and shut: a wink of complicity between men is enough for them to agree in their criticism, like the fourth-century tragic poet Carcinus: 'O Zeus! What good is it to speak ill of women? Is it not enough to say: "She is a woman?"' (Carcinus, *Semele* fr. 3, quoted by Athenaeus xiii. 559). This is all right just between men. The presence of women – above all, wives – compels a certain reserve and only the very tactless 'invited to a wedding feast, will rant on about the female sex' (Theophrastus, *Characters* xii. 6).[21]

20. Compare Socrates' words (see p. 142).
21. Women (wives) were normally excluded from banquets but nevertheless took part in wedding feasts.

GREEK MISOGYNY HAS A FUTURE

Although Semonides was able to borrow from his predecessor, the Pandora episode does not mean that he should be regarded only as a mere reader of Hesiod, or that his catalogue was just a pamphlet that found no resonance in masculine sensibilities. To measure the scope of such a text, we must bear in mind that the poet of that period adapted himself to the feelings of his listeners and, even if it were merely to amuse, the listeners' enjoyment revealed who they were and how they thought. The basis of its success (inferred from the fact that it has come down to us) comes from its violence, those zoological masks behind which lie the biting masculine sarcasms. The ancients' much greater proximity to animals had the result that their actual daily presence around them, combined with the common cultural imagery based on that familiarity, strengthened and revived the animal metaphor and explains its enduring nature.

Looking forward in time for a quick panorama, we find no end of eloquent echoes of these satires. For instance, in the sixth century, Phocylides takes up Semonides:

> The tribes of women have their origin in four creatures; one comes from the bitch, one from the bee, one from the hairy sow, one from the long-maned mare. The last is nimble, swift, a chaser (in both senses), a beauty. The one that comes from the sow is neither bad nor good. The one from the bitch is unsociable and wild. The one that comes from the bee is a good guardian of the 'house' and knows what work means. Pray, dear friend, that you will obtain a desirable union from the lottery of marriage. (Phocylides, fr. 3, *Bergk*)

The same goes for the whole misogynistic tradition of the Athenian fifth century, whether in tragedy, with Euripides to the fore (although Euripides' rapport with women obviously does not allow itself to be encapsulated in a simple definition), or in ancient comedy, with Aristophanes. Talking about the former, how can we sidestep the remark by Hippolytus who, against both women and gods, rejects love at the same time as maturity: 'O Zeus, why did you put those unnatural beings, women, amongst us, an evil that offends the light? If you wanted to perpetuate the human race, you should not have caused us to be born of them' (Euripides, *Hippolytus* 616–19).

Aristophanes deserves a greater hearing here. He is a representative of the common – traditional if you will – misogyny. He is a reactionary in the fullest sense, and even harks back to the shortcomings of the past. Whatever refers to the golden age is all well and good. That was a time of peace, plenty and sensuality. We should pay all the more attention to his discourse when he combines the two themes and makes us hear the voices of women who seem to condescend to the 'traditional' masculine idea of the feminine, when the themselves utter it.

> They squat before their grill pan as of old; carry burdens on their head as of old; celebrate the Thesmophoria as of old; cook their cakes as of old; they make their husbands' lives unbearable as of old; have lovers in their home as of old; buy goodies on the sly as of old; like full-bodied wine as of old; enjoy being poked as of old. (Aristophanes, *The Assembly-Women* 221–8)

Amazonomachy. Another version of the feminine in Greek imagination: the Amazons, who simultaneously correspond to the purest feminine archetype and its exact opposite. Here, on the left, the superman Heracles is winning against Andromache (armed as a hoplite). The black masculine bodies contrast with the Amazons' white bodies. Courtesy of Museum of Fine Arts, Boston. Reproduced with permission. © Museum of Fine Arts, Boston. All rights reserved

The woman as devourer of man and of riches inhabits masculine fantasies for a long time. In Christian times, Palladas of Alexandria bears witness to the vitality of topics encountered in Semonides and Hesiod: 'Woman is the wrath of Zeus; she was given to us in place of fire, a fateful exchange. For she burns man up with cares, she consumes him, she changes his youth into premature old age . . .' And again: 'Would that neither woman nor fire had appeared! At least fire can be swiftly put out; but woman is an inextinguishable fire, full of heat, who is always alight' (*Palatine Anthology* ix. 165 and 167).

We must call a halt to this anthology, the common fount of reproach and hackneyed defects bearing witness to the lasting nature of a conventional feminine which provides a stock of crude imagery fundamentally arranged along three lines. First, a key word, intemperance. Those who have no self-control are those who 'give themselves up excessively to sexual pleasures and the enjoyment of food,' says Aristotle (*Problemata* xxviii. 28. 7). Woman is a belly, starving for food and sex, which swells as others grow thin. Everything that surrounds her dwindles as she grows fat. Secondly, there is this evidence: woman is incapable of virtue (what do you expect, she has no mind), in other words, she has no resolution, no constancy, no perserverance, no courage, no love of beauty, and that makes her malicious. When she should not even dare to show herself (Pericles: the glory of women lies in the fact that they are not spoken about), she is still always heard and seen too much. Lastly, there is a concern that appears in Hesiod: her ambiguous and dangerous relationship with impurity is to be feared, it is dangerous 'to wash in water in which woman has bathed' (Hesiod, *Works and Days* 753–4). This fear is of a religious nature. Greek misogyny and its various avatars will continue to borrow from the phantasms born of masculine fears set against a backdrop of zoological images.

THE DONKEY KICKS OUT

'Swill-bag! Always stuffing yourself!', 'Couldn't care less, could you', clumsy, 'lazy beyond belief', wasteful, spends her time snoring so that one wonders how 'she does not tire her ribs out with sleeping' (Herodas, *Mimes* v). Who are they talking about? Women, of course. But *who* is talking? Women, female friends who find with satisfaction that they are in complete agreement, and bewail their sad fate – having to 'submit to the same yoke'. These are no longer the words of men about women, but the words of women about female slaves. These are portraits of their slaves by their mistresses, in the realistic playlets of the third century. And the pathetic clichés of misogyny are taken up by women themselves towards their servants. Free women rebuke slave women for the same stupidity – 'why are you looking

at me with your eyes out on stalks?' – the same idleness, the same piggishness, constantly threatening them with blows. It is true that there is another
even lower rung on the ladder, true that she can exercise her authority, even
if it is in the name of the higher authority of her husband . . .

Demeter and her daughter. The model mother-daughter pair – the intimacy of their relationship can be seen in the relaxed attitude of their bodies and their proximity (the mother's
left arm over her daughter's shoulders). [Votive relief in marble. Demeter and Persephone or
Kore – Acropolis Museum n° 1348 (*Pandora*, no. 84). 410/00.]

CHAPTER 2

Women of the epics

In spite of all the problems that raise their heads at the mention of the name, how can one escape Homer – source, origin, first witness? We have some 27,000 lines from which to set out in search of the first Greek women, finding a few heroines and many who are anonymous and silent. There are no 'lives' here, only silhouettes.

To talk of women in their entirety, the poets needed to contrast or bracket together only two conditions: that of daughter and that of wife. In hard-pressed Troy when anxiety over the fate of the men fighting brought the women to the Scaean gates: 'around [Hector], there came running wives (*alochoi*) and daughters (*thygatres*) of the Trojans [who] came to question him about their sons or brothers, their relatives, their husbands' (*Iliad* vi. 238–40).

So succinct when it came to women, Homer thus embraces at one stroke everything of importance in Trojan womanhood (men's daughters, sisters, mothers and wives).[1] Daughters and wives, because marriage divides this troubled breed into two, giving them two identities. The Greek feminine, as we shall frequently note, is almost as much a matter of age as of sex, and that is what modulates its relationship with man. But beyond this simple contrast between the married and unmarried feminine, the language of the poets, if we read carefully, reveals other unknown conditions of the feminine. We therefore have to pay careful attention to the words, the ones used to designate these girls, offspring, virgins, children, young wives, mothers, widows . . . all these women. Their words are not ours, nor entirely those which the Greek language continues to use. They are also words which are difficult because they refer to types of status that do not easily fit into our own present-day categories. But I shall not continue this discussion in the

---

1. Excluding, for instance, the non-free such as 'the women whose work is faultless.'

abstract, and in order to follow, even hesitantly, the Greek concept of the feminine in the epic, we shall take the heroines themselves as our guides, from *Iliad* to *Odyssey*, from model to model, following Briseis and Chryseis, then Nausicaa and lastly Penelope.

Women of the Iliad*: Briseis and Chryseis*

To enter the *Iliad* is to step into a quarrel; to follow the rise and be present at the breaking-point of Achilles' anger against a flagrant injustice towards him by king Agamemnon. The subject of the row is the possession of two women, one per hero – Briseis and Chryseis – an affair about women, in which one woman reflects the image of the other.[2]

LET US LISTEN TO THEIR NAMES . . .

To begin with, there are two fathers who are brothers and priests of Apollo: Briseus at Lyrnessus in the Troad, a town captured and sacked by Achilles, and Chryses at Chrysa in the Troad, a town captured and sacked by Agamemnon. Each has a daughter: the first, Hippodamia, whom the *Iliad* calls *Briseis*, and whom her father had given in marriage to Mynes, killed by Achilles at Lyrnessus in the Troad; the second, Astynome, whom the *Iliad* calls *Chryseis*, and whom her father had married probably to Epistrophus, killed by Achilles at Thebes in the Troad. Daughters of two brother-priest-kings, given as wives to two princes of the Troad and thus having changed 'house', they were captured and carried off as booty by two conquering Achaean princes. When we start the *Iliad*, all this is past history, and it becomes more complex before our very eyes. Chryses urges Agamemnon to restore his daughter to him (with the threat of a fearful scourge sent by Apollo). Agamemnon refuses. Then – a normal occurrence[3] – the plague falls on the Greek army camped outside Troy, forcing its leader Agamemnon to agree to hand over Chryseis; he agrees, but threatens Achilles: 'If Phoebus Apollo takes Chryseis from me, . . . in my turn, personally, I will come to your tent and carry off your pretty Briseis' (*Iliad* i. 183–4).

2. I am pleased to acknowledge my debt to the fine research undertaken on the girls in Homer by Stérenn Quéméner (*Oscillation de fille. Les noms de la fille dans la littérature grecque*, dissertation, Rennes, and continued today by her sister Gwenn.
3. The theme of a scourge sent by a deity who has been offended by a human failing is common in Greek myth.

Here is the insult, the spark that kindles Achilles' resentment and prompts him to abandon a struggle (the war against the Trojans) where his courage will be sorely missed. In this story, there is nothing to choose between the two women when the warriors are assessing them. And the mirror continues to throw back its reflection: the position they occupy, their beauty ('lovely cheeks'), the place where they live (the tent, the 'barracks' of the soldiers' leaders) and the role of 'warrior's relaxation' that they play for those leaders, all these elements are identical. Two cousins, so alike that, probably for that reason, post-Homeric tradition would enjoy distinguishing between them by making Chryseis a small, slender blonde, and Briseis a tall, elegant, white-skinned brunette, with shining eyes.

How does the narrator (and the narrator putting words in the warriors' mouths) describe these very similar girls? Their name and their condition? The subject is as complicated as can be, and so much the better. Here we have two girls who, to start with, in ordinary everyday fashion bear a 'true' Greek name, meaningful and capable of being 'dismantled.' The first is called Astynome 'the law of the town', the second, Hippodamia 'the tamed mare'.[4] But in the *Iliad* they have apparently changed them without our being told why, for they are no longer called by these names. Moreover, in their case, it is not a question of what normally changes women's identity, in other words, marriage.[5] This peculiar loss of their names will help us to a better understanding of the nature of the transition from girls to women (and inversely) in their story. The new names date from the moment when their respective husbands were killed, and a new man carried out the brutal capture of their body, before the curtain rises on the wrath of Achilles. The warriors never say Astynome or Hippodamia, the wives of certain defunct husbands, but Briseis and Chryseis, such strangely parallel words, phonetically and semantically, that it is hard to see this resemblance merely as chance.

Their names are resonant with meaning. First we discover a connection with their places or origin: there is a definite relationship between Chrysa (the town where Chryses is a priest of Apollo), Chryses and Chryseis, who is She-who-comes-from-Chrysa; as for Briseis, she comes from Brisa, on the nearby isle of Lesbos. So one way of interpreting these names is to translate them as feminine ethnics:[6] the Briseian woman, the Chryseian woman. The connection with the father is obvious: Briseis is derived from Briseus, is his daughter, and equally Chryseis is derived from, is the

4. On this name and type of name, see p. 61.
5. Marriage changes only the second part of the name, turning a daughter-of into a wife-of.
6. In Greek onomastics, 'ethnic' is an adjectival form used to designate both the place of origin of an individual and his political community: it may be a city or a people.

daughter of Chryses. Thus, Briseis and Chryseis sound like feminine adjectives formed from their fathers' names, and to translate Briseis as something like the Briseian Woman would give a correct idea of the result produced. To understand these girl-women's names, the idea of origin, of belonging, is predominant; in this way of talking about the feminine, lineage and home town go together. Lastly there is the root of each name and its meaning. Chrysa, Chryses, Chryseis – it is gold; Chryseis is the Golden Girl, which may be taken as a physical attribute: Chryseis is a blonde. However, as in Aphrodite's traditional epithet, 'Golden Aphrodite', the term 'golden' has many meanings: on the one hand, blondness and, on the other, gold with the erotic charge the Greeks connect with it, and then the idea of wealth. Briseus and Briseis come from *britho*, a verb used to express something that is weighty, is strong in its weight and, especially, is laden with fruits, with riches. The two girls are treasures.

IN SEARCH OF DEFINITIONS: GIRLS' NAMES

To identify Briseis and Chryseis, the narrator and warriors do not use only their names; they have at their disposal the fluid Greek categories of the feminine. This vocabulary is rich and ambiguous and, to try to obtain a clear picture, we must come back to their complex destinies which the narrator, involved in his real subject of the quarrel between the leaders, whittles down severely. They were (1) both daughters and virgins in their father's home, with one name; (2) having been given to a man, they were stripped of their fathers' names and assumed that of their husband; (3) after an indeterminate time (were they mothers?), they simultaneously found themselves widows, and violence placed them in the hands of men who could henceforward dispose of them as they wished. Despite this common history, the text does not employ the same categories to refer to their condition, and in these differences the reader manages to glimpse elements which may give a clearer view.

Greek thinking and language have many ways of describing, on the one hand, the feminine in relation to the man, and the various ages of the feminine; and on the other hand, the feminine in relation to the 'overall' feminine. As a result, the bard seeking to describe Chryseis and Briseis can delve into a rich storehouse of images. But it should be no surprise if the imagery does not completely match the summary of their story I have just given, or if this vocabulary does not convey *for us* clearly defined situations. Nor a surprise that one and the same heroine, Chryseis, is just as often called *pais*, 'child', as *thygater*, 'daughter' (as in 'daughter-of-'), or *koure*. As for Briseis, who is so close, it should be no surprise that she is twice called *alochos*, 'wife', twice *gyne*, 'woman', therefore adult, but conversely, seventeen times called *koure*. *Koure*? This is the Homeric way of saying what classical Greek would call *kore*, a word which dictionaries translate as 'girl' and 'maiden' (Liddell – Scott). If, therefore, Briseis, having been married, widowed and then taken prisoner, and thus a woman being handed between men, appears at the same time as a maiden, a *koure*, what *is* a Homeric girl?

Seeing the two cousins chosen by heroes such as Achilles and Agamemnon to come and live in their camp, the warriors, their masters' companions, must have regarded them only as two beauties who were most suitable to enliven a bed. And they were not the only ones: 'Thersites says to Agamemnon: Your tents are full of bronze, there are many choice women in your tents whom we Achaeans have given you, because you are the first among us all' (*Iliad* ii. 225–9).

It is in this context that the soothsayer Calchas describes Chryseis as *helikopis koure*, 'a bright-eyed virgin'. It is always rather pedantic to pick up a translator over a detail, but here we do so for a clearer understanding: for either Mazon in the Budé edition renders *koure* as 'virgin' to 'sound antique', or the word means what it says, and assuredly neither Briseis nor Chryseis is a virgin. They *were* at the time when their fathers gave them in marriage to their husbands but, in this instance, neither one plays the role of a virgin. Violence has allowed men possession of their sex, and that possession has the same value as if there had been a purchase; possession, obedience, enjoyment, is what Agamemnon clearly states about his bed and Chryseis: she must come running when he calls her (*Iliad* i. 29–31). Too carelessly taking the *koure* of Homeric language for a classical *kore*, which in effect designates an unmarried girl or virgin or both, is to miss an important part of the meaning of the word and its complexity. The *kourai* Chryseis and Briseis are sexual, amiable and attractive.

CHRYSEIS: CHILD AND DAUGHTER-OF-HER-FATHER

Briseis is her father's daughter, not only through her name, the Briseian, but also because she is very generally known as the *koure Briseos*, 'Briseus' daughter', an expression simultaneously combining the qualification of a sex, the definition of youth and the indispensable accuracy of lineage. As for Chryseis, one might say that she is simply a daughter. That is how the soothsayer describes her when he warns the Greeks that the god will not stop the scourge: until the 'bright-eyed *koure* is restored to her loving father' (*Iliad* i. 98). For her the gap is greatest between her 'social' status, her sexual role of prisoner-concubine, and the tender words used by the warriors and narrator to speak of her.

While it is never the case for Briseis, it seems strange to see a warlord's concubine described three times by the word *pais*, 'child.'[7] *Pais* indicates the closeness to the father (there is no mother here), but less to define kinship than to suggest a bond of affection. Take Troy and go home peaceably, says Chryses to the Achaeans, but above all, give me back 'my *beloved* child [*pais*]' (*Iliad* i. 20). In the scene where Chryseis is restored to her father by Agamemnon, it is not surprising to see Chryses receive his 'beloved child' with joy, but it is more revealing to hear a third party, Odysseus, describe her in the same way; this 'child' is nevertheless supposed to have come from Agamemnon's bed (*Iliad* i. 443–7). *Pais*, here, is thus less to do with age than sentiment. Rather like a father who continues to give his daughter (even when she is a widow) a name that speaks of their intimate relationship or, at least, the memory of the closeness of her early childhood.

The other word for Chryseis is *thygater*, 'daughter-of'. If Chryseis is one of the rare feminine 'children' in the *Iliad*, there is, by contrast, no lack of 'daughters', *thygatres*, and they are there for reasons that are mainly to do with the men, the heroes. The Homeric hero is made to oscillate between two opposites, that of a frenzied, paranoid individualism and that of his ties – his class and his 'house'. His strongest attachments are to his relatives. And here we have a whole world: with kinship, we enter a true system of symbols, described in a language with primordial significance. Assuredly, heroes can fairly often be born of a man alone: Glaucus, at the end of his confrontation with Diomedes, sums up his genealogy like this: 'In my case, Hippolochus brought me into the world' (*Iliad* vi. 206). But J. Redfield is right to insist on another unexpected facet: 'The hero (of the epic) is also born of a woman', and to emphasize that even in Homer one finds 'the idea that the innate qualities of an individual constitute a *maternal* heritage.'[8] Thus, the many *thygatres* in the *Iliad* are explained by the necessity for men to mention women *as well* when speaking of kinship. All these 'genealogical' girls are daughters-of-a-father, from the lowliest to the goddesses, even to the point where the latter are rarely designated otherwise: Thetis is commonly 'the *thygater* of the Old Man of the Sea', Aphrodite, Athena and the Muses are *thygatres* of Zeus; Hera is the *thygater* of Cronus. Reading this list, it is clear that the fact of being a divine *thygater* does not imply a unique sexual status. Neither Athena, nor the Muses, nor Hera – virgin, nymphs and wife – are on the same plane,

---

7. Out of dozens of occurences, *pais* is used only six times deliberately to designate girls (all the other uses are for both sexes or, rather, for the masculine alone).

8. J. M. Redfield (1975), *Nature and Culture in the Iliad. The Tragedy of Hector*, Chicago, p. 119.

from this point of view. Nor for mortals does the quality of *thygater* imply an exact sexual status. But it is precisely among the variations surrounding the caesura of marriage that the *thygater* is best defined.

In the pre-marriage period, the *Iliad* uses *thygater* most often in the plural; the *thygatres* of the *Iliad* define a collective group. All the Trojan women, as we have seen, are 'daughters and wives': *thygatres* and *alochoi*, that is, mothers and their daughters. When does one become one of the *thygatres*? At puberty perhaps. But this vagueness, like the plural, stops when marriage supervenes. Then, the *thygater* becomes an individual and turns into a *nymphe* in the singular. The path we will follow with Nausicaa will confirm it, the girl thus placed in her husband's possession will travel 'showered with gifts' to the house of her future spouse. The career of the *thygater*-wife should stop there, but her necessary presence in family trees means that she is 'extended' by childbearing and beyond; that is why we see the heroes, if not boasting about, at least revealing *thygatres* among their ancestors.

FROM GIRL TO WOMAN, FROM MARRIAGE TO DEATH

Two words are applied exclusively to Briseis: wife and woman. Wife. The first time it is used is to speak of her future: Patroclus promises her that she will marry Achilles. The second time, Achilles himself says that before Agamemnon took her from him, she had been his bedfellow and he had cherished her, since 'Every good and sensible man loves his *alochos* and takes care of her, as I loved mine with all my heart, although she had been won by the spear' (*Iliad* ix. 336). We will skip the confirmation that man gains possession of the woman's person by violence as well as by matrimonial transaction,[9] to point out here the first appearance of love. A man can therefore love (and perhaps love above all) a woman other than the one given to him in marriage by her father. Why, despite their quasi-identical situation, does Chryseis remain the *koure*-of-her-father much more than Briseis? Why, unlike Chryseis, do men reserve for Briseis terms that relate to the adult feminine?

From the very start of this examination of the Homeric vocabulary of the feminine, we have heard nothing but the words of men; never has either of the two cousins expressed herself, though we always hope that one or the other will break this feminine silence. It happens once only, and that is when we hear the voice of the *koure*-of-Briseus at the moment when the

9. As of any other body. Defeat makes everybody someone possessed by the victor, in other words, a slave.

Briseis. Without the two inscriptions which tell us their names, Achilles, on the other side, and Briseis, a flower in her hand, how would we know who they are? © British Museum

narrator slips in one of the two uses of the word *gyne*, woman. Patroclus is dead, his corpse lies in Achilles' camp. The Achaean leaders are reconciled and Agamemnon 'intends to make honourable amends and offer a vast ransom (to Achilles)'. The ransom certainly is vast, and the only transaction with which it could be compared would be the dowry of a precious *thygater*, those riches showered on the daughter when her father sends her to another home. To settle it, from Agamemnon's camp are taken 'the promised seven tripods, ten talents of gold, the twenty gleaming bowls, the twelve horses. Without delay, they bring seven skilful women whose work is faultless and, for the eighth, pretty Briseis' (*Iliad* ix. 264ff.) Agamemnon adds an oath to the transaction: no, 'he has never laid a hand on the *koure* of Briseis, neither for his avowed desire for her bed, nor for any other reason. She has remained untouched, always, in his camp' (*Iliad* ix. 274ff.).

With both wealth and virginity (or rather, abstinence, since for this widow it can be nothing else), Briseis here plays the role of a *nymphe*, an 'ordinary' young bride. Thus escorted, Briseis, 'like golden Aphrodite', arrives at Achilles' camp, sees Patroclus' body, falls across him, 'embraces him, utters piercing sobs, while at the same time, with her hands, she rends her bosom, her soft throat and her lovely counternance, and the *women* respond to her tears' (*Iliad* xix. 282–6; 301). Why, suddenly, is Briseis no longer the *koure-of-her-father*, with no further mention of him, and why in that instant does she acquire the maturity that makes her become a woman? It is because she finds herself involved in an event which goes beyond her: the death of the one who is dearest to her master and lover. At that moment a certain behaviour is imposed upon her, a task which is characteristic of the adult woman. She is too young for it to be one of those funerary duties specially reserved for the old female, consisting of pious purificatory attentions to the corpse;[10] her role is to mourn. On the death of the man so dear to her own man, in contrast with the silence which is always expected of her, she is given the duty of proclaiming her grief, if not for him, at least with him. The gesture has a ritual dimension: 'the *women* respond to her tears.' It is evident that the women here are crying out on behalf of the men who can only weep.

> O Patroclus, so dear to the heart of the wretched creature that I am, I left you alive the day I departed from this tent; and lo, commander of warriors, on the day I return I find you dead! . . . The man to whom my father and my worthy mother had given me I saw before my town, ripped by the piercing bronze, and the three brothers my mother had given me . . . (*Iliad* xix. 287–93)

Briseis also explains her particular attachment to Patroclus:

> The day when swift Achilles had killed my husband . . ., you did not leave me to weep; you assured me that you would make me the wife of the godlike Achilles, that he would take me away on board his boat to Phthia and would celebrate my wedding amidst the Myrmidons. (*Iliad* xix. 295–300)

How quickly these women pass from one man to another. Although she is indebted to Patroclus, this recent widow feels at least some attraction for the status of legitimate wife of a prince of Achilles' rank, even if he has killed her nearest and dearest, and, moreover, a liking for this godlike warrior. And that is how, from Hippodamia the wife, the widow, she becomes, if not the wife, at least the companion of Achilles and even, in later

---

10. The task of the aged woman whom Yvonne Verdier (*Façons de dire et façons de faire*, 1979) called the-woman-who-helps and who, in the Burgundy of yesteryear, attended to the dead as well as acting as midwife, and had her counterpart in ancient Greece.

sources, the mother of Achilles' son, Neoptolemus, while at the same time remaining the *koure*-of- Briseus.

FROM THE *KOURE*-OF-HER-FATHER TO THE DIVINE VIRGIN

Although later accounts reserve a destiny for Chryseis similar to that of Briseis, telling how her father deliberately gives her back to Agamemnon, and how she has Iphigenia and Chryses by him, it is in the *Iliad* that we find the answer to the question: why, unlike Briseis, does Chryseis remain the *koure*-of-her-father? It is because Chryses is still living whereas Briseus is dead. The difference is that, on the one hand, the bond has remained effective despite the violence that has occurred – Chryses acts, with divine assistance, to get his daughter back – but on the other, the death of Briseis' father has made her a sort of free electron, her father living on only in her name, like a coat-of-arms.

It is from this perspective that we can interpret the various ways in which the warriors speak of these women. As has been said, Briseis is far more *koure* than woman or wife, whereas Chryseis is a little *koure*, chiefly *thygater* and *pais*, never *gyne*. It is her father's presence that differentiates Chryseis from Briseis; it is he who makes her *pais* – he loves her – he who, concerned about her future because his authority over her has remained intact despite Agamemnon's bed, makes her *thygater*. Briseis has no active kin and, beyond the misfortunes of war, her name continues to remind everyone of her extraction; people continue to say where she comes from, Brisa, Briseus. As regards the girls, the poets tell us more about where they are from than who they are. The clearest parallel to be found of such a loss of an 'individual' name in favour of one that classifies is, later, that of people whom violence or purchase have caused to fall into slavery: slaves, too, were simultaneously stripped of their name and their freedom.

Athenian law of the classical period would preserve the deep-rooted traces of the exceptional strength in Greek culture of the bond between father and daughter. Even when the marriage was celebrated, the dowry paid to the husband, and when the daughter was living in her husband's 'house' under his guardianship, the father could take her (and the dowry) home again if for any reason whatsoever the daughter and/or father had cause to complain about the husband. This right of *aphaeresis*, as it was known, ended with the birth of the first child (first son?), a birth that definitely bound the wife to her new 'house'. This means that authority over the daughter was not immediately passed over entirely to the son-in-law and that the father retained the fundamental part; in which case, it could be said that his authority was stronger that the husband's, or that unlike the latter's, it remained alive, residual.

To conclude this examination of girls as daughters, the other Homeric *kourai* are the goddesses. One – Athena – will be enough and will serve as a model. In the three expressions which the *Iliad* uses for her, the word describing her is linked to that of her father: she is *thygater* and *tekos*, 'child', 'offspring', with the idea of being begotten, but mainly she is the *koure*-of-Zeus. It is worth recounting the story of her birth, which explains her special relationship with her father. According to Hesiod, Zeus had a wife, *Metis* ('Counsel' personified), by whom he was expecting a child: Athena. However, Zeus was persuaded to beware of the offspring of Metis because, after the birth of Athena, she would have a son who would threaten his sovereignty. Rather than take the risk, Zeus swallowed his wife; but as he digested the mother, he found himself pregnant with Athena. At full term, the latter sprang from the brain of her divine father, already adult and fully armed. And never would this perfect daughter of her father, the *koure*-of-Zeus, twice conceived, have any other form of the Greek feminine than *parthenos*, 'virgin' (a new word from our list, illustrated by the story

The birth of Athena. A subject much favoured by artists: the cephalic, cerebral and virile labour of Zeus, in the presence of astounded deities. Ah! says Athena, to be born of a father alone. © British Museum

of Nausicaa below); nor would she have any other relationship in the world
other than that maintained by a daughter-of-her-father, that is *completely*.
What distinguishes Athena from Zeus' many other offspring, is that she is
the first-born of his first wife. In what other culture could the image of the
daughter born of her father alone be so held up as an example? Leaving
aside the story of the threat to Zeus' sovereignty (a hackneyed theme),
would it be making too free with the sources to see in this myth one of the
common Greek male fantasies: creating children by oneself!

Three centuries later, in the *Eumenides*, Aeschylus centres the action
around a matter linked to the idea of relationships between parents and
their offspring. Whose is the daughter, whose the son? Clytemnestra has
killed her husband Agamemnon on his return from Troy in appalling circumstances. Her son Orestes avenges his father by committing an even
more horrifying murder: he kills his mother, and is thus brought before the
Athenian court of the Areopagus. There is cause for debate, for when it
comes to murderers of their relatives there are two kinds. Clytemnestra was
not accused; she had not caused her own blood to be shed. And Orestes?
When he killed his mother, did he not kill the one who had created him?
Did he have his mother's or his father's blood? Apollo and Athena argued
the case before the court. The former said: 'It is not the mother who produces the one who is called her son; she does no more than nurture the seed
that is sown in her.[11] The procreator is the man who impregnates her'
(Aeschylus, *Eumenides* 658–60). Apollo wants no other proof than his
father Zeus and sister Athena, engendered by Zeus' paternity alone. And
then it is Athena's turn to speak: 'I had no mother to bring me into the
world. So my heart . . . is on the side of the man:[12] without any reserva-
tions, I am for the father' (Aeschylus, *Eumenides* 736–8). Athena's vote is
clear, she 'has no concern for the death of a wife who has slain her husband, the guardian of the household', and sides with Apollo in appealing
for clemency for Orestes, the matricide.

Women of the Odyssey: *Nausicaa,* *the* Parthenos

Odysseus addresses Nausicaa: 'May the gods fulfil all your desires! May
they give you a husband, a 'house', union of hearts, a good gift! There is

---

11. There are other testimonies to feminine passiveness in the Greek concept of generation;
    but there is a contrasting idea which attributes sperm to the woman.
12. The text says precisely 'to the male', i.e. the male principle, which means moreover that
    there is nothing feminine in her.

nothing better or more precious than this, when man and wife live in a home in one accord: it is a great chagrin to the envious, a great joy to friends, and perfect bliss for the couple!' (*Odyssey* vi. 180–5)

Another *koure* is Nausicaa, the princess who lives in the strange, non-violent, neighbourless and utterly virtuous world of the Phaeacians. When the poet leads us there, 'Odysseus the divine, overcome by fatigue and sleep is slumbering' on the shore. Nausicaa comes from the town 'with her *amphipoloi*' to do the laundry for the royal 'house', a task that is assigned to her.

It does not take a moment to get to know Nausicaa, she is so sponta-neous. She is the daughter of the king of the Phaeacians, Alcinous, and his wife, Arete. Alcinous, king and father, and Arete, mistress of the 'house' and mother – each has a role and is a model, like the ideal couple they make. On the death of his older brother, Alcinous married the latter's daughter and 'revered her more than any other was venerated among those who run the 'house' under a husband's rule'. Homer emphasizes the qual-ities of the well-named Arete ('Virtue'): 'She was always held in honour by her children, Alcinous and her people . . . She has so much good sense, . . . nobility!' (*Odyssey* vii. 65–70).

All speak of Nausicaa in the same terms: sometimes *thygater*, occasion-ally *pais*, most often *koure*, and lastly *parthenos*. As with Briseis and Chryseis, none of these names is used without a reason. She is *thygater* only when it is a matter of stating her lineage clearly: she is daughter of her father, but also of her mother. When they introduce her, the narrator and Odysseus make her the offspring of Alcinous. She herself, when speaking of herself, introduces herself to Odysseus as the *thygater* of the king. So much for the genealogy. Like Briseis and Chryseis, she too is often referred to as *koure*. However, and remarkably for the reader who has come from the army camps of the *Iliad*, she is never the *koure*-of-Alcinous; her filial relationship is spec-ified only by *thygater*. True, the situation of Phaeacia – that world outside the world – implies that there is no need to be precise about her origin; where else could she have come from, whose offspring could she be? *Koure* is often associated with an epithet emphasizing her beauty: she is 'the girl with the beautiful eyes'. She is also *pais*, and it is always her father who calls her this, loading the word with the same affectionate connection already noted for the *paides* in the *Iliad*. She is *his* 'child.'

Thygater, koure, pais, all these words serve to indicate Nausicaa's sex, her kinship and the affection that surrounds her, but they are not absolutely specific to her and do not really reveal her age, that is, how her sex is judged in her day. The story we read, the effect she produces on Odysseus and the one she receives in return, and the strange proposal her father will make to this unknown foreigner say it clearly: she is in a tightly circumscribed state, a time that is difficult to live through, the particular social and sexual status of the *koure*, when she has become 'beautiful' and has not yet been taken by a man, that of *parthenos*. Obviously, it is a state which is subject to transformation. For Nausicaa, this pre-nuptial period will not last: 'Your marriage draws near . . ., you will not be a *parthenos* much longer' (*Odyssey* vi. 33–5). 'The noblest Phaeacians' have begun the matrimonial championships, which the aim of winning her, and her marriage appears to be sufficiently imminent for Athena to use this pretext convincingly to urge her to ask her father for permission to go and wash the linen of the 'house' ('you will have to wear your finest garments, and provide your entourage with them'). The narrator invests Nausicaa with an impatience to see the end of this latent pre-marital period, which might become one of guilt; her father is only too aware of it, even though both father and daughter discreetly avoid mentioning Nausicaa's desire to take the plunge.

'BEAUTY' OF THE *PARTHENOS*

Odysseus addresses Alcinous thus:

> Then I beheld your daughter (*thygater*) and her *amphipoloi* playing on the shore, a true goddess in their midst. I entreated her, and her spirit showed a nobility not be expected from someone of her age: for that age is often lacking in reason. (*Odyssey* vii. 290–3)

Nausicaa, young and already 'sensible' and what a beauty. We would perhaps tend to play down the epithets applied to her 'lovely looks', her 'white arms', which are so standard and far removed from our own appreciation. But we would be wrong, because they are what distinguishes the heroines we are allowed to see from the anonymous crowd of other women, the concealed ones. Comparison with the divine is common. These girls are quasi-divine in a superhuman context: for instance, Nausicaa is in the midst of her *amphipoloi*. The comparison lies in the first (certainly clever) words of Odysseus emerging from the bushes: 'You must be Artemis, daughter of the great Zeus: stature, beauty, bearing, it is she!' The *parthenos* in a sudden revelation. At the start of the scene, while the linen dries on the shore, the narrator shows her 'leading the chorus', and then continuous without a break:

> Like Artemis going across the hills . . . delighting in her boars and swift does; around her, the daughters of Zeus the Shield-bearer, the Nymphs

The scene on the beach as viewed in the fifth century BC. A 'looking' game. Athena, visible or not, between Odysseus emerging from the waves (but is supposed to be veiling his naked-ness) and seeing Nausicaa, her legs towards the exterior but looking towards the interior; her *amphipoloi* are already elsewhere. Staatlichhe Antikensammlungen und Glyptothek München

of the fields play; Leto[13] exults, for higher than all the rest can be seen the face of Artemis, easily recognizable though the others are so beauti-ful! Thus she excelled among her *amphipoloi*, the untamed *parthenos*. (*Odyssey* vi. 101–9)

We have come across these *amphipoloi* on several occasions. To get a better idea of the expressiveness of those group scenes – the human as well as its divine version – we must ask ourselves who are these enigmatic women who correspond to the Nymphs in the divine domain. Nausicaa's mother Arete also has *amphipoloi*; and the translator finds it difficult to choose a word that is suitable each time the term appears: in the palace he calls them 'chambermaids' but, depending on the circumstances, they become the queen's 'companions' or even, outside the palace, simply 'women'. The word is plural, the *amphipoloi* form a train of women, and appear most often in the service of the mistress of the house, normally receiving their orders from her (never from men). Their age is in keeping with that of the one they accompany, which would explain the diversity of their occupations. If Arete's *amphipoloi* are *gynai*, 'women', those who

13. The mother of the goddess.

follow Nausicaa are '*kourai* with pretty curls.' In this context, the image of Nausicaa becomes one of a ringleader-mistress-organizer at the centre of a group of girls of the same age; it is the image of a chorus, the fundamental setting for both the celebration of the gods and the education of young females.[14] They can, of course, have other occupations, but the characteristic of their particular cummunity of age and sex, its most specific expression, is the chorus of the *parthenoi*.

No one is surprised that a *parthenos* princess on the verge of marriage is playing ball. Nausicaa is at the head of a chorus who could just as well sing, dance and pray, in the style of Artemis accompanied by the Nymphs, a *parthenos* in the midst of divine *parthenoi*. She occupies a well defined

A feminine chorus. Discovered in the Corycian cave at Delphi, these vestiges of a Boeotian terracotta present eight nymphs in a chorus on a wheel, at the hub of which is the god Pan (at home in such surroundings) as a member of the chorus: a divine image, and a ritual image of the feminine chorus. Archaeological Fund Service, Athens

14. See the fine book on this topic by C. Calame (1977), *Les choeurs de jeunes filles en Grèce archaïque*, Rome: Ateneo, translated as C. Calame (1997), *Choruses of Young Women in Ancient Greece*, Lanham, Rowman and Littlefield.

position, she is their leader, the *choregos*.[15] Like Artemis, Nausicaa is the 'beauty' among the 'beauties', the flower who stands out from the centre of the bouquet. At the centre of the circle formed by all these *parthenoi* with their 'loosened veils', she predominates, even in height (Odysseus:

Torso of Artemis. A young woman walking, wearing boots and a quiver. This is how the famous trunk seen by Odysseus as he emerged from the waves was represented in the Hellenistic era. © Photo RMN – Hervé Lewandowski

15. The man or woman who directs the chorus; by extension, the one who bears the costs of its performance.

'You must be Artemis, daughter of the great Zeus: stature, beauty and bearing, it is she!'). There, Nausicaa is 'beautiful'. The laundry done and spread out on the shore, 'they bathed and rubbed one another with fine oil', then 'all untied their veils to play ball.' The evocative setting charms the imagination of the reader-listener, and dazzles Odysseus, whose appearance in the middle of the game causes her companions to flee, Nausicaa alone 'erect, standing her ground.' Then Odysseus, having taken care to 'veil his manhood' with a 'leafy branch', speaks a couplet in praise of her. Is she a goddess or mortal? 'My eyes have never seen the like, man or woman.' This may seem both conventional and perfunctory. We are often thwarted in our search for the Greek female body, which has nothing at all to do with the prominence, the permanence, even the exhibition, of the male body, that of the warriors and athletes. What glimpse do the poets give of this beauty? Slender ankles, white arms, shining eyes and then her hair ... And one wonders what prompts stirrings in the other's body. With Nausicaa things are different; the image is certainly fleeting but makes its mark. The only comparison that springs to Odysseus' mind to describe this body is an image preserved in his memory, of a sight he had once witnessed on Delos, near the altar of Apollo, and that spectacle was a ... palm-tree. 'I saw such beauty: the seedling of a palm-tree rising skyward.' Not even a full-grown palm-tree, but a seedling, an offshoot of a palm-tree. This is puzzling, even if one notes the fact that the palm-tree is the tree of another *parthenos*, Artemis, and that more than any other it is *orthos*, 'straight'. True, the image can be found elsewhere: Achilles and Telemachus are also (desirable) young shoots. But where does it originate, and what is desirable in a body that resembles the trunk of a palm-tree? Luckily for our understanding, Odysseus says to her: 'As I was then in ecstasy before it, for *never had such a trunk* arisen from the ground, so now, as woman,[16] I look upon you with amazement' (*Odyssey* vi. 167–9).

So, what delights Odysseus is that a woman is a trunk or the trunk is a woman or, rather, a girl-becoming-woman. The palm-tree is straight, vertical, meaning also direct, true. The idea is that of the vigour of this sapling-girl, her élan, her youth, all this grips him.[17] Greek 'beauty' – that of boys as well – has a great deal to do with age. The same botanical vocabulary conveys both age/strength and belonging/separateness, for although the

16. The sole use of *gyne* for Nausicaa, meaning something like 'feminine being.'
17. The palm-tree reappears in an erotico-aesthetic context in the *Song of Songs*, 7, 7: 'How fair and how pleasant art thou, O my love, among delights! Thy stature is like a palm-tree, and thy breasts like clusters of grapes. I said: I will climb the palm-tree, I will grasp its boughs ...'

offshoot presents itself as wonderfully self-sufficient and appears to spring up from the soil, it has nonetheless issued from the same roots as the trunk. Odysseus puts it this way: 'As you must pour joy into their delighted hearts [those of parents and brothers] every time they see this beautiful offspring dance!' (*Odyssey* vi. 155–7). 'Offspring' translates *thalos*, 'young shoot', 'one that blossoms, flourishes.' It is the sexual and biological image of the *parthenos*: the attainment of a certain stage of development, on the point of blossoming, like the girl of that age. Although Nausicaa still belongs to her father's 'house', she also knows she is available; at any rate this is how the spectator understands it. Then the *parthenos* is irresistible, and not everybody controls his libido like Odysseus. How many erotic attempts are there on such young shoots by men, heroes, gods? An etymology has been suggested for *parthenos* giving the origin of the word as the idea of protu-berance, thus the age of the *parthenos* would be when the breasts start to develop. We find the same image in the botanical metaphors for the sexual parts of men and women as the broad bean and the barley grain. For instance, at puberty, breasts, like testicles, are called beans; the clitoris is called a barley grain, a word also used for the glans. In all this, there is the same idea of swelling, of a turgescence that can be rolled between the fingers.

THE TAMING OF THE *PARTHENOS*

The youthful élan and vigour which make up beauty signify an age, that of the *parthenos admes*, an expression repeated twice and meaning the *parthenos* 'with no master'. *Admes*, literally 'untamed', can be equally applied to animals (especially domestic animals like the mare) and, by analogy and metaphor, to humans. Girls, including those who have not yet reached puberty, are often collectively designated by the names of animals, being called 'she-bears', 'fillies', 'heifers' and so on. Their own names are often a reminder of this 'primitive' animal nature: for instance. Briseis was first known as Hippodamia ('tamed mare'). The idea that in the *parthenos* lies hidden a wild animal which has not yet been subjected to the process of civilization corresponds well with the Greeks' conception of feminine evolution. The tamer of the wild female is the husband; it is by taking the *parthenos* into his home as his wife that he civilizes her.

Like all her fellow-candidates for marriage, Nausicaa is going to have to bow her neck, feel on her nape the weight of the hand of the 'lucky mortal whose triumphant gifts will bring (her) to him!' It will be up to him to destroy as best he can, by force or persuasion, any residual incivility or rebelliousness in the *parthenos*, and to make her leave the world of

Polyxena at the fountain. The daughter of Priam and Hecuba has left Troy to fetch water, accompanied by her brother Troilus; her hydria is filling. Outside the 'house' the most terrible perils await the *parthenos*, and here take on the aspect of a famous lover: Achilles in person, who is lurking. © British Museum

childhood, playing ball, dancing and Artemis.[18] The process of taking the wildness out of her is aimed at bringing her to shoulder the responsibilities of her new 'house', adopting the virtues demanded by her new responsibilities while at the same time becoming the bedfellow of a man – in other words, discovering other constraints, those of seduction/love, desire, pleasure: Eros and Aphrodite are not *only* tender. This is what it is like to be tamed, placed 'under the yoke', even if it is said that the chariot of the 'house' should be pulled *together*. Nausicaa seems to have no fear of all this; she wants to be married and is venturesome. Nevertheless, apart from the fact that, as a loving daughter, she obeys her dear father, what does she know of the programme that lies in store for her?

18.   On this aspect, see P. Brulé (1996), 'Des osselets et des tambourins pour Artémis', in *Clio. Le temps des jeunes filles*, no. 4, 11–32.

DAUGHTER OF THE 'HOUSE'
AND A DAUGHTER'S 'HOUSE'

For the *parthenos*, the whole point of living is the wedding; she prepares for it. When it comes to Nausicaa's marriage, let us do as the Phaeacians do, let us talk about it. It is *the* big affair of the royal 'house', of Phaeacia itself. The laundry must be done for this occasion. The matrimonial competition has already begun. Details of this type of rivalry will be seen more clearly when we visit Penelope, suffice it to say here that claimants have already come to display themselves and their riches before Alcinous. Odysseus is well aware of it and, in his praises, envies 'the lucky mortal whose triumphant gifts will take (her) to him!' The winner can only be a man of high rank; Athena has told Nausicaa: 'You will not have long to remain a *parthenos* (everyone is in a hurry!): the noblest men from here, among us Phaeacians who are your kinfolk, are fighting for your hand' (*Odyssey* vi. 33–5).

So everything is going normally, for the moment. For, shattering the best founded conventions, here is the virtuous king, receiving Odysseus (bathed, anointed, perfumed and clothed thanks to the king's daughter) at the palace, and declaring without more ado, 'Ah! if only . . . being who you are, and thinking as I am thinking, you took my child and became my son-in-law, and stayed here, I would offer you a 'house', possessions . . .' (*Odyssey* vii. 310–14). Is Alcinous talking marriage? Why does he not say simply that he is giving Odysseus Nausicaa to have as his wife? Are we to understand that this is a matter of a certain form of union, in which one 'keeps (in one's home) [a man] with the title of son-in-law'? Moreover, what sort of behaviour is this, not to take any account of the matrimonial competition already engaged in by the Phaeacian nobles to gain possession of

Rite of passage of the *nymphe*. A metaphorical image of the nocturnal procession of the *gamos*: the social and religious rite of passage of the partially veiled *nymphe* from her childhood home to that the well-defended house of her husband. The gods are also present: Apollo with his laurel-wreath and Artemis with her bow. Note too the difference in age between the bride and groom. © Photo RMN – Hervé Lewandowski

Nausicaa? Why Odysseus, more than another? And if the proposal concerns the gift of Nausicaa, what about the rest, is it her 'house' that Alcinous is thus offering to Odysseus, and what are the 'possessions' which he is prepared to grant along with her?

Greek marriage is virilocal (the woman comes to live with her husband) and monogamous (he can have only one wife as guardian of the 'house' and mother of legitimate children). Now, when the king makes this proposition, Odysseus already has a real 'house', at home in Ithaca; this 'house' is somewhere else, doubly so in that Phaeacia is outside the world, and Alcinous does not want Nausicaa to go there. Furthermore, Odysseus' bed is occupied; the reader-listener of the *Odyssey* knows it (even if Alcinous is unaware, since Odysseus began the account of his misfortunes only with Calypso); nor could he make Nausicaa his concubine. To enjoy Nausicaa, there must be no violence, as with Achilles and Agamemnon, no purchase – the shipwrecked mariner is out of funds. Alcinous expects nothing from Odysseus, he is giving him everything, his daughter and his riches; and Odysseus would give nothing in return. Quite simply, he is 'handsome and like-minded', he is pleasing to both father and daughter, and is sufficiently glorious for them to try to keep him. The royal and paternal power is such that it can settle Odysseus in lands that would distinguish him from the ordinary (as the sons of Alcinous are settled); if Odysseus accepts, the father keeps his daughter near him and binds his son-in-law to Phaeacia, by granting him his daughter's sex. The matter would take quite another turn if Nausicaa had no brothers: then recourse to a man from elsewhere, who would enter the 'house' of Alcinous, would not be purely a fancy on the father's part, but a burning duty. Every 'house', in fact, must constantly work to secure the coming of an heir/successor.

> Let the wife give her husband, who is committed to the path that leads away from youth, the son he so greatly desires, and may keen affection warm the paternal heart; for nothing is more odious, at the hour of death, than to see our fortune fall into the hands of a strange master, an intruder. (Pindar, *Olympians* x. 86–90)

There is an urgency when there is only a daughter in the 'house'. Odysseus cannot take Nausicaa away to his own home, not only because Penelope is already there, but also because he has not yet bought her from her father. But let us stop ruminating; after hesitating for a time over his reply, Odysseus declines Alcinous' generous offer, and there is no union with Nausicaa. We shall never know what lovely children they might have had; and our retrospective dissatisfaction cannot be altered just because some romantic followers of Homer added that Nausicaa married Telemachus.

Penelope: A One-man Wife

Doubt and ambiguity predominate in the image of the captive-concubine-cousins of the *Iliad*, because of their mobility and a sort of indeterminate quality – moving from child to woman to wife – just as in the case of Nausicaa, who is a *parthenos* 'in transition'. But the emblematic figure of Penelope in the *Odyssey* poses fewer problems of definition. That is what commonsense and the dictionaries tell us repeatedly: 'The wife of Odysseus, whose fidelity to her husband, for whom she waited twenty years while he was at the Trojan War, made her universally famous in the legends and literature of Antiquity.'[19] 'A faithful wife – unmanageable,' said George Brassens; but even if his questionable thoughts hit the right note, Penelope is more than that. She is the *mother* of Telemachus, the *mistress* of her husband's 'house' following his departure for Troy and – is this merely secondary? – a peerless weaver.

Leaving aside all that Homer will add or contradict, Penelope is the daughter of Icarius; and Odysseus is the son of Laertes, king of Ithaca. His

Penelope and Telemachus. Penelope – Homer's model of fidelity, prudence and ingenuity – appears to weaken under the burden of her cares: her son, her possessions and the memory of Odysseus. In the background stands the royal loom on which for ten years she wove by day a shroud for Laertes and then unravelled it by night.

19. P. Grimal (1986), *The Dictionary of Classical Mythology*, trans A. R. Maxwell-Hyslop, Oxford: Blackwell, pp. 354f.

father has handed over to him the monarchy and his 'house', with his home and land: the royal portion, with all the riches that are within the 'house' and on the land. After Homer, it would be said that Odysseus had at first tried to obtain Helen of Sparta from her father Tyndareus, but faced with exceptional competition from powerful rival claimants, he had given up seeking the fair Helen's hand.

THE MATRIMONIAL STAKES

In the *Odyssey*, Odysseus' marriage is well in the past and a few words from Penelope's lips are enough to evoke it (the poets' listeners are well aware of how marriages take place). Two questions arise: why get married; but primarily, how?

The procedure is rather like a contest. Rivalry sets at odds men whose whole aim is to obtain the consent of another man, generally the father of the hoped-for prize, the one who has authority over the girl they want for their 'house' and in their bed. Like the others, Odysseus will have only one woman. By this we must understand one *wife*, since on the one hand, the 'house' of a hero can also contain concubines and female captives (like Agamemnon who, despite having Clytemnestra as his wife, also has Chryseis) and, on the other, the 'external' life of the hero is not necessarily miserable. When the father has chosen the victor of the contest, his daughter will go to share this husband's bed.[20] But if 'houses' give their daughters like this, must not other 'houses' act reciprocally? Thus all these 'houses' described by Homer simultaneously give their daughters to the others and demand some in return. This is an idealistic, theoretical way of looking at things, because there are also daughterless houses which cannot take part in this movement. All the same, this is a far less serious situation than that of a 'house' which lacks a son, because it then becomes imperative to introduce a man – a son-in-law – into it by any means at all, if the line is not to fade away, honours to the dead cease and the 'house' fall to the distaff side, that is die out.[21]

So here we have a vast exchange circuit between 'houses', in which the *thygater* plays a major role, without however constituting the entirety of this flow. The Homeric epic is a world irrigated with presents, where gifts of all kinds travel between all kinds of partners – from the people to the

---

20. Several words indicating 'wife' (*akoites, alochos*) mean no more than sharing a bed with someone.
21. An expression that clearly reveals the despair of 'houses' at being reduced to female heirs only (the distaff as a characteristic attribute). As women were not allowed to own or manage land, how could the 'house' be enabled to continue?

king, from kings to other kings, from men to the gods – and for all kinds of reasons – gratitude, gifts in return, violence, love or self-interest. They are functional gifts, too, because they are instrumental, expected.[22] The aims and means of matrimonial competition are contained in these itinerant riches. With the help of such gifts, those who aspire to the father's daughter can show off their status and exhibit their prosperity, an indication of their rank. Everything is there to be seen and touched. Everything is golden, lush, costly, loaded with potential, whether it is a matter of dwelling, clothing or sustenance, in what the contestant physically brings for the father to assess. Like the other suitors, Odysseus obviously brings transportable riches to display before Icarius' eyes and let him weigh in his hand. What a spectacle to see these 'presents' go in procession before the door of the 'manor', best embodied in the idea of necessarily 'fat' herds of cattle and sheep, in innumerable quantities. All this for the father. Then, for the woman, the aspiring spouse adds 'still dazzling' gifts, to clothe her sumptuously and adorn her magnificently. Once all that has been assessed, as Penelope says: 'the one who offers most . . . will become the husband' (*Odyssey* xvi. 392), the highest bidder sways the father's decision and wins the daughter's 'hand'.

The father falls upon his new possession of 'countless presents', and will add the winner's livestock to his own herds, all in exchange for a single chattel. A sign of her father's rank, the girl is on the way to her new 'house'; she represents a perfect vehicle for displaying the excellence of her 'house' of origin and the value her father attaches to her (like Chryseis, Briseis and Nausicaa, Penelope is the *koure*-of-Icarius); his prestige increases with the value of his daughter. This 'circulating capital' is also useful to the one who sets it in motion.

> Hector and his companions bring the woman with the bright eyes, from sacred Thebes and the external springs of Placia, gentle Andromache, in their boats across the briny seas, with many gold bracelets, purple garments, finery of every colour, innumerable silver goblets and ivories. (Sappho, fr. 44)

Enriched by both her father and her new husband, the girl takes with her from one 'house' to the other the strongest evidence by which the opulence of the 'houses' can be recognized. But why buy a girl? In other words, why marry? For the taker the reply is quite simple: because he wants her in his home, because he loves her and/or because he wants to have children by

---

22. See E. Scheid-Tissinier (1994), *Les usages du don chez Homère. Vocabulaire et pratiques*, Nancy.

her. But for the giver the answer is more difficult: you cannot love your daughter very much if you will pay for her to leave.

BRIDE PRICE: BUYING AND SELLING

So then, women can be given, bought and won, even if only to make them work. Women like Arete's and Nausicaa's *amphipoloi* work hard and, for certain tasks, are irreplaceable. A king may also take them for his bedfellows. One can even assess one's fortune in terms of women. Remember the ransom paid by Agememnon, the 'seven women skilled in faultless work . . . and, for the eighth, the pretty Briseis.'

Matrimonial transactions set in motion a 'transhumance' of wealth – the flocks brought by the suitor, the 'dazzling gifts' of the future husband, garments and jewellery (theoretically for the bride, but as she will live with her husband, these riches are merely for ostentation, hardly have they come out of the coffers than they are put back in them), the 'dazzling gifts' of the father, which form the true 'payback' of the transaction. They legitimize the marriage and the children-to-come, and are the basis of the alliance between the 'houses'. It all counts: both the price paid by the taker to purchase the girl, and the sum added to his daughter by the father to display the value he sets on her and the interest he bears towards the 'house' of his son-in-law. All goes well if each reckons the two transfers are of equal worth. But there may come a time when, for whatever reason, the bond between the woman and her new 'house' must be broken, and the wealth brought by the woman must follow her to her new destiny. That is why Telemachus complains at the idea of having to 'reimburse Icarius' if he sends his mother back to him (*Odyssey* ii. 133).

But, again, why sell one's daughter? The theory of reciprocity springs to mind here, the idea that one must give back, even over and above, if one has received. Of course, the overall view of the way society functioned which emerges from such matrimonial practices presents the picture of a generalized circulation of women and riches, presupposing what economists would call an atomicity of supply and demand, in which each 'house' must participate on pain of seeing the system seize up. I doubt, however, whether this globalizing view was taken by the fathers in Homer's world: the transaction takes place with *this* 'house', *this* father, for *this* daughter, and taking the daughter of a 'house' in no way implied that one was obliged to give one in return. The intensity of the father-daughter relationship (beloved like Chryseis and Nausicaa) suggests that more powerful motives were needed to bring fathers to part with them. Penelope is an adult woman, a wife, possibly even a widow (nothing is known of Odysseus' fate at the time), yet she continues to be called the '*koure*-of-Icarius'. If there is doubt that the father's motivation lies in a contribution to general harmony, where is it to be found?

It is found in the hope of the daughter's offspring, a hope that changes perspectives. These children belong less to the husband than might *a priori* be supposed; Homeric marriage forms a veritable alliance between the two 'houses', and maternal kinship is by no means negligible. But should we not also explore in another direction? Would the father pay (also) to rid himself of a useless sex, mouth, being? It is rather contradictory, but we have seen to what extent Greek misogyny could have early roots. Then, there is virginity. It is dangerous to keep in one's home this time-bomb of a *parthenos* who laments, 'Sweet mother, I can no longer weave this cloth. For I am overcome by desire for a young man because of slender Aphrodite' (Sappho, fr. 102). Does not Nausicaa reproach a *parthenos* friend who, although she has 'father and mother', goes off 'against their will, running around with men, without waiting for the wedding to be celebrated' (*Odyssey* vi. 286–8). There is a translator's euphemism in the French ('courir avec', Berard); the verb says clearly 'making love'. Nausicaa is thinking of innocent *parthenoi*, of herself, of her excursions from the palace to do the washing, of her companions who flee and of her meeting with the ship-wrecked man. It is then that a father intending to marry off his daughter realizes how the urges of a *parthenos* may doom her not to find a suitor.

As regards the man who needs a woman to produce children and look after his 'house', or the one who seeks both to rid *his* 'house' of a useless and dangerous sex and mouth, and at the same time to obtain grandchildren, marriage – which is moreover an alliance between two 'houses' – is above all a masculine market.

WHAT ARE THE 'IMPORTUNATE SUITORS' DOING IN ODYSSEUS' 'HOUSE'?

All is not going well in the 'house' of Odysseus. Everyone has doubts about the master, many believe him dead, but no one knows for certain. Telemachus is still a beardless boy and can neither enter into possession of the 'house' nor replace his father as king – neither inherit nor succeed. However wise Penelope may be, she is only a woman, meaning that she can enjoy neither pre-eminent authority over the people nor personal owner-ship of riches. Meanwhile, the 'bold suitors' invade the court and palace rooms, laying on many banquets which are swallowing up the 'manor's' stores. And the son groans: 'They are all courting my mother and devour-ing my 'house'. She, without rejecting a nuptial bond, which she abhors, does not dare to put an end to it' (*Odyssey* ii. 130–1). But, even taking into account that Telemachus is a minor, what are these aspiring suitors hoping to obtain?

Quite simply, they are casting longing looks on one they consider to be a widow; it is obvious that those who 'are devouring the 'house'' want to go to bed with the mother. But how? By violence? Penelope, who knows her brutal environment, is aware of what dark plans may germinate in their brains and, in front of Antinous, whom she suspects of such designs, exposes their plots: 'Today, without payment, you eat his 'house' [that of Odysseus], pay court to his wife [*gyne*] and want to kill his son!' (*Odyssey* xvi. 431–2). Kill his son? That would be the end of it all: with Telemachus dead, Odysseus' 'house' would be without a potential heir or successor. Penelope would thus find herself merged with this 'house', identified with the riches that go to make it and should remain with it. A 'house' like this, over which a lone woman – even one of Penelope's calibre – is in charge, is in a calamitous condition: it has fallen into the distaff line, a sort of feeble destiny, a feeble impasse. The men of the 'house' and close kin do everything in their power to avert this threat, 'for nothing is more odious to us, when death comes, than to see our fortune fall to a foreign master, an intruder' (Pindar, *Olympians* x. 88–90). What a dying 'house' needs is a man, a son-in-law; so that should some misfortune overcome Telemachus, the faithful Penelope would change character and become a woman seeking a husband, a seductress, for the well-being of the 'house'. And who knows what her thoughts are? The 'bold suitors' would then have 'nothing more to do than bed the widow-queen in order to obtain everything.'

Without violence? In reality, the 'bold suitors' are wagering on two counts: they are furious that they cannot go too far too fast by killing Telemachus; but for a long time they have been playing the other game, the usual customary one of rivals in matters of matrimonial strategy.[23] They send 'countless flocks' back and forth in front of the manor of Ithaca, and proffer riches likely to seduce Telemachus (and his mother) so that, once he attains his majority, he will hand her over to the highest bidder, and she will finally leave with the victor, accompanied by the riches which her son will restore to her. In this scenario Telemachus plays the role of the father of the coveted daughter, since in Greece a son can give his mother in marriage. But two obstacles prevent the contest between the 'importunate suitors' coming to an end: Telemachus' youth and the doubt that hangs over Odysseus' survival. The same conditions, the absence of her natural

23. The tangle of this situation has been unravelled by C. Leduc in 'Comment la donner en mariage?' in P. Schmitt Pantel (ed.) (1991), *Histoire des femmes*, Paris, pp. 259–316; translated as 'Marriage in Ancient Greece', in P. Schmitt Pantel (ed.) (1992), *A History of Women in the West*, Cambridge, MA, pp. 233–94.

guardian, Odysseus, and the difficulty of her potential guardian, Telemachus, make Penelope a woman with a free choice, an extraordinary situation:

> Shall I stay with my son in order to safeguard everything, my posses-sions, my servants and my great and lofty dwelling, respecting my hus-band's bed and the people's good opinion? Or shall I follow one of these Achaeans? (*Odyssey* xix. 525–8)

Telemachus' version is: she can 'stay . . . look after my 'house''; Athena's version is: she can 'if her heart aspires to marriage, go home to her father'. Thank goodness, amid all these vicissitudes, the bond with her father per-sists. She will return to Icarius, and the 'dazzling gifts' which accompanied her when she was given to Odysseus will have to be restored to him. Then, as twenty years earlier, the four-footed riches will parade before Icarius' manor, and the second part of the alternative suggested by Telemachus will be fulfilled: 'My mother? . . . her heart is torn between two desires: to stay or follow the Achaean of her choice' (*Odyssey* xvi. 73–6); here, or at her father's. But why must she leave the 'house'? Because she cannot challenge any of her son's privileges, on his majority, he will inherit and succeed his father.

PENELOPE IN HER 'HOUSE'

Yes, the good Penelope who has waited for Ulysses for such a long time is faithful, but she is also prepared to 'follow an Achaean', a suitor. Athena, the goddess with no husband, deplores women's liking for a new house:

> [to Telemachus] You know what kind of heart lies in a woman's bosom: she wants only to increase the 'house' of the one who marries her; but she has no memories of her first children and the husband of her youth! She does not worry about them . . . (*Odyssey* xv. 20–3)

Is the 'so good' Penelope fickle? Remembering the widows who so quickly become the highly appreciated concubines in the camps of the *Iliad*, are we to conclude that the bards endow women in the epics with a very short memory? It cannot be said that we hear much of Briseis and Chryseis lamenting the fates of their murdered husbands. Could the Penelopes be more attached to marriage than to their husbands? Shame on such nasty thoughts. For the time being, Penelope is content with what is already quite considerable: being a mother, a *despoina*, guardian of the 'house', a respected wife, like Ariste, and 'tuned in' to 'her people'. Odysseus' absence puts her in a special position: it is not 'under the rule of a husband' but on her own that she 'runs the 'house'.' However, in this matter the authority of the man is both pre-eminent and formal; for everyone recognizes that it is up to the wife 'to take care of the home'. When Telemachus throws his tantrum on the subject of authority and reproaches his mother for her public interference, he sends her back to her daily duties: spinning and weaving.

> Go back to your own quarters, return to your tasks, your weaving and your distaff, and order your women to get to work: words are men's affair, and mine first and foremost, for here power lies with me! (*Odyssey* i. 356–9)[24]

The woman carries out her tasks on her own, or with the help of *amphipoloi* (Penelope has some) and the active support of a *tamia*, a stewardess for the 'house' and a nurse for the children. Demeter boasts what she can do for the king of Eleusis, Celeus:

> Gladly I would hold a newborn infant in my arms, and would be a good nurse to him; I would keep an on the 'house', set up the master's bed within well-built apartments, and instruct the women in their work. (*Homeric Hymn to Demeter* (ii) 141–4)

Demeter is well versed in the duties of a wife: the running and economy of the 'house', which includes satisfying the basic needs of its members (close family, more distant relatives and servants), and caring for children. The woman in the epic plays two roles at once: she directs, as regent, controlling the places and people who come under her delegated authority, and she works. Penelope is a model spinner, but chiefly weaver? Of course. But in this she is no different from other heroines: for instance, Hecuba, queen of Troy, weaves a *peplos* (cloak) for the goddess Athena, as Andromache does for her husband; even Helen, whom one might think better endowed for other activities: no one knows better than she how 'to fill her basket, when she spins, with such accomplished work; no one, interweaving the threads with a shuttle ... draws a closer woven cloth from the long strands' (Theocritis xviii. 32–4). An almost divine dexterity and absence of fatigue – these are the distinguishing features of the heroines, for in other respects they resemble the poor ordinary mortals, both free and non-free, who spin and weave and weave and spin as long as they live.

---

24. Compare xxi. 350–3.

GIRLS AND WOMEN IN THE EPICS

In the epic, the same distance separates heroines from ordinary women as the one between Nausicaa and her *amphipoloi*: identity and anonymity. But is it merely a matter of identity? 'Odysseus' world' is not filled only with camps and palaces, life does not consist only of fights between warriors in the fields, and boats lost on the return trip, and gods do not appear out of nowhere to sort out the choices made by humans. The unnoticed world of the *amphipoloi* and, beyond, the shadowy figures of the outcasts also follow social usages; what can they have in common with those usages which govern the world of the heroines? To ask the question is to go from fiction to reality, and as we lack any documentation for this period except that of the epic tradition, nothing enables us to either affirm or deny it. It is a notorious crux for historians not to be able to reply to the question: does the society described in the Homeric poems give a picture of a real society? For the Greeks themselves, the reply is unambigous: Homer tells the truth about the past. Without being dogmatic, the epic text plays a founding role, gives depth to the common past, a geography, a sacrality of practices which stamp with the seal of antiquity what later practices will borrow from them. For us, and in the absence of any real likelihood of archaeological verification, the only possible line of reasoning must proceed by induction. The facts are fairly clear: insofar as we find in later centuries a number of customs, practices, ideas and rules of law that are, if not identical, at least similar, to those of Odysseus' world, we must suppose that it had a reality (without denying its uniqueness or forgetting the 'literary' nature of the source). Thus the feminine element of the Homeric poems presents many aspects and colours which later Greek femininity will illustrate.

Epics refine attitudes too much for life not to appear condensed and shortened; so, leaving the great past of Homer for the classical period, let us put first things first in our quest for Greek women: the body. Setting off in search of this lost continent is to listen to new voices, those of specialists: biologists and doctors who are learned in regard to the qualities and differences of the sexes. But will it really be the body which speaks?

CHAPTER 3

On the body and sexuality

What a change of tone and era: to pass from Homer to Aristotle the biologist and the doctors who are known as the Hippocratics means leaping a gap of three or four centuries and encountering vastly different views on the world. Different, but certainly not as opposite as modern acceptance of terms like biology and medicine might lead one to suppose. If the quest for the rational defines Greek biology and medicine as ventures in the 'scientification' of knowledge, what we read remains most often 'unscientific.' We see in operation less a reflection delving deeply into observations *in vivo*, with a gradual adaptation of thought to reality, than just one more product of the imagination; in this instance, the masculine working from an *a priori* conception of the feminine. Reading Hippocrates or Aristotle, we realize the extraordinary distance that separates them from the customary picture of Greece, homeland of Reason, and the devastating effects of their ideological interpretation of the body. Which, *a contrario*, justifies the interest this literature holds for the historian of different types of society.

> Nature created a strong sex and a weak sex so that in the latter the spirit of watchfulness is born out of fear, and in the former the spirit of hardiness out of courage, so that the one contributes things from outside and the other ensures the safety of those inside; and in the division of labour, one is fitted for the sedentary life and lacks the strength for life outside, while the other, less suited for tranquility, flourishes in activity. (Ps-Aristotle, *Oeconomica*. i. 3. 4. 1,334a)

The world is polarized, and here the forces that organize it are those of sex and gender. From the outset, here is the application of their principal procedure for an ordered interpretation of the cosmos. 'Nature', 'divinity', 'custom', and 'law' command human beings 'to try to accomplish . . . [their] respective duties to the best of their ability.' Evoking 'nature' is to pronounce obvious truths, such as this: pondering 'Why is it more serious to kill a woman than a man?', Aristotle comments, 'Yet the male sex is better "by nature" than the female sex' (*Problemata* xxix. 11). There is general accord between providence and the rules that men establish for themselves. 'Custom declares beneficial those occupations for which the deity has endowed each person with the most natural abilities.' Like Hierocles, everyone finds himself in this sexual division of the world. 'It is the man's job to see to the fields, the market, errands in the town; the woman's to work with wool, make bread and carry out the tasks of the 'house' (Ps-Aristotle, *Oeconomica* i. 3. 4).'

In the classical era, commonsense, well represented by Xenophon in his *Oeconomicus* (see Chapter 5), contrasts men and women in their social functions, in absolute terms. Their fundamental dissimilarity is first expressed spatially: one occupies the interior, the other the exterior.

Let the 'Specialists' have their say

By the classical period the Greeks had long been looking at the world in this 'polarized' fashion and the contrast between the sexes played a dynamic role in this interpretative model.[1] But the thickest dossier belongs to the practitioners and theorists of biology in the fifth and fourth centuries. Two great collections of texts give a substantial amount of space to females, women and femininity. First, there is a corpus of treatises collected under the name of Hippocrates (in fact, by various doctors), in which, without going as far as speaking of a uniform doctrine, commonly held ideas have an important part. Women, their biology and ailments are well to the fore, with some dozen treatises out of sixty dealing with gynaecology. The other group is formed by the biological works of Aristotle who, although not himself a doctor like his father, is particularly versed in biology and does not hesitate to use comparisons drawn from the vegetable and animal kingdom to justify his reasoning in areas that are sometimes as far removed as political science, morals or metaphysics.[2]

---

1. This is the interpretative path I proposed following in *Les Grecs et leur monde* (1998), a little work on the interpretation of Greek texts.
2. The texts used throughout this chapter belong to Artistotle's biological treatises: (*Generation of Animals* and *History of Animals* and the Hippocratic corpus in the translation edition of Émile Littré, or in the Budé edition.

FEMALES AND MALES

Let us begin with Aristotle and his zoological treatises. In his search for woman, the question of the place of animals in relation to humans crops up immediately. Rightly or wrongly, we attribute specific characteristics to the human race, and it is doubtful if we would resort to a manual on beekeeping to study the difference between genders in humankind. In very modern fashion, not for a moment does Aristotle doubt the unity of the living world: from animals to men there is no break of continuity, and if the human race merits special treatment it is not because of any difference in nature, only in the degree of intensity of this or that quality. Man, being the most accomplished of animals ('the only one in which the natural parts are arranged according to natural order'), provides the yardstick for the world. It follows that, for the historian trying to decode the sexual contrasts that structure humans, it is not only legitimate but often more enlightening to examine first those that show up within the animal world. Moreover, in the Greek idea of the sexes (human and animal), the respective position of the two genders in relation to animals is different; woman even reaches the animal superlative: she is *the* female of females. But if human and animal interact on the feminine side, the masculine side is kept well apart. The gap that separates the woman from the masculine model brings her closer to the other antonyms of the Greek man: the young, the old, slaves and Barbarians . . . The behaviour of females as recounted in zoological treatises has its roots in biological and psychological commonplaces about women, and thanks to them we shall have a better understanding of the material in the misogynistic bestiary in the style of Semonides in which the qualities of females serve as a blazon for the 'breeds' of women.

'Even among the molluscs, when one spears the cuttlefish with a trident, the male comes to the aid of the female, whereas the female flees when the male is hit' (Aristotle, *History of Animals* ix. 1 608b). Hardly have we entered the field of the sexing of animals, when polarization crops up again. Courage is male and, so still more, masculine. The verification? There is only one word, *andreios*, to render both 'courageous' and 'virile'. There is a fine example of this variable distance between the two human genders and the animals: with regard to courage, even the best of women will never attain anything more than masculine cowardice. Everyone knows that each gender owes its specific features to its own *physis* ('nature'). There is a close coherence between a given physical make-up – flesh, humours and so on, specific to each sex – and its moral qualities. Aristotle develops the idea that the contrast between the free man and the slave is at the same time the consequence of, and reveals itself by, a different *physis*, which makes the body of the former differ significantly from that of the latter:

Nature itself is anxious to mark the difference between the bodies of free men and those of slaves: the latter are strong for the tasks necessary [to their condition], the others, of erect stature, and unfitted for such activities [productive tasks], but suited to political life. (Aristotle, *Politics*, i. 5. 1,254b, 25)

Nature intends to mark clear differences: there are bodies which are bent (for hard work) and pale (for working in workshops) – those of slaves – and there are erect and suntanned bodies, to speak in public, give orders, live in the open air – those of citizens. We are made to do what we do, to be what we are. These perspectives on the servile body in its contrast to the free body throw light on the concept of the feminine body: the very substance of these two bodies, as well as their appearance – softness and pallor – are comparable, because the two natures – feminine and servile – are close. The effect of this kind of interpretation of the woman-man scale of differentiation does not end there: the strict and absolute distinction between the genders in Greek countries is in contrast to a lack of differentiation among the Barbarians.

[There] the woman and the slave are on the same level: the reason is that among them there are no natural leaders whom nature has destined to command, and that conjugal union there is that of a male slave with a female slave. (*Politics* i. 2. 1,252b, 5)

Now, there is nothing gratuitous in what nature (or the deity) does; everything is conceived to suit functions, 'nature always seeks a purpose.' Functionalism reigns supreme. So anatomy adapts to activities but, conversely, activities match dispositions. If males have harder bones, it is because 'endowed with a more violent temperament . . . [they] have to indulge in war.' Forms and functions are therefore predetermined: if stags, boars and cocks have antlers, extra teeth and spurs, it is because 'the male is stronger and more courageous' and the female more timid (Aristotle, *Parts of Animals* ii. 9. 655a).

SEXES BACK TO FRONT

Generally, everything is for the best in this sexual harmony of the world, everything seems to fit neatly in place in this picture of the genders, their defects and virtues, and learned taxonomists check that the files are in the drawers and the drawers are working . . . But it can happen that this fine overall concept presents serious difficulties to the learned scholar (like Aristotle). Indeed, if females are, as they should be, fearful and cowardly, what is to be made of the hen-partridge, which is prepared to sacrifice herself for her chicks, or the she-bear, which 'seems more courageous than the male'? Never mind – if observation of reality does not quite match what the general schema presupposes, it is always ideology, not reality, that wins in the end. We shall get a better idea of the constraint exerted by the *a priori* conception of the sexes if we examine a few exceptions. Among the inversions, there are the really paradoxical cases of the she-bear and she-leopard, which are said to be more valiant than the males (Aristotle, *History of Animals* ix. 1. 608a, 33), for this abnormal 'virility' of the female is found among species which the Greek bestiary sets precisely among the most feminine. The she-bear is an extreme example of maternity: boasting four teats, she enjoys the extraordinary faculty of being able gradually to shape the body of her cub with her tongue in order to endow it by stages with the morphology of its species. Like the bitch, she too is capable of fighting to defend her young: in other words, she can change into a male. The she-leopard is at the other extreme of the feminine: her exploits are those of seductress (a kind of mare-woman). Thus we have two females, with two superlative qualities appearing at two extremes of the spectrum, but which have in common that they enhance their own female character, coming out on top, so to speak. This is the logic of 'an upside-down world',[3] where it is 'normal' for courage to be acknowledged in females.

Aristotle admits it: 'The generation of bees poses many problems' (*History of Animals* v. 21. 553a). To begin with, it is a purely biological question. Considering that it is impossible for bees to reproduce without copulation, where does the brood come from? Is it born of another creature? Does it come from outside? These are desperate hypotheses. Might the difficulty arise from a false interpretation of the sexes of the hive's inhabitants? Of the queen, the drones and the workers, which is male and which is female? Going against what seems obvious to us nowadays, Aristotle maintains, 'it is unlikely that the workers are female and the drones male.' Because 'nature does not endow any female with the weapons for combat; the drones have no sting whereas all the workers have one.' The coexistence of two natures, female and armed, in one and the same being is impossible.[4] Here we have a demonstration by anatomy. The other alternative also presents a problem. 'Nor is the opposite any more likely, that the workers are male and the drones are female' (*History of Animals* v. 21. 553b) because of the social role of the genders; in fact, 'no male is in the habit of caring for the young, but that is precisely what the

3. An expression used in this context by Y. Garlan in a lecture given at Rennes.
4. Of course, there is Athena, but she is a goddess, and the Amazons, but they are imaginary too . . .

workers do.' So here is behavioural evidence. All this is deemed to prove that 'bees are not born of copulation'. How does one come to terms with the workers' sting, a fundamental contradiction to the general representation of the living world in a clear dichotomy of the sexes? Not for a moment does Aristotle cast doubt on the validity of a conception of the world that is beyond him; he prefers to deny reality. The sexes are therefore not divided between the inhabitants of the hive as common opinion holds: the workers could not be male and the drones female, because the workers take care of the young. Thus the drones are not completely male and the workers not completely female, so, to get out of the dilemma, Aristotle imagines dioecious bees like plants, having the 'male sex alongside the female sex' (*Generation of Animals* 31). A sort of third androgynous gender, like that used by Aristophanes for a nice little piece of fantasy anthropology which we shall see later.

Nevertheless, life takes it upon itself to cause the sexes to deviate from the rails on which they were launched. For instance, in the chicken world: if, by some extraordinary happenstance, a cock is defeated by a hen, lo and behold, she acts like a cock, even undergoing physical transformations that will henceforward show her to be a cock: her comb and tail stand up and she develops little spurs. Conversely, if she fails to care for her brood, the cock 'busies himself in her place in caring for the chicks' and stops acting like a cock: 'he no longer goes "cock-a-doodle-doo" and loses all desire to cover the female' (Aristotle, *History of Animals* ix. 49. 631b, 8). It is an easy step from role-swapping to morphological modifications; and the opposite is true. A tangible proof that the alteration of the being brings about a change in appearance is mutilation. If a male is castrated, he 'alters to the point where he resembles a female', his morphology and voice are *feminized*. Eunuchs 'undergo deformations that change them into women, in effect . . . their movements become less pronounced and they degenerate as completely as do castrated males among the other animals' (Aristotle, *History of Animals* viii. 2. 590a).

WOMEN AND MEN: CONFLICTING VOICES

The voice is by no means least in the secondary sexual characteristics, for it is the organ of command. Aristotle, unrepentant taxonomist, makes the distinction in his political writings between the various powers which man exercises within his 'house': as husband over his wife, because he has been given a contract of authority over her; as father over his children, since they are his issue; and as master over his slaves, because inheritance, purchase or violence have made them dependent upon him. It is the voice of the father, the despot and the master which transmits his wishes. Outside his 'house',

in the common masculine arena, it is also the organ for exercising his
political prerogatives, including the power to command his fellow-citizens.
The abilities of the citizen's body, assiduously maintained by physical exercise ('upright stature', see p. 77) both facilitate and explain its rhetorical/
political use in the setting of the city, while at the same time allowing him
easy and calm domination over his nearest and dearest and his slaves. The
opposite extremity of this strong voice, which enunciates justice, truth and
order, is obviously occupied by the feminine, in other words, by a weakness
which utters moans and groans, and a lack of civility which stirs up trouble. How commonplace is this masculine criticism of women's voices; let us
recall the bitch-woman whose husband cannot 'stop her barking' even
when they are someone's guests. 'Ah! male grasshoppers! Aren't they lucky
to have females who were not given any kind of voice at all?' (Xenarchus,
fr. 14 K–A, quoted by Athenaeus xiii. 559a). The same applies to the voice
as to 'hair, limbs, muscles and joints': it is deficient like that of the young,
the old and the sick. There is an obvious explanation: 'Woman can move
only a small quantity of air. This small quantity moves rapidly: now, rapidity is conveyed in the voice by a high-pitched sound' (Aristotle, *Generation
of Animals* v. 7. 787a).

The best proof is that the deep voice is good and the high-pitched bad:
'The deep voice seems to be the prerogative of a stronger nature . . . and in
singing the low sound is better than the high-pitched.' And yet, is it not said
that among cattle the voices of cows and calves are lower-pitched than
those of bulls? (Aristotle, *History of Animals* iv. 11. 538b). Certainly, but
that is precisely because, being more powerful, they are able to breathe
more speed into the air stream (too bad if, in this explanation, the rapidity
of the air has changed the sex). Only deep in exceptional cases and almost
always high-pitched, the voice of females is inferior to that of males. For
the woman, there is the same correspondence between voice and position:
it is at the opposite extreme to the inaccessible masculine, and resembles
that of those closest to her, those who people her upside-down world – the
young, the sick, slaves and even, in some well-chosen speeches, craftsmen,
Barbarians and old people. 'Woman is like a sterile male' (Aristotle,
Generation of Animals i. 20. 728a). This kind of algebra would suggest
the existence of categories likely to have several faults at once: for
instance, woman and slave, woman and Barbarian. Certainly, in the same
way and in the same exploitation of class, the racist feels no awareness of
community of class with one who belongs to another religion or another
community.[5] The dominated can dominate: the slave world reproduces the
same hierarchy of type as the world of the free. Speaking of the bodies of

5.   As a former *pied-noir* worker from colonial Africa made abundantly clear to me.

children and of sterile males to explain why women do not produce sperm, Aristotle adds: 'The child has a feminine form.'[6]

This interpretation of the world presents no more than the appearance of symmetry: the negative route that goes from the castrated male to the feminine should, in fact, logically be balanced by a symmetrical route from the castrated female[7] to the masculine, but there is never any question of it. Amputation of the feminine principle, and above all of her sex, not only never produces the masculine, but acts in reverse: it distances her even further from the masculine. *Every regression is therefore female.* If we speak of symmetrical opposites referring to the two sexes, the two genders ('Similarly, in the union of male and female there needs to be harmony,' *symmetria*, says Aristotle in respect of humans (*Generation of Animals* iv. 2. 767a 20)), we are initially encroaching on their ground, but that does not prevent them from failing to conform to the properties ascribed to them. The symmetry and polarity on which this rhetoric is based are illusory: the female is not really the antithesis of the male, but rather an inferior version of him. More generally, 'for beings that are born, the male is best'; the birth of the female is 'a lapse of nature' (*Generation of Animals* iv. 2. 767b 8). So why be surprised if the concept of the female turns her into 'a sort of natural mutilation', a eunuch creature? All this is explained by what goes on inside the body.

OF HUMOURS AND THEIR EFFECTS

The interior of the body is the concern of doctors. Living in their own world, they put on their 'ideological filters' (how could they do otherwise?). Because they are close to sick bodies, because they examine organs and assess their qualities and defects, because they repeat and adapt their patients' accounts, for them the sexual dichotomy of the world is still more significant. It begins with the flesh.

I say that the flesh of women is more porous and lighter than man's, which causes the woman's body to draw moisture from the belly more quickly and in greater amounts than the man's. (*Women's Illnesses* i. 1, Littré vol. 8)

Softness on the one hand, density on the other, as in animals. This flesh is often compared to wool, capable of absorbing a good deal of moisture.

6. Greek eroticism finds room to apply itself here.
7. Rare in modern livestock breeding practice, castration of females was performed in ancient times, especially on sows.

Men are not totally lacking such porous tissue, however, but they have it only in a few places, like the glands, whose function is to absorb bodily moisture. The more feminine one is, the more porous one is. This can be verified, of course, in the breasts: 'Women produce milk, men don't. In women the quality of these glands is their extreme porosity, like that of the rest of their body . . .' It is not only the very nature of the feminine and the masculine which is basically in question, but also their development. Thus, 'the man remains compact and hard . . . [and] work [and physical exercise] strengthen his body, with the result that he contains nothing that would cause him to retain excess fluid' (*Women's Illnesses* i. 1, Littré vol. 8).

Commonsense and doctors are in total agreement: man moves around, acts, creates, is faced with external aggression, and must therefore have courage in order to react. The more courageous he is, the more he is a man; muscular and bronzed, he spends his time outside (on horseback, in the fields, in the town), his wife is soft and pale, she is an inside person. But that can also be taken the other way. Here we are at the heart of the Greek operation of Greek ideological filters. If we interpret correctly, the principle has changed. It is said that women are soft and cowardly because they are women; that if they are soft it is because they stay inside doing nothing. Then it is claimed that if they stay indoors, it is because their cowardice makes them watchful. Anatomy adapts to activities, but conversely activities match anatomical and physiological dispositions, and one can no longer easily distinguish cause and effect. One proof, among others, of this correspondence between seeming and being is the impossibility for a woman of adapting to a new regime. Plato, who would like to institute for them the same public collective meals as those enjoyed by men, anticipates great difficulties.

> How could one try to compel women to eat and drink in full view? There is nothing that this sex would find more unbearable, accustomed as they are to keep in the background and the shadows, they would resist with all their might if one tried to drag them by force into the light. (Plato, *Laws* vi. 781c)

GENERAL PHYSIOLOGY

We are immediately told the essentials: that what sets women's bodies apart can be seen in their flesh; everything arises from this excess of moisture. It circulates in the body and serves to make what is essential: blood (as well as other humours). Because she is very 'moist', woman is also very 'bloody' and this excess of blood causes her problems. Luckily for her health, she has periods, which enable her to get rid of part of this excess blood. Luckily, too, the blood is used to nourish the foetus while she is pregnant, so that is another way of using it up. The prime mover of internal transformations is coction, a basic thermodynamic operation according to Hippocratic notions. It is by coction that food is passed to the blood, and from the blood to the other biological liquids such as menses, milk or sperm. Abiding by the rules of good polarity, if the bloods of the two kinds differ, it is because (you've guessed it) the masculine power of coction is greater, as man is hotter and woman colder.

> The blood of females differs from that of males. In fact, it is thicker and darker in females than in males of the same health and age, and there is less blood in the peripheral parts of women, but more internally.[8] Of all female animals, the woman has more blood, and as for what is called the menstrual flow, among the animals it is women who produce it more abundantly. (Aristotle, *History of Animals* iii. 19. 521a–b)

Generally speaking, female blood interferes with what is sacred: like other manifestations of biological life, such as birth or death, sexual relations and rape, periods taint the woman and distance her from communication with the immortals. Through a contagious effect, it also distances men, even indirectly.[9] Female blood is endowed with an astounding intrinsic power, some idea of which can be gleaned from this example borrowed from Aristotle:

> When menstruating women glance at a completely clean mirror, a bloody cloud forms on the surface. (Explanation) When menses are produced, the change that occurs in the eyes is concealed from us by a blurriness and bloodshot inflammation, but it exists (the *physis* of sperm and menses is identical) and the latter set the air in motion, and this produces a certain alteration in the air touching and near the mirror, transmitting an alteration like that which it is undergoing: this air acts on the surface of the mirror. (Aristotle, *Parva Naturalia* ii. 459b–60a)

It is breathtaking stuff. Eyes find themselves 'in the same state as any other part of the body during periods', in other words 'particularly veined' and thus, through them, the blood of the period sets the air in motion, a movement that is transmitted even to the bronze of the mirror, tarnishing it. It is hard to know what to admire the most: the reasoning of The Master

8. The polarity is graduated: 'The woman's body draws moisture from the belly more quickly and in larger quantities than the man.'
9. See pp. 20–9 for feminine connections with the sacred.

of the Lyceum or the destructive power of women on metal (Pliny also describes the blood's disturbing effect on the cutting edge of a blade and the shine on ivory; it blackens flax, causes rust and increases the foetid smell of copper (*Natural History* vii. 15)).

Blood represents the female, and therefore woman; it is her signature and its amazing regular emission best characterizes her physiology.[10] Even if periods are regarded as difficult, they are indispensable, the sign of health and fertility; in any case their absence causes all kinds of illnesses and problems, and the essence of Greek gynaecology aims to restore their regular return. It is all still a matter of *physis*: if for one reason or another the blood is unable to flow out, it flows back towards other parts of the body where it accumulates, causing damage. This is particular the case for the *parthenos*. Doctors believed her intact hymen to be the origin of this retention of excess blood. Indeed, when excess blood descends at the *menarche* (first period), it cannot flow out from the body because the 'exit orifice' is closed. It therefore returns to the diaphragm and the heart, compressing them. This is the mechanism that gives rise to the appearance in the *parthenos* of the 'sacred disease' (epilepsy) which assails them and reveals itself, among other ways, by the display of a morbid desire that drives the poor afflicted girls to suicide. They hang themselves or throw themselves down wells. The throttled body of the virgin tells of the revolution of her blood. And the doctor thunders against superstitions and charlatans; no, the girls will not be cured by making the sickness pass into the 'bodies of wild goats', or by offering garments to Artemis: 'I *order* that *parthenoi* be married as quickly as possible if they are suffering from this. Because if they become pregnant, they will regain their health' (*Young Girls' Illnesses*, Littré vol. 7). As quickly as possible – what does that mean? At puberty? Even before? That is not impossible if the hymen is to be ruptured *before* the menarche. We shall take another look at the question of the very early marriageable age for girls.

Finally, when the retention of menstrual blood occurs in adults, difficulties also reveal themselves in mental derangements: attacks of restless wandering, hurling obscenities, and slovenly behaviour.

REPRODUCTION

Contrary to Aristotle, the doctors believed in the existence of feminine sperm. For both sexes, it resulted in an overall harmony both of the

10. Is the body that has not yet experienced regular emissions of blood truly feminine, and
     is it still when it no longer does so? See pp. 17–20 for the effects of this rhythm on
     women's religious life.

humours produced and of anatomy. Sperm was thought of as the residue of the action of coction on the blood; thus, given that masculine thermodynamics is more effective, masculine sperm is 'better cooked.' There is the same overall idea for sperm and periods in boys and girls:

> With the creation of the sperm, the flesh and epidermis become porous, and the veins open more than previously; for in boys, as the veins are slender, the sperm cannot pass; the same explanation applies to girls' periods. The way is opened at the same time for periods and sperm. (*On the Nature of the Child* xx. 2, Littré vol. 7)

Both being residues, these biological liquids thus have parallel functions. If, for Aristotle too, the *physis* of menstrual blood and that of the sperm are identical, if periods are to women what sperm is to men, in the case of women it is a matter of 'sub-sperm', 'impure', not 'cooked' enough or even 'not cooked at all.'

> It is necessary for a being to exist which engenders and a being from which the engendered being emerges (and for that biologists contrast the male as prime mover and agent with the female as the passive recipient); she cannot contribute seed to the male seed, only some matter. Female is the being that generates by itself, which is why the earth has the attribute of a feminine nature and the name of mother, and the sky, the sun and other bodies of the same kind, the name of generators and fathers. (Aristotle, *Generation of Animals* vii. 1. 716a)

An exact 'supernatural' image of this idealized concept of reproduction is to be found in the fundamental divine couple of Hesiod's theogony-cosmogony. After the Earth had reproduced herself identically and all by herself ('without the help of tender love')[11] by creating Uranus ('Starry sky', her lover-son), the latter, by covering her completely, continually impregnated her. Even the name Uranus, derived from the verb 'to urinate', clearly expresses the meteorological procedure of this impregnation: he rains on her. In this second phase, he is the vector, the movement; she is the point of application, the recipient, the body, the substance. It is the same image as that of the passive earth, which supplies the matter and awaits the seed, contrasted with a male principle, which is penetration, movement. In a well-known prayer in the Greek religion, the faithful, addressing Zeus with their faces turned towards the sky, implore him 'Fall as rain', then with

---

11. Thus proving that she is not just 'matter' which is 'self-engendering', but is also, by her reproductive self-sufficiency, 'movement.'

faces turned towards the ground they address Demeter, 'Conceive!' What is this matter which, according to Aristotle, is not sperm? It is both the substance of periods and primordial 'matter' (it was from this 'matter', that is to say, from herself, that Earth 'without the help of tender Love' created Sky, all by herself). Do not these respective attitudes – to enter the other, to remain within oneself – replicate a large part of the social images of the two sexes' position in the world? 'So it is necessary for the female to contribute a body, a certain quantity of matter, whereas that is not the case for the male,' wrote Aristotle, and he continues, 'The body is provided by the female and the soul by the male, for the soul is the essence of a particular body' (*Generation of Animals* ii. 4. 738b). As if we could possibly have doubted it, the soul is masculine (here we are very close to Semonides and the woman who does not belong to humankind – see pp. 31–2. What is the relationship between sperm and the soul? The reply is simple and the overall concept coherent:

> The female is like a mutilated male ['impotent', 'crippled' and one obviously thinks of that regressive idea of the castrated male, the eunuch] . . . and periods are a seed, but not one that is pure: one thing alone is missing from it, the principle of the soul. (Aristotle, *Generation of Animals* ii. 3. 737a)

ON THE EMBRYO AND THE RELATIVE SPEEDS OF DEVELOPMENT OF FEMALE AND MALE

'Sperm is a residue and by its emission causes dryness' (Aristotle, *On Longevity* v. 466b). As coction consists of a distillation which is an elimination of water, it is recommended that one should not overindulge in intercourse; a little is good for the health, but too much ages you and makes you thin. 'Lustful animals, which have a lot of sperm, grow old quickly' (ibid.). This follows from the basic law of thermodynamics: as males and men are hotter and produce less residue, 'generally speaking, they live longer than females' (ibid.); women, because of their lascivious nature, produce a lot of sperm and live shorter lives (Hippocratics).

But let us trace to its origin the parallel history of the two sexes from the time of their conception. To start with there is the difference in the sperms. 'The seed of the female is weaker and moister than the male's; it is inevitable . . . that the female embryo solidifies later than the male' (*On the Nature of the Child* xviii. 8, Littré vol. 7). On the other hand, the male embryo has issued from 'a stronger and denser seed than the female embryo.' Masculine density on one side, lack of structure and feminine flabbiness on the other: it is the same old song and obviously a matter of coction.

This masculine advantage is borne out in connection with the postpartum late discharge of blood called *lochia*, their duration corresponding to that of the formation of the embryo and which must emerge according to the number of days: if the *lochia* are forty-two days for a girl, thirty are enough for a boy. The speed of intra-uterine development also differs from one sex to the other: while forty days after fertilization, the masculine embryo is already showing distinct parts and moving, the feminine embryo has developed little. This is because (in women) 'the similar remains longer in a state of similarity and takes a long time to acquire distinguishing features' (*Of the Eight-month Foetus* ix. 6). In other words, it is because the forces of polarization and the processes of discrimination are inadequate in women, whereas male tissues rapidly free themselves from an undifferentiated state in order to specialize. To blazes with histological details, the feminine has got off to a bad start.

Nevertheless, even in this world that is so well mapped out, something unexpected occurs: the feminine makes up for her tardiness. 'Subsequently, however, once they have emerged from their mother, girls become pubescent, have sense . . . more quickly than boys' (*Of the Eight-month Foetus* ix. 6). These are the doctors talking. Without denying that they could have made exact observations, it is tempting – knowing to what extent their ideological spectacles made them interpret physiology from the starting point of customs and vice versa – to read this medical 'truth' as making their notion of feminine 'nature' fall in line with social usages. It is particularly a question of the customs governing the matching of the spouses' ages to marriage, which I will examine in more detail in Chapter 4. At her first marriage, the wife is very young and her husband fairly old; the age gap may be as much as fifteen or twenty years. This means that if the girl is married at an age close to puberty, her husband's is well behind him. In theory, marriage requires the stage of puberty and also, in men's view, implies a certain degree of maturity so that the wife can oversee the 'house'; but the massively disparaging conception of the feminine hardly encourages this to be expected in a young girl. So? Well, in order that she can nonetheless marry young, as custom dictates, and in order that 'nature' does not suffer as a result, there must be a biological justification to allow for it and thus, developing more quickly than a boy, a girl must become a woman both on the sexual plane and by the early acquisition of 'sense'. She travels towards her maturity more swiftly than the boys of her own age, boys whom in a way the Greek matrimonial system keeps in reserve.

On the one hand, being more 'bloody', more generative, more lustful, women die younger, and on the other, they outdistance men by an earlier puberty and wisdom. Is this a contradiction? Not at all, as the preceding quotation states: although girls outstrip boys to puberty, on the other hand, they 'age more quickly . . . because of the weakness of their body and diet.' Aristotle places the age difference between the generative possibilities of the two sexes at twenty years (fifty and seventy years) Aristotle, *Politics* vii.

Table 3.1 **Balance sheet of the opposite sexes**

Areas of difference	Women (and females)	Men (and males)
Place in the animal world	Closer to females than to males	The most accomplished of males
Place among humans	Closer to slaves and Barbarians	Ideal form; erect stature
Internal polarity	Centripetal	Centrifugal
'Natural' ambiance	Interior; sedentary	Exterior; active
Moral disposition	Tenderness; weakness; timidity	Strength, bravery; stamina
Sensuality	Lustfulness	'Normal'
'Natural' occupations	Feeding and care of the newborn; preservation, care and preparation of foodstuffs; wool-working; supervision of domestics vision of domestics	Agriculture; war
Interior space	Left; low	Right; high
	Backward	Forward
	Ill, bad	Well, good
Flesh	Moist, loose, flabby	Dry, compact
Skin	Pale, white	Tanned, dark
Voice	Weak, deficient, high-pitched (bad)	Strong, deep (good)
Appetite	Excessive	Moderate
Blood	Thick, dark, abundant, centripetal	Clear, light, centrifugal
Sperm	Much, imperfect sperm	Small amount of concentrated sperm
Coction of the blood in sperm:		
heat	−	+
movement	−	+
Embryo (in the first weeks)	Unformed, late, no movement, no differentiation	Early, mobile, differentiated
Puberty	Early	Later
Lifespan	Short	Long

16. 1,335a). Their diet must therefore be pretty bad, and their body much inferior to the man's for them so obviously to lose the advantage that their early development had ensured for them at the outset. They wear out more quickly.

Becoming aware of the scope of their failings, and taking in at a single glance such a deep dichotomy, one may wonder if what separates man and woman is more radical than what, for example, separates man from dog. If the degree of seriousness of an idea can be measured by the fact that Aristotle envisaged it, it is not too harebrained:

How is it that woman does not differ specifically from man, although the feminine and the masculine are opposite . . . Why are the male and female not different species, although that difference in sex is essential . . . and is not accidental like colour . . . but it is *qua* animal that the animal is male or female . . . As for the sex, male or female, these are modifications peculiar to the animal; but these modifications do not touch the essence; they are only in the substance and in the body. (Aristotle, *Metaphysics* x. 1,058b, 20–5)

Sexuality

POLYMORPHOUS LOVES

What path is to be followed in search of love? In the streets you complain of the lust of the courtesan thirsty for gold. Love a virgin? Your misplaced tenderness leads to prison or a proper marriage. I have little appetite for the forced banter, the obligatory intoxication that a wife inflicts on us. The adulterer's bed is loathsome, a stranger to love, on a par with the criminal passion for boys. A pretty widow? She is perverse, greedy, even wilier than a prostitute. The modest woman? Hardly has she given herself in love when she feels the sting of pitiless repentance and regards with horror the act she has just committed; with some residual modesty, she beats a retreat until the message that puts an end to the affair. Your slave? All right, if it pleases you, but resign yourself from the start to being her manservant. Your neighbour's slave? You will be arrested and punished for an infringement of his property. What can you do? Scorning the Laïs of former times, Diogenes was right to prefer his own fingers. (*Palatine Anthology* v. 302, Agathias Scholasticus)

Let us begin with men, and with sexual versatility – something that seems very Greek to us and very human to them. The broad range of aspects of their sexuality can be approached along three lines. First, there is a clear, although tacit, contrast between the sexuality of procreation – within marriage – which is the 'political' sexuality of citizens in the sense of having legitimate children for themselves and for the city, and the sexuality of recreation, normally outside the 'house' (but not necessarily so), which has no other (tacit) purpose than to assuage the lust of at least one of the partners (or of the citizen, if one of the partners is not). Then, there is a wealth of possible combinations among amorous and sexual partners in relations of the second type: they can be of the same sex and age (male and female homosexuality), the same sex and different ages (pederasty) – above all for men – and they can be of different sexes. Thirdly, there is the fairly complex implicit or explicit hierarchy of the values attributed to each kind of

Zeus seizes Ganymede. Intrusion of divine pederastic desire (it is Zeus himself) in a group of *paides* at play, of whom Ganymede is the pick of the bunch. Ah, the *pais kalos*! Antikenmuseum Basel und Sammlung Ludwig, Inv., 418. Photo Claire Niggli

relation that involves personal 'tastes': it can be better to love a boy than a woman; the love of women for men is less good than that of men for children. In the matter of homosexuality, for example, it is better to be masculine; even better are masculine relations between an adult and a child in codified roles and positions. Plutarch (*Eroticus* 751c) quotes this line from the reformer Solon: 'Until one falls in love with a sweet young boy in his prime, desiring supple flanks and a sweet mouth . . .' Greek eroticism sets up pederastic eroticism as its model. Despite the difficulty this presents, we must try to imagine that even heterosexual relations, even in the conjugal bed, borrow from its example. But the hierarchy goes further still: not everyone has the right to the perfection of pederastic relations, only citizens can enjoy them. This perfection is forbidden, for example, to slaves, freedmen and male prostitutes, who could not with impunity cast an eye on pretty boys. Lastly, while female prostitution, which in any case often involved slaves, has no moral importance, it goes beyond the bounds of vileness to debauch free women, the wives of citizens and citizens themselves.

In a book devoted to Greek women, it is without any paradox essential to allow pederastic relationships their full part. In fact, a large proportion of sexual life, that of the relationships of Greek women, is dependent on

Pederastic eroticism. Rendezvous amid the vines: disparity in ages. Courtesy of Museum of Fine Arts, Boston. Reproduced with permission. © Museum of Fine Arts, Boston. All rights reserved

what for the most part eludes them: the love between a man and a child of the same sex. Fortunately, the work of historians over the past thirty or so years has enabled pederasty to be restored to its true dimensions, both day-to-day and institutional. However, perhaps not all the consequences of the place it occupied have yet been measured, and the whole picture of Greek sexuality needs to be modified in order to fit in with this versatility in the expressions of masculine lust. It is a sexuality in which men seem to pass comfortably from a male to a female partner, successively but also simultaneously. For them there was little or no compartmentalization according to particular tastes: a true 'polysexuality'. In its course, it follows a path that leads from a pederastic relationship in the role of *loved one*, to venal heterosexual affairs, then to conjugal love with, again, possibly a pederastic relationship in the role of *lover* and relations with a concubine and a few *hetairai*. At certain ages, certain partners are rare. Girls of boys' age are kept shut in. The age-gap at the time of marriage creates a marked lack of symmetry in which Greek homo- and heterosexual loves are shaped. A man's liking for pretty boys and the interest he may have for one in particular are not in contradiction with his loving his wife.

Looking at the way they lived, the Greeks themselves must have been surprised by, or at least interested in, the interchange in the possibilities of 'mix and match' available to them through their polysexuality. From this view of things, all the conditions combined to give rise to an anthropology that was both physical and social. As often happened with the Greeks, they accounted for it by means of an aetiological myth – in this instance, the one of amorous desire. The subject is to be found in Plato's *Symposium*, but the writer ascribes its paternity to Aristophanes; so it is hardly surprising that the origin of sexes, genders and love is expressed there in a fanciful manner.

FANTASY ANTHROPOLOGY

A very, very long time ago, man's nature was not two but three, and beings were round. The male 'was an offspring of the sun, the female of the earth and the gender that was the product of both one and the other was an off-spring of the moon.' The problem was that these creatures were very subversive, to the point where they were intending to mount an attack on the gods by piling some mountains on top of one another. Zeus had to put a stop to it. One extreme solution would have been quite simply to wipe them out; but then there would have been no more sacrifices, no more offerings ... Gods without men – that's no kind of life for the divine! So Zeus planned to reduce their harmfulness by cutting them into two; and if they did not behave themselves, he would cut them again.

Therefore, when primitive humans had been doubled by this cutting, each piece, missing its other half, tried to unite with it again. Embracing and intertwining with each other, because they wanted to merge into one being, they ended by dying of hunger and the inaction caused by the fact that neither wanted to do anything without the other ... And when one of the halves died and the other survived, the surviving half sought another and intertwined with that. (Plato, *Symposium* 191 b)

This endless search for the same, through these halves of a man or a woman which the surgical cut had set free, made them monomaniacs and halted the fertility of the species. It was necessary, therefore, to shift the reproductive organs from behind, where the preceding operation had placed them, to the front, so that the two genders could procreate, the one in the other, 'in other words, the male organ in the female.' That done, all was now ready for the chariot of the Eros of Aristophanes' day: the pairing of the sexes would be able to stem from this aetiological myth. This is what we have come to, we human beings, cut in two 'like flatfish', with our sex more or less in the front, perpetually seeking our other half. The rules that govern the determination of solutions are very like those we have been taught regarding the genetics of Mendel the Monk's smooth and wrinkled peas: the story of the double and single dose. If you have the kind with a double dose, the result if homosexuality; and if you have the kind with a single dose, the result is heterosexuality. But let us not go too far too fast. Zeus' aim was the perpetuation of the species. Since those two surgical operations, each half is always in search of its complementary half; if, for example, such and such a male half comes from an androgyne, it embarks on a desperate quest for its matching other half, a woman: 'it is from this species that most of the husbands who deceive their wives come': they are too 'philogynous'. In the same way, women who love men and are adulterous come from this species (the androgyne): they are too 'philandrous'. In this set-up, when a man meets a woman, they have a child. And that is all right, because if it is a man who meets a man, that is just too bad, but even better, such men finding 'satiety in their relations ... calm down and turn to action', ceasing to wear themselves out in passion alone. But our list of possibilities is not yet complete:

Women who are a portion of woman pay no heed to men, their inclination takes them rather towards women, and from this type come lesbians. Those men who have a portion of male seek males and, as long as they are children, they love men,[12] take pleasure in sleeping with them, and uniting with them. (Plato, *Symposium* 191c–e)

Here we have a surprise. When, interpreting other cultures from the point of view of our own, we picture the male homosexual as effeminate (a rather worn image, but still current in common opinion), here the opposite is revealed. In Greek lands, those who love men are 'by nature the most virile.' Aristophanes defends them against those who, wrongly, call them indecent: 'it is their boldness, their virility, their male air,[13] which makes them hold dear the one who resembles them' (Plato, *Symposium* 192 a). So boys love men all the more because they are more boyish. The pederastic partner has not reached puberty, and it follows that their virility is without doubt all a matter of upbringing. In the same trend, do handsome virile boys scorn what they regard as being most opposite to them: whiteness, softness, femininity? Anyone who glances through biological literature on male courage knows the gap that separates virility from cowardice. These same male boys, 'becoming men', in fact change their role, following the normal scenario of Greek pederasty, in which at puberty and after they pass from the role of the passive *loved one* to that of the active *lover*. At last, fully adult, 'marriage and fatherhood . . . are of little interest' to these males who 'love boys'; if it were only up to them, women could go to blazes. Moreover, 'let him perish, the first to get entangled in the ties of marriage, and the second, and the third, and even the fourth, and those who follow him, to the very end . . .' (Menander, *Empimpramene* fr. 119 K–A, quoted by Athenaeus, xiii. 559e–f).

The major objection to this is, of course, the city:[14] 'The law alone obliges them.' The law, but not nature, as we can see. The Greek man is schizophrenic. Now – curiously the comparison is made by Aristophanes at this point – *pederasts* too can make good citizens. 'When they are completely developed, the boys of this kind are the only ones to show themselves men by taking part in politics.' Another kind of virility?

It is customary to make light of these words of Aristophanes, who mocks more than he should. However, there is no need to argue that this aetiological myth should not be taken seriously. Not, of course, as a belief, but as a version of the concept of sexuality. It is almost the same assessment as that of the *Iambic on Women* by Semonides: the humour, which is its

12. They prefer them to girls (at any rate, not free ones) and to women. This leads to confusion; in the eroticized relations between child and adult, the one who loves, who seeks out the loved one and gets pleasure from the other's body, is the adult.
13. It will be recalled that the same word in Greek, *andreia*, is used for virility and courage.
14. Not the only one, however; reasons for a couple to have children are on pp. 160–4.

prime aim, is all the keener because the viewpoint to be found at the origin of the story is close to the one held by the audience.

DYED-IN-THE-WOOL BACHELORS?

What do you choose if all the solutions offered to a man are bad? The sophist Antiphon gives a detailed list, taking marriage as his observation point.

> One day, one night – and that is enough to begin a new life, a new destiny. Marriage is a great risk for a man: if the union is ill-matched, how can be extricate himself from such an accident? (Antiphon, fr. 49, D–K)

Do not let us believe for a moment that Antiphon is expressing the slightest concern here for the wife; he is speaking of his own problems:

> A divorce [the Greek word *ekpompe* speaks of 'expulsion'] is a bad solution which makes enemies of friends, those who had the same heart and mind, those who have found him acceptable and have accepted him . . . (Antiphon, fr. 49, D–K)

The wife has disappeared from the debate, but all the regret is concentrated on the consequences of the split on relations with friends. Before Claude Lévi-Strauss, Antiphon sees marriage more as an alliance – a 'horizontal' link – than as a contract with the aim of reproduction. What then? Must one preserve these social relations at the cost of a household hell, when 'believing that one is acquiring pleasure, one has married trouble'? Nevertheless, and we shall verify it again, without being exaggerated or flaunted, conjugal love does exist. Let us remember Achilles and his 'every normal man loves his *alochos*' (see p. 49). 'What can be more pleasant . . . for a man than a beloved woman? What can be sweeter, above all in one's youth?' confides the same Antiphon (fr. 49, D–K). Was it all just a pretence and is he at last going to reassure us? 'But this very state which includes pleasure also includes, in close proximity, sorrow: joys do not go alone, but unhappiness and trials accompany them' (Antiphon, fr. 49, D–K).

Let there be no misunderstanding; Antiphon does not ascribe these sorrows to infidelity, to an idea of marriage as the tomb of love. The paradox is even more forceful. Just as in striving to win victories in the great athletic competitions, or fulfilling great intellectual works, 'great pains and sufferings' are required,

> For myself, if I had a second body, another me, I could not live, so great would be my concern for its health, for earning its daily living, for the

opinion people would have of it, for its wisdom, its honour, its reputation. What would it be like if I had another me who would be such a subject for concern? It is clear that a woman, when she is not loved, causes a man as much worry and torment as he could have for himself, whether it is a matter of the health of two bodies, a living to be earned for two, of wisdom, of honour. (Antiphon, fr. 49, D–K)

Whether he loves her or not (whether she loves him or not, the alternative is missing . . .), that changes nothing; the burden is too heavy for the man to have to live for two. What makes the husband suffer in his body and soul is the fear he has of seeing his wife undermine the necessary qualities which give him his worth in society: *doxa*, 'good opinion', *sophrosyne*, 'self-control', *eukleia*, 'glory', 'reputation' (the two latter, reiterated). It is painful to risk losing one's image because of the behaviour of a wife. It is better to go without one.

But what if there are children? Then life is full of worries, the soul has lost the joyfulness of its springtime; it even shows in the face, which is no longer the same. (Antiphon, fr. 49, D–K)

WOMEN AND MEN: GENDERS OR SEXES?

Doctors and comedy-writers are very close when they are talking about the female sex. The only nymphomaniacs are *nymphes* . . . Sexual disturbances, personality disorders, loss of self-control, hysteria: all are maladies deriving solely from the feminine genital apparatus, troubles of which they alone are the victims. True, we were warned in advance; females are more 'bloody', more generative, and more lustful, and the female of all females is woman. 'Those illnesses known as feminine: the uterus is the cause of all these ailments' (*Women's Illnesses* 57, Littré vol. 8). As the reproductive apparatus is the whole woman, her entire health passes through it. It is a kind of twist of fate: there, in the cavity of their body, in their belly, they have a curious organ which is more than an organ – it is an animal. Everyone knows this; even Plato: 'What is called the matrix or uterus is, in women, like a *zoon* (animal) possessed with the desire to create children' (Plato, *Timaeus* 91c).

It is therefore a mobile animal, with its own needs, and over which (a rare echo of masculine leniency?) woman has no great control. This zoomorphic representation of the womb is coherent, and a whole panoply of organs is ascribed to it which justify its autonomy: two mouths, one lower, one upper, a neck, lips. In its entirety it can communicate, which is why, when the woman is seated on a pot, if the odour of the scent (contained in it) comes through her mouth, one may say that she can conceive and that the womb is still healthy. If the odour does not penetrate, she must not lose heart: when she goes to bed, she must apply Egyptian perfume to herself on some wool. The next day she must examine the uterine orifice to see if it is straighter. (*Women's Illnesses* ii. 146, Littré vol. 8)

This 'person within a person', as R. Joly has called it, is endowed with an olfactory sharpness beyond the normal, and smell forms a favoured way of approaching this inaccessible creature. The image of the *zoon*, roaming in its bodily cavity, is so vivid that it goes beyond the medical circles; we have only to continue the quotation from Plato's *Timaeus*:

When the womb remains sterile long beyond the due season, it becomes dangerously irritated; it moves in all directions within the body, obstructs the passage of the breath, hinders respiration, thus putting the body in dire anguish and causing it to suffer other illnesses of every kind.

The reason for this turbulence which may give rise to suffocation? For want of sexual relations which keep it moist, for want of a pregnancy which locks it into the lower part of the body, the *zoon* suffers, it dries out. Now that it has reached the polar opposite in a moist ambiance, the difference itself sets it in motion; whereas by moistening it, sperm heals it.

If women have relations with men, they are fitter; if not, they are less well. Because in coitus the womb becomes moist, not dry; when it is dry it contracts violently and more than it should; and in contracting violently it makes the body suffer. (*On Generation* 4. 3, Littré vol. 7)

Hysteria is the illness of desire. It brings on a general state of despondency marked by silence (clenched teeth), deathly pale complexion, panting breath, a stupor that is almost a loss of consciousness. The only tension perceptible is like rigor mortis. The woman is in the grip of a desire for strangulation: 'Stifled down below, the woman seeks a way out higher up, by hanging herself', writes L. Bodiou.[15] Insofar as only intercourse or pregnancy can enable women to avoid this march towards the noose, virgins, on the one hand, and those who have ceased regular sexual activity – young

15. This appears in her book on the blood of Greek women, to be published by the Presses universitaires de Rennes.

widows and recent mothers – on the other, are the ones under threat. The doctors are quite clear in their advice.

> This is what the widow must do: the best thing is to become pregnant. As for young girls, they are advised to marry. (*Women's Illnesses* ii. 127, Littré vol. 8)

> I recommend that young girls experiencing such occurrences should marry as quickly as possible; indeed, if they become pregnant, they recover. (*Young Girls' Illnesses*, Littré vol. 8)

Shaking hands with traditional misogyny and the doctors' analyses, comedy-writers agree on the same portrait of the woman who has a bodily illness. We have only to listen to Lysistrata, one of Aristophanes' most representative heroines, trying to force men to make peace and hatching a plot aiming at nothing less than an international sex strike. At the very first contact with her co-conspirators, she worries about the outcome of the venture; not because she doubts the result that a strike on love-making will have on the men, but rather because she doubts her companions' strong-mindedness when faced with such privation: will they not be the first to succumb to their libido? 'Ah! ours is a fine sex, never thinking of anything else but getting their little hole stoppered!' In fact, one of the delegates complains: 'Having to go without a fuck, (no) dear Lysistrata . . . Nothing is worth that!' (Aristophanes, *Lysistrata* 137: 133–5). Aristophanes is wily enough to have this uttered by a woman. There we are then, there is no getting away from it, they are all mad about their bodies. Females on heat, incapable of concentrating on anything but their urges. The vocabulary of comedy tells us to what extent woman's sexual desire does not have the same intensity, even the same nature, as that of man.

To express sexual attraction, where a man is concerned, comedy uses verbs that may be described as 'human', such as *philein*, 'to love.' It is only for women that much stronger expressions appear, for example, *anathyan*, the first meaning of which relates to a sow on heat. The same idea surrounds the declension of terms coming from *kaprios*, 'boar', hence: *kapria*, 'sow's womb', *karaïte*, 'to be in rut', but is also used of women, *kapraô*, 'sow' or 'debauched woman.' There is the same variation around *skuzaô*, 'to be on heat', used of bitches and mares (Aristotle), but also of women (Cratinus and Phrynichus).

On the comic scene, the sow in question is the woman, most often a lewd old woman, and the expression crops up again with revealing regularity in several authors of ancient comedy: Pherecrates, Hermippus and Aristophanes. Its use is proverbial: 'Lust reclaims the old woman.' When this frenzy for coitus is coupled with drunkenness, that takes the biscuit: rutting sow, drunkard and witch, old women, prostitutes . . . they are the worst things you can say: old hag and whore. In parallel, comedy spreads the idea, passed on by the doctors, that although men also certainly find pleasure in intercourse, they should not overdo it because it dries them out. A fragment from Aristophanes puts it nicely, describing two scrawny types: 'Look at those two there, making love like a couple of moths!' On the part of women, the admission is simple: they enjoy being made love to. Without going as far as that famous *hetaira*, Laïs, who died of it, excess in this matter is undoubtedly feminine, particularly – if we have understood it well – the aged feminine: the young man in Aristophanes' *The Assembly-Women* is not up to it, but is obliged to 'make love day and night to the old woman' (*The Assembly-Women* 108–9). Obviously, this excessive female libido awakens masculine fears that we have already read about in Semonides and Hesiod centuries earlier, those of the female belly which wears the man out. Listen to the two old men exchanging their points of view on the future of the world after women have assumed power:

> Something for people of our age to fear is that, having taken the reins of government, women will then compel us to screw them. – And if we cannot? – They won't give us any dinner. – Oh well, by Zeus, comply; you can dine and screw at the same time. (*The Assembly-Women* 465–70)

The fear of not being able to satisfy the old girls, anxiety about hunger – they are old fears, of ravenous masculine and feminine bellies, but we know who are the guilty ones.

MASCULINE WAYS OF MAKING (OR TALKING ABOUT) LOVE WITH A WOMAN

How do men express their sexuality? Quite evidently, men put the intensity of their lust on public display. Everyone can see that the town is full of *phalloi*, of all materials, colours, sizes, but always exaggerated. Masculine sex is all-invasive; it is seen and heard, if in nothing more than the vocabulary of ancient comedy. The verbal inventiveness, evidenced by comedy, regarding human sexuality is quite extraordinary. It obviously owes a great deal to the creative gifts of the poets, those 'kings of words' (but we know almost nothing of possible borrowings from spoken language and slang). It presents a picture of the sexual organs and act in a perspective that is fairly uniform, dynamic and joyful. With the exception of a rare constraint placed upon one of the partners, the sexual act is a pleasure and takes place in a cheerful atmosphere. Verbs and expressions convey the idea of the man's movement towards the woman. It is a direction described with the help of terms borrowed from the immediate environment. We are in Athens, a maritime city if ever there was one, and much of the imagery strikes a chord with sailor audiences. To fuck is 'to ram', as the warship does when aiming its ram to pierce the adversary's hull and 'to caulk' (the old woman is a rundown boat and the young man confides that 'he has been caulking her for quite a while'). It is also 'to steer' and to 'manoeuvre a boat.' All sailors are matadors of virility, for instance: 'My husband – a real Salaminian, my old man – manoeuvred me all night long', and the commentator on this passage explains that the Salaminians (from the island opposite Athens) were held to be great sea-dogs, much talked-about oarsmen and also lovers, returning passionate and ardent to the conjugal home. In the same vein as that of the oarsmen, we have the example (extreme, naturally) of Adonis, in Plato the comic poet, where the hero, loved by both Aphrodite and Dionysus, has to satisfy them both at the same time: 'Aphrodite manoeuvred the oars with him on the sly, and Dionysus did the same.'

The audience responds to expressions borrowed from the acts of every-day life. Here, food plays a leading role: 'to press' (the grape); 'to remove' (the seeds from a pomegranate, 'to de-seed'); 'to debug' (a play on words with *koris*, 'bug', and *kore*, 'maiden', 'girl', 'virgin', hence 'to take her virginity'; 'to grind', 'to crunch' (bread, sweetmeats), 'to crush' (women). Still stronger, we have 'to sack or plunder' ('a woman enjoys being plundered'); we also have 'to lean on', 'to press against' (a slave 'presses his mistress all night long on the perfumed bed'), 'to pierce'. Domestic life obviously provides its share: 'to poke the fire' (in *Peace*, among the happy prospects brought by the truce, the hero anticipates 'passing his life in the midst of peace, with a lady friend, poking the fire'). Agricultural life and its tasks, regarded as masculine, offer a number of suggestive comparisons, at least for the most demanding: 'to plough' is an image we find in the context of a father's handing over his daughter to his future son-in-law ('I hand this girl over to you for you to plough her to beget legitimate children'). To dream of ploughing is to dream about a woman; to dream of seeds is to dream of children (Artemidorus, *Interpretation of Dreams* i. 451). This imagery goes together well with others: for example the feminine sex is often referred to as 'meadow', 'plain', 'garden'. We have 'to harrow', whence 'manhandle or maltreat' ('you well and truly manhandled me'), 'to hoe' in the phrase 'having fun hoeing' ('If, seeing a little girl, anyone desires her and wants to have fun hoeing her'), and 'to drill a hole', 'to dig in', 'to sow seed'.

The setting for the 'sweet life', born of peace and the satisfaction of primary needs (those that satisfy the stomach and sexual organs), is nature in close contact with its produce: 'to gather fruit', chiefly the 'fig', one of the linguistic substitutes for the female sex ('to pluck a fig'): 'In a dream I saw Isocrates' concubine, Lagiska, and I plucked her fig' (Strattis, fr. 3 K–A). It is no great exaggeration to say that the essence of Aristophanes' philosophy is summed up in: 'To live a happy, carefree life, and pluck figs'). We also find 'to pick grapes': the proud Opora is there before them, and the chorus of ploughmen ask, 'What shall we do to her?' 'We shall pick her grapes,' replies Trygaeus, whose name means 'Grapeharvester'. This closeness to nature also explains comparisons with the animal world, and with birds and their tails: 'to act like a bird', 'to act the wagtail' ('Bend over to the rhythm of the wagtail').

THE VIOLENT RETURN OF MISOGYNY

This vocabulary is a 'polite' way of putting masculine love for a woman, imparting an image of bliss to the act of love. Heterosexual pleasure does not take second place in comedy. But beneath the wild variety of words and the first impression of broad jokes runs an omnipresent underlying theme: violence.[16] In fact, the range of verbs is constantly disturbing: 'to ram', 'to squeeze', 'to grind', 'to crunch', 'to manhandle', 'to beat', 'to rummage', 'to break down', 'to wreck', 'to fight against' . . . As usual in Aristophanes, even women use these terms – for instance the woman (accompanied by slaves and a man) who cries, in a sexual context, 'You want to use violence on me?' Elsewhere, in a reversal of the roles, Chemes says to the young man, 'Don't be afraid, [the old woman] will not force you.' Indeed, in *The Assembly-Women*, in the name of 'feminine communism', they have decided that if a man desires a woman, 'he will not have her unless he has first "had a stab" at an old woman.' A fragment of Alcaeus mentions the complaint of a husband: 'He used violence on my wife' (fr. 29). Aristophanes also uses many verbs meaning 'to carry off', 'abduct' or 'to force in order to carry off': for instance, 'to throw to the ground' for carrying off a girl. He and his colleagues also make much use of 'to beat'. What is worse, certain scenes presuppose that the idea of violence is contained in that of the relationship itself. When she hears the young man announce that he wants to knock on her door, a girl understands that the door in question is her sex. When Praxagora claims not to be afraid that the archers will mistreat her, she justifies it because she 'has experienced a good number of "knocks".' Of course, this is farce; of course, there is no question of sliding carelessly from this vocabulary to an idea of sexuality

---

16. The number of examples is such that J. Henderson's excellent book *The Maculate Muse: Obscene Language in Attic Comedy* devotes a section to them.

Every kind of power over a body. Violence, sadism? The man lifts the woman's legs (she does not struggle) and prepares to strike her with his sandal. Is she a prostitute, a slave, or a prostituted slave? On the left, another man intervenes or eggs him on. Munich, Arndt coll., Attic cup by Antiphon

in which physical violence plays the leading part, but there is no smoke without fire. And a great deal of iconography bears witness to this aspect of affairs. The place and image which Greek thinking reserves for woman and her body put her alongside those of the slave. Without fantasizing over the attitude of the master with a whip always to hand, relations with slaves obviously allowed much room for blows and beatings.

Woman as object? The expression has become so common that it has lost much of its power of evocation. However, in Greek antiquity, what better way is there of conveying the place of the feminine body in sexual relations? All means are good when it comes to 'justifying' getting possession of this instrument of pleasure: the violence of war, such as placed Briseis and Chryseis in the hands of Achilles and Agamemnon; purchase; inheritance; renting, which in the classical city put the slave in the hands of the master (or those of his neighbour, like the character in Aristophanes declaring his pleasure 'on surprising Thratta, the pretty woodcutter, Strymodorus' slave, as she was stealing wood, and seizing her bodily, lifting her up, throwing her to the ground and taking her cherry' (Aristophanes, *The Acharnians* 272–5); the wage that puts the prostitute at the disposal of her client; and the contract, sanctioned by custom and law, which makes the guardian/husband the exclusive user of the wife. As regards the sexuality of reproduction, the achievement of the plan for the succession of the master of the 'house' ends up in the same control of the feminine body. At all times and in all places, she is put in a relationship of subjection, dependency and submission which makes her – the term is banal but the outcome inevitable – an object in the man's hands.

In the *Interpretation of Dreams*, a kind of manual for those who interpret dreams, the writer Artemidorus, addressing his fellow-interpreters, recommends them to pay great attention; they must 'take careful note of every detail', and he gives this example:

> A man who had a sick son dreamed that he penetrated his son and *took pleasure in it*. The son lived:[17] in fact, we may say 'possess' and 'penetrate' and 'have had' him: the interpretation is drawn from the detail 'take pleasure in'. Another man whose son was ill dreamed that he penetrated his son and '*found it painful*', and the son died, for we may equate 'be corrupted', with 'be penetrated' and 'dying': the interpretation is drawn from the detail 'found it painful.' (*Interpretation of Dreams* iv. 4. 248)

Between one dream-figure and the other lies the entire distance between active and passive; the usual contrast in eroticism, as it is in domination. 'To possess' is to 'keep' or 'hold' a being, an object, in order to take advantage of it. Speaking of a body, to 'fuck it' and 'make the most of it' amount to the same thing. As for 'penetrating', this is *perainein*, and to 'penetrate something' also means 'to have sexual relations', but more broadly, it means 'to bring something to its end', 'to a successful conclusion', 'to result in'. Still in Artemidorus:

> To have sexual commerce with one's slave, woman or man, is good: for slaves are the possessions of the dreamer. So that indicates that the dreamer is gaining from his possessions, and that they will probably increase and become more sumptuous. (*Interpretation of Dreams* i. 78. 88)

All the indicators are positive, thus to possess his son in a dream *with pleasure* is the sign of a gain, therefore of life.

'To be penetrated', *perainesthai*, is obviously the contrary, involving a 'corruption', a 'taint' but, even more, it is 'destruction' or 'death'. The

17. Contrary to the 'normal' diagnosis given before in the treatise for the son 'who is not yet five years old, that indicates death for the son . . .' The text then makes the distinction between the son from five to ten years, then the son over ten and, finally, the son who is 'a grown man.'

terms of the alternative are the exact opposite of one another: possession-enjoyment-life versus submission-taint-death. But in another passage Artemidorus shows that the social aspect is relative, both to gender and to wealth. On the feminine side, we see what men can extract from the dreams they ascribe to women: 'As for being penetrated by someone you know, for a woman, on the one hand, it is an advantage, whoever may penetrate her.' On the masculine side, one can either penetrate or be penetrated:

> For a man, on the other hand, if he is penetrated by someone who is richer or older, that is good, for one customarily receives from such people; but if it is by someone younger and poor, that is bad: for it is usual to give such people a share of what one has. The same meaning applies if the one penetrating is older and poor. (*Interpretation of Dreams* i. 78. 89)

FEMINIZATION

There are also men who are not comfortable in their male role, and Greek life was quick to confirm this: two phalanxes of soldiers face to face with nothing to come between the deafening assault of the enemy group and the imagination of each one who can already feel the blade piercing his tender flesh. Everywhere there are citizens who would perhaps be citizens just like the rest if *everyone* was not aware, in the city, that on the day of such and such a battle they threw down their shield to flee more easily, presenting their back rather than their breast to the enemy. Fear is feminine. In Sparta, a city that was more male than the rest, there was much talk of these 'tremblers', (*tresantes*), shown up by direct physical confrontation in combat, and they were condemned to lose their political rights.

Elsewhere, rejection took other forms. In Athens, Cleonymus, reputedly a coward, was made a scapegoat by Aristophanes to the point where, in a scene from the *Clouds*, he ended up by declining (in the grammatical sense) his name as if it were feminine. Not surprisingly, he is described as fat ('flabby'), a greedy pig (classic misogyny); he is a bogus male, a eunuch, in short, a woman. To shirk the solidarity of combat, is to demean oneself, to feminize oneself. In Aristophanes' works there are several similar figures of men who are said to be 'inverts'. Objects of disapproval and scorn, they did not have an easy life. This was especially the case for adult males who took the passive role in the homosexual couple. Those who are sodomized are base and/or absolutely dominated. Those who take pleasure in it, are merely objects to be buggered and are said to enjoy it, they are less than nothing. Iconography is a great help here. Heterosexual anal penetration is never represented in the setting of conjugal relations, but always with prostitutes. The woman bending deeply forward proffers her backside to her partner who is standing. The scene often makes quite clear the social nature of the relations by showing money being handed over and the context of masculine brutality that accompanies it. This posture is also popular in pederastic relations, where the backside is endowed with all kinds of charms, 'is humanized': the same imagery is used for it as for the feminine sex – the fig and the rosebud are seductive.

These two erotic figures, both hetero- and homosexual, are matched by the same image of domination, the same power exercised by the adult male. Buggery is domination. Proclaiming it, as today, was to insult and at the same time to condemn the other to a loss of honour. In such cases it is obvious who is the one 'with balls' and who, as D. Cohen puts it, 'drops his trousers', who 'masculinizes' and who 'feminizes' himself.[18] An Athenian picture of the mid-fifth century reveals it at a stroke in a political context. In it we see a Persian soldier bending over while an Athenian hoplite (a heavily armed infantryman) comes up behind him, his erect phallus in his hand. Those Persian buggers, we've fucked them! The victory referred to here is that of the Eurymedon in 466 BC. The equation is made easier by the fact that the Barbarians, particularly the Persians, were thought of as flabby, cowardly, effeminate.

> At Gortyn, on Crete, when a man was caught in adultery, he was brought before the magistrates and, after he was convicted of his misdemeanour, he was crowned with wool. This crown denounced him as a depraved, effeminate, 'handsome hunk' fancied by women. (Aelian, *Miscellanies* xii. 12)

Here is yet another fine example of the danger of transposing one's own mental categories to the culture one is examining: where in our customary terms of reference the womanizer, the ladies' man, tends to be placed in the virile category, the Greeks likened him to the feminine. It is a comparison based not on opposites but on similarity: the seducer, in feminine fashion, is the plaything of his urges. And the punishment exaggerates the crime. Wool is totally feminine, it goes with softening, the loss of healthy tan, the absence of muscles resulting from being kept indoors; it is dampening in itself and through the absence of movement which it implies. There is no end to its degeneration. Look at Heracles. The undisputed perfect male but, once given up to his devouring passion for Omphale, there he is spinning wool at her feet. Spinning, good God, what an antithesis.

18. D. Cohen (1991), *Law, Sexuality and Society*, Cambridge: Cambridge University Press, p. 184f.

The process of feminization works through softening. This is at the heart of the matter and the world, history and sociology are interpreted in this way. It was a common refrain in Athens to cite the habits of Ionia (western Asia Minor) as testifying to a slackening of morals because of the increase in easy living and a general sloppiness: the men there wore fine linen and adopted ambiguous attitudes, all of which were judged to be too feminine in comparison with the very male habits of Greece proper – a rustic life and physical exercise. In this sexualized geography, agreeable Ionia was most in contrast with male Sparta. Athens was somewhere between the two. The Greeks asked by what process of transformation this had come about, as is shown by the curious story of the Salmacis spring of Halicarnassus on this coast of Asia Minor. The geographer Strabo wondered why it was claimed that the water from this spring had a 'feminizing' effect (Strabo, xiv. 16). Vitruvius knew its reputation for turning 'normal' men into 'passive homosexuals', a certainly masculine but totally depraved extreme of erotic excess, making a man play a feminine role. Vitruvius denies that the water had an effect on sexuality (*venerio morbo*), contrary 'to the false rumour which has spread this opinion all around' (Vitruvius, *On Architecture* ii. 8. 11). The proof was that one could see the Carians, Barbarians driven back by the Greeks into their mountains, attracted by this water, drinking it alone or in groups and changing their way of life, which had previously been brutish and based on banditry, into that of Greeks, well-ordered and civilized. The spring of Halicarnassus, that was where the 'process of acculturation' could have been transmitted. It softened the Barbarians' spirit by means of the delights of civilization. Nor does Strabo believe that absorbing those waters causes effeminacy: 'The true cause . . . lies rather in wealth and a dissolute lifestyle' (xiv. 2. 16). Greek historiography, with Thucydides to the fore, regarded it as proved that the historical process of the gradual abandonment of weapons, the introduction of nudity in athletic competitions and, generally speaking, a gentler urbanity, originated under Ionian influence. And since Ionia meant wealth, luxury, refinement of morals, flimsy (erotic) fabrics and famous courtesans (whom we shall get to know better in Chapter 5), Ionia also meant feminine.

The Athenians [of privileged classes] were the first to lay down their arms . . . living freely [they] turned in the direction of a new refinement [*trypheroteros*, 'delicate', but also 'flabby', 'effeminate']. Not long ago[19] . . . to give an air of luxury [*abrodiaiton*, 'delicate', but also 'flabby' 'effeminate'], elderly people wore long linen garments and held back the

19. Thucydides wrote at the end of the fifth century.

locks of their hair by inserting gold clips shaped like cicadas. (Thucydides, *History of the Peloponnesian War* i. 6. 3)

This notion of a lifestyle and customs progressing in the direction of a greater gentleness in human relations is connected with the feminine end of the spectrum. Thucydides perceives an evolution which undoubtedly began in the wealthy classes. Other signs show that Athens experienced such a gradual 'feminization', for instance the 'pictorial movement' in the painting of the second half of the fifth century which so often chose its subjects in the 'house' and especially in scenes where female characters predominate.

FEMININE WAYS OF MAKING LOVE?

Active or passive? It all depends on the partner. In mercenary affairs, women often take the active role, as is borne out by a series of amorous epigrams accompanying the offering of a whip, by some women, to Aphrodite.

> This polished whip and these shiny reins are offered by Plangon under the portico . . . when at a mounted trot she had triumphed over the ardent Philainis in the evening, when the mares begin to whinny . . . (*Palatine Anthology* v. 202, Asclepiades or Posidippus)

This competitive spirit fits in well with the amorous posture which these professionals make their speciality, but Plangon has not said it all. What is the client's cane used for?

> Lysidike consecrated to you Cypris, her horsewoman's whip, the gold spur from her beautiful leg, with which she has worn out many a mount lying supine; but never has her own thigh been bloodied, thanks to the agility of her movements; for she reached the end of the race with no need to be urged on . . . (*Palatine Anthology* v. 203, Asclepiades)

To satisfy customers' tastes for a passive pleasure, Lysidike enjoys that prime quality for whoever wants to 'hold out' physically and achieve pleasure with an economy of movement; this spares her those strokes of the whip with which clients favour the *pornai* (prostitutes) in these circumstances. Violence again.

To listen to Aristophanes' Lysistrata, war is a calamity that takes away our men ('Where are our kids' daddies?') and our lovers. To cap it all, the defection of one of Athens' principal allies, Miletus, deprives us . . . of what? What shortage is Athens suffering? Soldiers, shields, bread, wine? None of that. Since this diplomatic setback, 'we haven't seen a single one of those eight-inch *olisboi* that offer us a leathery relief' (Aristophanes, *Lysistrata* 109–10). Two images stand out regarding masturbation in Greece. The first is the very masculine one of Diogenes the Cynic, the resolute protester who 'wants a communal pool of women, denies the value of marriage, advises free love at will and according to the inclinations of each person', and shocks because he deliberately masturbates in public. 'Would to heaven that it could likewise be enough to rub one's belly to appease one's hunger' (Diogenes Laertius, *Lives of the Philosophers* vi. 69). What was scandalous was not the masturbation but the absence of modesty. We can go further. It seems that beyond the particular matter of exhibitionism here, there is the question of the act itself. Common morality, certainly, was scarcely bothered by the licit or illicit nature of obtaining pleasure from one's own body as one might wish. More subtly, it is rather a question of how. In the same way that one does not carry one's own burden but has it carried by someone else, and that one does not read but has someone else do the reading, it is assuredly more pleasurable to be masturbated than to masturbate; conversely, how humiliating to masturbate someone else, one of those 'bodily tasks' that figure in the prostitutes' repertoire.

The other image is that of dildoes, familiar in literary allusions and paintings. Very large, often adorned with an eye at the tip (zoomorphic, anthropomorphic), sometimes represented with wings at their base, they are seen in paintings, gathered in bundles in baskets but also being manipulated by naked women. Paintings show some scenes of masturbation and reciprocal feminine fondling, but when it comes to dildoes the list is much longer. But how is the importance of such an instrument to be measured only on the strength of the various allusions that are made to it? It is one of the typical objects in the life of prostitutes, but also of other women, including wives.

Another feature deserves attention: the use of the dildo does not seem to involve isolating oneself. At all events, women speak about it freely. They offer it around to one another, as for instance in the mime *The Girl Friends* by Herodas: Metro tells Coritto that she has seen a magnificent scarlet *baubon*[20] at the home of 'Nossis, Erinna's daughter', who herself had 'received it as a present from Euboule, Bitas' wife', and they exchange addresses:

---

20. The dildo is called *olisbos* and *baubon*. It is also the name of a slavegirl who, by displaying her sex, had managed to make the goddess Demeter laugh when she was searching for her daughter Kore.

Manipulating a dildo? There are jars full of these *olisboi*! © Photothéque des Musées de la Ville de Paris ou PMUP

Metro: . . . Who made it for you? If you love me, tell me . . . I beg you, my dear Coritto, tell me the truth, say who made it.

Coritto: All right. No need to beg me. Kerdon made it.

Metro: Which Kerdon? Tell me. For there are two of them . . .

Coritto: Neither of the two you're talking about Metro . . . This one works indoors, to sell on the quiet. But his work, what work he does! You would think Athena herself had a hand in it . . . For myself, when I saw them (for there were two when he came, Metro) my eyes popped out of my head. Men (just between you and me) don't achieve such hardness. And not only that, but the softness – simply a dream! Straps that one would swear were wool, not leather! You will look in vain, no woman will ever find a nicer cobbler. (Herodas, *Mimes* vi. 16–50)

Here we are away from Athens, and in the third century, and women are certainly enjoying a greater freedom of activity, but all this 'life' around the dildo is somewhat surprising. One begins to have doubts. Could it be that dildoes existed only in the minds of men who could imagine no feminine sexual pleasures other than those they constructed around fantasies connected with penetration? They can be seen in operation, and even so effectively that they make certain feminine ways of sexuality incomprehensible to men. For instance, evoking lesbian sexual relations, Artemidorus, in his *Interpretation of Dreams*, uses the word *perainein*, 'to penetrate', and differentiates the case in which a woman dreams that she 'is penetrating' another from the case in which a woman dreams that she 'is penetrated' by another. This is how far masculine representation of the world goes and how watertight the partition is between the sexes. True, these masculine imaginary constructions exist, but so do dildoes. Where should we stand between these two equally untenable extremes: should we believe in an astonishing masculine permissiveness or in a pure and simple invention? It is more probably the result of exaggeration. With regard to men, scenes of masturbation appear quite often in paintings, in both homo- and heterosexual contexts. In the latter instance, the men are being masturbated by women, frequently *old* women; they are having themselves made love to. Unless our survey is in error, although no man is to be seen anywhere paying any attention to the genitalia of his partner, everywhere there are women anxious to pamper theirs.

Women are troublemakers, feminine words promote chaos. The theme of devastating female sexual urges goes together with that of intemperance, and thus with infidelity. All the women in comedy cheat on their husbands: 'They are in common accord, and have a lover, like an hors d'oeuvre, ready to hand.' If, however, women of the times are far more often victims of infidelity than men, it is apparently because masculine opinion considers that this uncontrolled abandonment to lust is a far more feminine than masculine way of behaving, and the Greeks see two reasons for this. The first is that, despite a seeming symmetry at the outset, women experience much greater difficulty than men in controlling themselves. They are the victims of an inadequate mastery of their body. This is an obviously paradoxical judgement when, in parallel, we are constantly witnessing Greek women's tendency to be retiring and withdrawn, as they are expected to be; thus, on the wife's death, when her husband is having her epitaph carved, it is precisely this self-control which is one of the virtues he praises. Paradoxical too, because husbands demand of their spouses that they shall be able to substitute for them in every way in the 'house'. But that changes nothing in the opinion which asserts, and reasserts, that what is required is a natural beauty without make-up, modesty at all times and in all places, silence and, if not complete enclosure, at least concealment of the body. And what does it matter here if it is not

The intimate lives of young women. Is this scene concerned with hygiene or is it a very rare image of feminine homosexuality? Cup from Tarquinia by Apollodorus

altogether proven that everywhere all wives and daughters of citizens remained at home, did not speak to men from the outside world, did not go to the agora to buy or sell, and emerged only in exceptional circumstances to attend funerals, fetch water, visit the sanctuary of the goddess of childbirth and the major festivals where men needed them; in short, what does it matter if the practice was more flexible – ideology says it all clearly.

WHAT GOES ON INSIDE?

The second reason why abandonment to lust is seen as more feminine than masculine stems from an existential concern. The enigma begins with the body and develops with the sensations it brings; the Greek man also worries about the strange behaviour of woman. He has fantasized more than he should about all that and, as often happens, the expression of this fantasy has taken the form of a myth, that of Tiresias.

> Tiresias . . . saw . . . snakes coupling. He wounded one and, immediately, changed his appearance. From being a man he became a woman, and coupled with a man. But Apollo told him by an oracle that if, in the same way, he wounded the other, he would once more become as he had been. Tiresias was careful to do as the god had told him, and thus regained his former nature. One day when Zeus was arguing with Hera, maintaining that in the sexual act the woman experienced more pleasure than the man, whereas Hera held the opposite view, they decided to put the question to Tiresias, given that he had experienced both states . . . Tiresias answered that, if there were ten portions (of pleasure), the man enjoyed one only and the woman nine. Angered, Hera put out his eyes, blinding him. But Zeus granted him the gift of soothsaying and a lifespan of seven generations. (Phlegon of Tralles, _Mirabilia_ iv. FGrH 257 F36 IV)

A myth is not a belief, but it cannot be denied that all this is coherent. It goes together with the 'bloody' woman, and her proximity to animals. Yes, men acknowledge feminine pleasure, 'biologists' even hold that it is indispensable to impregnation. According to Aristotle, one of the reasons why some imagined that 'for her part, the female emits sperm during coitus', was that they were wrong about the nature of the liquid she releases at that moment: it is not 'sperm, but a local secretion peculiar to every woman' coming from the uterus. The emission of this liquid is expressly linked to the pleasure felt ('comparable to that of males'). But not all women feel it with the same intensity (do not produce the same amount of liquid). The more they have 'a pale complexion and (are) of strictly feminine appearance', the more they enjoy it; furthermore, at the other extreme of womankind, 'among brunettes of masculine appearance' (Aristotle, _Generation of Animals_ i. 19. 727b–28a), none at all is emitted. This is within the logic of the representation: the woman is the most 'bloody' of females, the coital secretion is the privilege of the womanliest of women and relies on the pleasure experienced, and this is all the greater because the female is more 'bloody'. Among the Hippocratics, the orgasmic model stays moulded on the masculine example, it is vaginal and borrows from the ejaculatory scenario:

> Among women, as the vagina is rubbed during coitus and the womb is in movement, [she] is seized as if by an itch which brings pleasure and

warmth to the rest of the body. The woman also ejaculates starting from the (whole) body, now in the womb (and it becomes moist), now outside, if the womb is wider open than it should be. (*On Generation* 4. 1–3, Littré vol. 7)

Looking at it from the procreative perspective alone, the doctor fervently recommends the continuance of relations: 'Because habit excites desire, the veins are opened wide. And if the man's seed converges directly with that of the woman, conception will take place' (*Women's Illnesses* i. 17, Littré vol. 8). In this system, the woman depends on the man:

The woman has enjoyment from the start, throughout the time of coitus, until the man leaves her. If she has orgasms, she ejaculates before the man and her enjoyment is no longer the same; if she does not achieve orgasm, her enjoyment finishes with that of the man ... It is like throwing cold water on boiling water: the water stops boiling; similarly, the man's sperm falling into the womb quenches the heat of the woman's pleasure. Pleasure and heat flare up when the sperm falls into the womb, then end. It is like throwing wine on to a flame: at first the flame blazes and increases when the wine is poured, then it is over. Similarly, in the woman, the heat rises on contact with the man's sperm, then it ends. The woman's enjoyment in coitus is much less strong than the man's, but it lasts longer. (On *Generation*. 4. 1–3 Littré vol. 7)

Is it because the subject of the Hippocratics is procreation that they do not mention the clitoris? Yet under the various names of myrtle bud, pip, barley grain and *nymphe*, both the organ and its effects were known to their contemporaries.

Often the woman conceives without experiencing pleasure during coitus: and when, on the contrary, her pleasure has been no less great, and the man and woman have kept in time, there is no impregnation, and the discharge known as menses does not take place as it should. (Aristotle, *The Generation of Animals* i. 19. 727b)

The pleasure has shifted: 'in copulation, [women] feel pleasure by contact in the same place as males ... the liquid they emit does not come from there' (ibid. i. 728a). Aristotle thus clearly disassociates the process of impregnation from the feminine experience of pleasure.

CHAPTER 4

Joys and miseries of married life

First of all for an extravagant price we must buy ourselves a husband who will be master of our body, an even more burdensome misfortune than the price. For therein lies our greatest risk: was the bargain good or bad?

To divorce one's husband is dishonourable, and, once wed, a woman is not allowed to refuse him. (Euripides, *Medea* 232–7)

Take for your husband the one your parents choose. (Stobaeus, iv. 23. 7. 1, W–H)

After the constraints, or pseudo-constants, of misogyny and biology, our interest now turns to the social fabric, and chiefly to what forms its essence: the 'house'. This 'house' is the entity in whose heart lives the free woman, the wife and daughter of the citizen. Of course, there are other women, free and non-free, both outside and inside the 'house', but there is no 'real' woman, no 'useful' woman outside this institution, as there is no true 'house' without a woman. Chapter 5 will be devoted to the woman in the 'house', but for now, we shall look at the functioning of this system insofar as it relies on the movement of women from place to place. Our example will come from the very top, with an evocation of the 'house' of Pericles, one of the most celebrated in classical Athens.

Through both his parents, Pericles came from a 'house' and family of the highest rank. Indeed, Xanthippus [his father] . . . had married Agariste, the granddaughter of the Cleisthenes who drove out the sons of Pisistratus [the tyrant], bravely overthrew the tyranny and established laws and an admirably moderate constitution ... (Plutarch, *Life of Pericles* 3. 1–2)

Regrettably, Plutarch stops there in this chapter of the private life and geneaology of Pericles and immediately goes on to what seems to him more important in taking stock of his personality, the young man's upbringing and training. Only further on, when it is a matter of Pericles' relations with his concubine Aspasia, does he feel obliged to return to his private life and speak of his wife and children: 'He had been married to one of his relatives, who had first been married to Hipponicus, by whom she had had Callias "the Rich"; she had given Pericles two sons, Xanthippus and Paralus' (*Life of Pericles* 24. 8).

The fact that the subject of such a text – the biography of a 'great man' with an important political role – is *a priori* far removed from concerns of a private kind, gives even more value to these short passages in which, as if by chance, three fundamental characteristics of Athenian marriage in the classical period are mentioned. Neither Plutarch nor others tell us the name of the woman who married the most famous man of his time and had two sons by him. Is this by chance? No. It is a tacit rule, and these rules are the best observed: certain women, the wives, daughters and mothers of citizens are not named; in other words, they are the women of 'houses', under the authority of a father, husband or brother. When a man feels the need to designate one of them, he identifies her by default, by means of the kinship she has with the one who exerts that authority over her, the one who is legally responsible for her: her *kyrios* or, generally and chronologically, her father, then her husband and then, possibly, her son. When the first disappears he is replaced by the next. This convention of silence about names does not apply to prostitutes, slaves ... or the dead.

Pericles marries a relative. The end of the chapter will show to what extent the term endogamy applies to these people. There is nothing surprising in the second marriage of this wife (we are not told if she was the widow of her first husband), because this feature is not peculiar to her alone ... and also because she has not yet finished with it all. In fact, continuing our reading, we learn that after the birth of the two boys, 'life together [for Pericles and his wife] having become painful to them, [he] passed her on, with her full consent, to another husband' (*Life of Pericles* 24. 8).

If our arithmetic is right, that makes it her third; she goes from one 'house' to another and possibly has children (only boys are worth a mention). Before returning to this anonymous wife, let us finish the short sequence of Periclean biography presented by Plutarch: at that point 'he himself took Aspasia [a woman outside the system of 'houses', so her name is given] for his companion and loved her dearly.' In more prosaic terms, he replaced a legitimate wife in his 'house' with a concubine.

D. Passed from hand to hand: A turnover in women among the great families

The anonymity of the wife in masculine discourse poses thorny problems for historians trying to identify her with the help of the meagre remains of various fragmentary genealogies. One of the *plausible* reconstructions of Pericles' ancestors ended by proposing a *possible* name for this anonymous woman: she might be called Dinomache. However, as nothing is certain and to remain in the spirit of my sources, I shall from now on designate her as D. Table 4.1 shows the probable family tree of Pericles and D. as the work of historians has been able to reconstruct it (all the people written *in the same way* in the coming tables belong to the same lineage).

Table 4.1

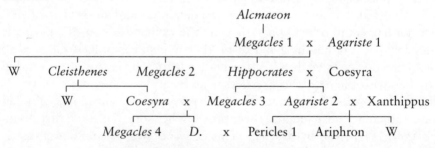

Note that W stands for an anonymous woman.

All these matching names – the Alcmaeons, Megacles – all descendants of the same ancestor, form a line, that of the Alcmaeonides, which was famous in the Athens of that period. Descendants of the same Alcmaeon,[1] Cleisthenes and Hippocrates marry their children to each other and D.'s grandfather is the paternal uncle of Pericles' mother. Going down a generation, on one hand Coesyra and Megacles 3 have two children, a Megacles 4 and this D.; on the other, Agariste 2 and Xanthippus have three children: Pericles 1 (the one we know), a brother Ariphron and an anonymous sister. D. marries our Pericles 1, in her second marriage; she is his relative, says Plutarch: to be precise, they are respectively the granddaughter and

1. Although all the male descendants of Alcmaeon really belong to the line, the women form part of it only as daughter-of until they marry; then, passing into their husband's house, their children belong to the lineage of their spouse.

grandson of two brothers, and are second cousins. Working backwards, let us complete the astonishing matrimonial career of D., taking a look at her first marriage. She had married at her first wedding Hipponicus, by whom she had Callias 'the Rich'. Table 4.2 shows the simplified reconstructed family tree.

Table 4.2

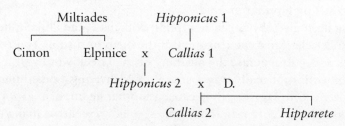

Callias 2 is 'Callias the Rich', according to Plutarch. Rich, certainly, and very important. The family to which he belongs, the Ceryces, is one of those about whom enough is known to be able to say that they combined the majority of elements which, in that epoch, imparted true prestige to a line. Wealth? There is no doubt about it. Was it not said of his father, Hipponicus 2, that he was the richest man in Greece? His wealth was derived mainly from mines. Another Hipponicus, the son of Callias 2, had 600 slaves working for him in the silver mines of Laurium[2] in the territory of Athens. Prestige too. From time immemorial, this Ceryces family had held the outstanding privilege of filling the office of *daidouchos*, one of the two principal priests of the Eleusinian mysteries, that most important manifestation of religious life in Athens. Political power also: the family regularly provided magistrates, *choregoi*[3] and ambassadors (to the Great King, and to Sparta). As for Hipponicus 2's maternal origins, they were not bad either: Elpinice and her brother Cimon were descended via their father Miltiades (the victor of Marathon) from the important Philaïdae family.

Princes in all the known worlds marry princesses, and as there was no apparent reason why marriage should not be used, here as elsewhere, as a means of social elevation, D. must not have been out of place in this milieu. Indeed, she was the descendant of a no less illustrious family: the Alcmaeonidae. What clearly gave them the advantage compared with the Ceryces was political prestige. People were indebted to them for having

2. The mines of south-east Attica which partly contributed to the fortune and power of Athens.
3. Wealthy citizens who took responsibility for a liturgy, consisting of paying the costs of rehearsal and performance by a choir.

actively challenged and then overthrown the tyranny of Pisistratus and the Pisistratidae in the sixth century. As far as wealth is concerned, although not attaining the magnificence of the Ceryces, they do not seem to have had much to complain about. Herodotus records that the ancestor, Alcmaeon, became the richest man in Greece, thanks to Croesus' generosity to him, and that a Megacles of the sixth century contributed money to the rebuilding of Apollo's temple at Delphi, which was by no means negligible. In short, D. was on familiar ground.

Having been given by her father to Hipponicus 2, the Philaïd, he passed her on to Pericles for some reason after the birth of a son.[4] To say 'passed her on' is not to exaggerate the meaning of the Greek word and the image associated with it; it really was a matter of 'delivering' something, 'handing her over'. With Pericles, D. became a mother again, of two sons, then, if we read Plutarch correctly, the couple seemed to feel that living together no longer suited them and decided by common consent to separate in a kind of divorce by mutual agreement. As she had not finished her reproductive career, Pericles passed her on – again that verb – to another as a legitimate spouse. Pericles acted magnanimously: he helped in transferring D. to a new 'house' (the last, as far as we know), and added to his wife's dowry. The last husband must have been highly content, and perhaps in his eyes that compensated for a slight lack of freshness which having been the wife, successively, of Hipponicus and Pericles might suggest. Let us look, in Table 4.3, at the continuation and (for us) the end of this matrimonial history.

Table 4.3

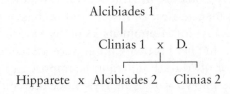

Once this matrimonial path was trodden, it seems that, although D. remained anonymous for so long, she was nonetheless a person of great price in the history of Athens. The granddaughter of the eminent reformer Cleisthenes, the wife of the richest man in Greece and then of the man who gave his name to his century, to end her reproductive career (at least as far

4. Perhaps there were other children, especially if they were girls. A good many daughters and women, without any special role in history (in the vaguest sense of the word), do not appear in lists and, therefore, in genealogical reconstructions.

as we know) she gave birth to two boys, one of whom during his lifetime continued to rouse conflicting passions, and has been of interest to historians ever since: the handsome, impetuous Alcibiades. Leaving aside the prestigious image of his family, the Eurysacidae (descendants of the Homeric hero Ajax), I will call to mind just one aspect of the biography of this famous offspring: 'Clinias (D.'s husband) fought with glory at Artemisium on a trireme[5] equipped at his expense, and later he died fighting the Boeotians at Coronea' (Plutarch, *Life of Alcibiades* 1. 1).

Before Clinias died, he had already appointed Pericles and his brother Ariphron as guardians of his children Alcibiades 2 and Clinias 2, if he should come to grief, and he had been wise to make provision. Aged about five, Alcibiades thus joined the 'house' of his mother's former husband (had she given her advice? Pericles had probably been informed and had consented). The boy had nothing to complain about in the matter of wealth. Pericles, who legally managed his fortune for him until he came of age, did not have the reputation of a spendthrift – quite the contrary. And then, he would have all that his marriage in 422 brought him.

And who married Alcibiades? Or rather, whom did Pericles agree to accept as the wife of his ward? It could only be the daughter of one of Athens' richest citizens: Hipparete, a daughter of Hipponicus, the Ceryce we have just seen. In the interim, D.'s first husband, whom she had left on his own, had married a nameless woman (perhaps he had passed D. on to Pericles with the idea of marrying her). For his part, the older of Pericles' children, Xanthippus, married a daughter of Teisander, a representative of the senior branch of the Philaïdae. As C. Mossé says, Pericles must have needed a good dose of non-conformism to 'break with these practices' of consanguinity, whose economic and political reasons are easy to fathom, 'and repudiate his wife to live with a foreign woman.' We do not know what became of D. afterwards. She was still alive and very wealthy when Alcibiades was about twenty. After that, nothing more. She had done more than her share of providing boys in several 'houses', and that was what really counted.

This close-knit tracery of matrimonial relations is truly amazing. It might be said that high society still works like this – how many examples are there in the courts of modern and contemporary Europe? But in the same way that, confronted with one such as Nausicaa, we can only come up with the anonymous *amphipoloi*, in the fifth century there are no examples to set against this so-called aristocracy, and consequently nothing to tell us (but nothing to deny) that the poor did not practise the same social

---

5. A warship with three banks of oarsmen – the most effective warship – for which the richest Athenians were obliged to provide most of the necessary finance.

endogamy. All we have are a few clues to make us think that this intermarriage, on the social as well as the genetic plane, was a very Greek form of alliance. It was thus that, *mutatis mutandis*, these customs of the 'upper crust' appeared among the 'bourgeois' and lower classes of Athens, and that leaving the *Lives of Illustrius Men* of the fifth century for the defence pleas of civil lawsuits in the fourth (and thus for more modest circles), we find a fair number of features in common with the matrimonial customs we have just seen: numerous remarriages and endogamy. This is what Plutarch repeats, making it a rule of behaviour of the Greeks compared with the Romans: 'For what reason do they, the Romans, not marry their close relatives?' (Plutarch, *Roman Questions* 108, 289d). Read from the Greek viewpoint, in other words conversely, one of Plutarch's replies certainly contains some truth: Greek endogamy may have been caused by the wish to limit alliances and kinships to the point where the two ideas merged.

The facts, therefore, are merely anecdotal and if we are to understand them better, we must examine the strategic rules governing these matrimonial practices. Everything revolves round a figure of a dynamic social geometry – the 'circulation' of women, itself closely connected with that of wealth (that may be seen from the genealogical tables above). The woman-wife, passing from man to man and leaving the 'house' of the first to enter that of the second, grafts herself onto a line, as Penelope had done when she came from Icarius to enter the 'house' of Odysseus. Thus, in Table 4.2, the movements of Elpinice and D. are remarkably symmetrical. Each woman, belonging to a definite line – Elpinice to the Philaïdae, D. to the Alcmaeonidae – comes into a corner of a family tree symbolizing a patrilinear structure which is characterized by, among other things, the repetition of names from one generation to the next. D's entry into the lineage of the Eurysacidae in Table 4.3 presents the same image. If we regard the lines as coherent wholes, we see that they exchange mobile elements, daughters and women who (for a certain time, like D., or for life) become wives. For instance, the Alcmaeonidae send spouses to the Ceryces, the Eurysacidae and the unknown line of Xanthippus/Pericles, to end up sending them to themselves, such as the one named Coesyra. Branches detached from their own paternal trunk, the women-wives will, in turn, produce fruit elsewhere. The deep-rooted reasons for this situation are to be found in the legal definition and social practice of Athenian marriage in the classical period. It is therefore best to examine them as a whole, the better to interpret the story of D.

Marriage in the classical era: An agreement between two men

LEGAL AND SOCIAL ASPECTS

Marriage. The word and concept seem to speak for themselves. Nevertheless, the idea we have of it does not really fit with Greek reality. We associate it with a life in common based on a lifelong agreement. Not so the Greeks. Love and marriage for us are inseparable ideas. Our era and our western world cannot imagine marrying without love. How could one do otherwise? We may well concede that, purely through chance, the husband and wife in a Victorian marriage might love each other, but it seems incongruous; and it was somewhat the same in classical Greece. Love, if there was any, would be a bonus. Or because it *was* the custom to love; because, as Achilles says, every 'normal' man loves his *alochos* (see p. 49). However that may be, the question is a minor one: the main reason for marriage was to make a woman one's legitimate wife in order that she (because she enjoys an unambiguous origin) might produce legitimate children.

Greek marriage contains two crucial moments, which may be quite distant in time. First, there is the conclusion of a contract, the purpose of which is the handing over, the granting, of a daughter[6] coming from a 'house', by the man who has authority over her to another man, so that she goes to live in another 'house'. This gift takes place at a ceremony called *ekdosis*, the 'handing over.' Even without pomp, it requires the presence of witnesses; but nothing changes in the life of the betrothed until the tangible celebration of the marriage: the *gamos*, the content of which we shall examine. On the legal level, the central element of this transmission is extremely simple. It is a matter of an agreement between two men concerning the person of the girl. The first is her *kyrios* (guardian), most frequently her father, and this position confers on him the power to give her to another. As for the girl, it is quite clear that she has no say in the matter and is not necessarily required to be present. (Things are different when it comes to a remarriage – we saw Pericles pass D. on to Clinias, asking for her opinion.) Various fourth-century comedies have preserved the essentials of the dialogue exchanged in such circumstances by the two contracting adult male citizens.

---

6. *Daughter*, because the fundamental legal and social questions of Greek marriage first regulate the problems posed by the transfer of a *parthenos* (the way in which D. is wed very late in her life makes a clear distinction).

The father: I hand over this girl to you so that you may 'plough' her to beget legitimate children by her.

The son-in-law: I take her with pleasure.

The father: And I add this dowry of three talents.

The son-in-law: This also I accept with pleasure. (Menander, *Perikeiromene* 1,013–14; *cf. The Samian Woman*, 897–901)

In its astonishing simplicity, this act puts into effect a fundamental transfer, that of the weight of authority exercised by the man over the girl. She passes from her father's authority to that of her husband. An over-hasty jurist might argue that, by handing over his daughter, the father puts the taker in a position to exercise over her a coercive power that is the mark of marital authority. Yes, but only after a certain time . . . In fact, things have not changed since those *thygatres* in the *Iliad*, who were so close to their father that, even after their marriage, widowhood and capture by warriors, they always returned to him and were always identified with the help of his name. From the epic heroines to ordinary women the same strength of the father-daughter relationship can be seen. Perhaps not enough attention has been paid to what is said precisely in the dialogue of the contract. This girl has not been *given* by her father, she has been *handed over*. Should the husband behave badly towards her, should she complain and her father hear about it, he can take her back into his own home, making use of a pre-emptive right of the former 'house' over the new one. Of course, if the wife has become a mother, she is conclusively attached to the new 'house' (though we have seen how someone like D. can still be mobile), and that puts an end to the remnants of paternal authority.

In the classical era, matrimonial competition has disappeared and Odysseus no longer comes to parade before the house of Icarius in order to win the beautiful girl, but this absence is not a sign of the development of the matrimonial institution, and thus of the wife. There is no longer any reciprocity, the future husband no longer buys the daughter from her father; the only movement is made by the father towards the son-in-law, or rather the father's 'house' towards that, existing or yet-to-come, of the son-in-law. And assuredly, he is not in any hurry to get married.

DOWRY

For a marriage in correct and proper form, the father is not content to give his daughter – that would not be enough. Although he may not shower her with 'dazzling gifts' like the epic kings, the idea is still the same, even among the poor: a daughter is not given or received except with wealth. Wealth to send her on her way, and wealth to receive in return. Of course, one can always take a woman home and sleep with her, whether she has been bought or has come of her own free will; one may even install her in one's home, have children by her – look at Aspasia . . . But that will never be a legitimate marriage, producing legitimate offspring. No dowry, no official marriage – that's the rule. As with all rules, there are exceptions: Socrates for instance. I will refer again to his concubine, Xanthippe, but he has a second woman in the 'house', an 'official' one. This woman was Myrto who, despite being the granddaughter of a 'great man' of yesteryear (Aristides, an important strategist of the beginning of the fifth century), was 'doomed to spinsterhood because of her poverty' (Plutarch, *Life of Aristides* 27. 3–4, quoting other sources); Socrates had graciously agreed to 'take her in', although without a dowry. It was a generous gesture on his part, unusual and therefore worthy of being recalled.

Condemned to spinsterhood through poverty: it is easy to see by what mechanism the dowry formed a barrier excluding poor girls from the matrimonial market. But at first glance, the effect it could also have on men is less apparent. The contract between giver and taker is symmetrical, and the girl's parents also make a choice of their son-in-law. As popular wisdom has it, 'money attracts money', and a poor man cannot envisage the arrival in his possible 'house' of a girl plus her dowry. The city is threatened by this spinsterhood of the poor, and is sufficiently concerned to set up funds to provide a dowry for the most deprived marriageable girls. Traces of this anxiety are to be found in utopian constructions like that of Plato in the *Laws*, where civic equality as well as a ban on the dowry practice will result in the 'poor having little risk of growing old without taking a wife and marrying off their daughter because they lack resources' (Plato, *Laws* 774c). But he is also concerned about another consequence of the dowry system, its role as social marker, perceptible even within the 'house' in conjugal relations. He is afraid that the woman may play on the superiority that she would gain from a dowry contribution out of proportion to the wealth of her husband: '[In our city of the future] money matters there will lead fewer women to uppishness and husbands to a base and demeaning servitude' (Plato, *Laws* 774c).

Fathers have a struggle to endow their daughters, and who receives the dowries of the poor? And the dowries of the rich? It is a veritable market, with supply, demand and matching of the data provided. It could be said to be a fact of reality, but the result is a social endogamy we have already seen earlier. D. would certainly not have contradicted the adage that one marries in one's own circle.

Wealth? The Greeks made a distinction between two kinds: the visible – the 'house' in its material aspect, house, land and everything that gives them existence and makes them productive, like tools and slaves – and the invisible: money, sometimes the income from an asset. A daughter is more like money, she is mobile; a man is more like the land, stable. Furthermore, a man is a member of the political community, and it is by way of an exclusive connection with the land that, in general throughout Greece, one is a citizen.

Riches, but how much? It is obviously very variable. In the pleas of fourth-century lawsuits[7] (where not the poorest Athenian citizens fought their battles), the highest known dowries are twelve times the amount of the lowest.[8] To give a more concrete idea, the average daily wage of a building worker rose to 1.5 or 2 drachmas in the same period so these dowries are the equivalent of from 500 to 8,000 days' work (or over twenty years' labour, working every day). When one considers that the largest known dowry, of the Hipparete we have just seen, reached 20 talents, that makes 80,000 days. But what is its relative value? According to the same calculation, the share of the father's wealth taken by the dowry varied from around 5 per cent to over 25 per cent: for example, the father who gave his daughter a dowry of two talents subtracted 14 per cent of his fortune. For *one* daughter. Now, it seems to have been customary to endow any other sisters with equal amounts, so, with two (or more) daughters, the financial problems could be serious. Fathers were terrified by the prospect of seeing the share of dowries increase from 15 to 30 and 45 per cent of their total wealth. If the family had too many daughters and they were all to have a dowry, the 'house' would not have enough invisible wealth available, and would then have to sell part of the other, 'visible', property in order to provide a respectable dowry (which it was a point of honour to do). And that could not be done except to the detriment of the masculine inheritance. It would have been necessary to think beforehand (*well* beforehand) and bring up only a pre-planned number of daughters. The other solution would be to endow only the daughter(s) one wished to endow and let the rest waste away in the dark depths of the household, because people like Socrates, who would take them as they came, were thin on the ground.

It will come as no surprise to learn that the dowry which the father throws in with his daughter is not for her. So where did it go then? Its

7. C. Leduc, 'Comment la donner en mariage?', in P. Schmitt Pantel (ed.) (1991), *Histoire des femmes. L'antiquité*, Paris, pp. 302ff; translated as 'Marriage in Ancient Greece' in P. Schmitt Pantel (ed.) (1992), *A History of Women in the West*, Cambridge, MA, pp. 278ff.

8. One talent = 60 minae and one mina = 100 drachmas.

journey holds quite a few surprises; and when following it we are helped by L. Gernet's phrase: the dowry follows the woman *like her shadow*. Whatever her social path after she has left her 'house', whether she returns to her father or whether he or another remarries her once or more, as with D., throughout her lifetime her dowry always goes with her. If *she* is not the holder (it is her dowry, but she cannot touch it), nor is her husband. He has custody of this dowry, can have the use and profit of it, can derive every possible advantage from it, but he must return it intact when the woman moves. We have already seen Penelope's situation. As a widow, she would return to her father and Telemachus would then have to reimburse Icarius for all he had paid out. Dowry rests on an economic principle which in the end is very modern: the capital does not belong to you but you try to make it bear fruit while drawing interest from it. However, it may happen that the husband's business is bad or he may prove dishonest when the time comes to return the capital. Prudently, the father, guardian of his daughter's interests (and, indirectly, of his own), therefore makes the necessary prior arrangements so that he can regain control of the dowry later, even if the husband is insolvent or underhand. The stratagem consists in taking out a mortgage in advance on the husband's assets.

And the final destination of this 'pile'? It is added to the rest of the (paternal) inheritance and goes to the son or sons. D.'s dowry, increased by the contributions of successive husbands (or at least that of Pericles), went to Alcibiades and Clinias. Table 4.4 shows how this works.

Table 4.4

```
    W1  =  M1          W2  =  M2
        |                   |
      W3          =         M3
              ┌─────┴─────┐
            W4           M4
```

In Table 4.4 M1 endows his daughter W3 for her to marry M3; if nothing untoward happens, W3's dowry will go to her son M4. But when M3 has to give W4 a dowry, he cannot use his wife W3's since he cannot commit the capital; as a good paterfamilias he must therefore use the dowry he inherited from his mother, W2 (as M1 had done for W3). A husband does not endow his daughter with his wife's money. The way this works is in harmony with a kind of permanence of the values of the dowry over several generations, the ideal being to endow one's daughter with the same capital as that inherited from one's mother. From one generation to the next, the paths of money cross. They return to the same sex every other generation. What might be termed the pecuniary descent follows this route: on the left

– father → daughter → daughter's son; on the right – paternal mother →
son → son's daughter. As for the visible assets – chiefly house and land –
they obviously follow the masculine line and go, for example, in a direct
line from M2 to M3, then to M4. This means that the possessions of M3,
for instance, go to W4 and M4, whereas those of W3 go to M4 alone. In
the geneaological trees, money and land cross paths, and this cross-traffic
is typical of the way marriage and inheritance functioned in Athens.

Accustomed as we are now to the inferiority and social subordination of
the female, we run the risk here of missing the opportunity to point out for
once a symmetry of roles, underlined by the emphasis on the female line of
descent. In any case, the dowry system is of signal interest to women. Having the backing of their dowry forms the best guarantee of finding a home,
and then of finding another. Of course, this insurance is not absolute and
obviously depends on its total amount. But a woman is not married *only*
for her dowry. Although money may well form the main element of choice,
other arguments may come into play: the friendly relations one has with
her *kyrios*, his reputation and that of his 'house' and, more generally, the
desire to ally oneself with such a 'house'. For the woman, it is all or nothing. Marriage ensures that she will have a roof over her head, status and
sustenance. Women with no 'house' are in great danger in the city.
Assuredly, children are the support of their parents and, indeed, that is one
of the main reasons for having them. But children may disappear . . . Then,
for the woman, everything depends on her age and what stage she has
reached in her reproductive career. Conversely, the rules for passing on the
dowry form a brake on the social standing of men; indeed, fathers sometimes have to wait for their mother to die before they can give their daughter a dowry.

THE AUTHORITY OF FATHERS AND HUSBANDS

Something that happened to the wife of Alcibiades opens up other hori-
zons. '[Alcibiades] had married [Hipparete] the sister of Callias[9] with a
dowry of ten talents' (Plutarch, *Life of Alcibiades* 8. 3). A colossal dowry!
That was the original contract, and in fact it led him to 'demand ten more
talents on the death of Hipponicus.' In this instance, marrying the daughter of Hipponicus meant hitting the jackpot. Andocides, a contemporary
(and adversary), specifies that Alcibiades claimed Hipponicus 'had promised to add this sum when his daughter bore Alcibiades a child, no doubt *a
son*' (*Against Alcibiades* iv. 13). With all we have learnt of Greek fathers'

9.   See Table 4.3.

special relationships with their daughters and daughters' offspring, there is nothing beyond the bounds of imagination in this anecdote, but it signifies the true reason why a Greek father gives his daughter in marriage: the father of a daughter agrees to a man providing him with grandchildren. But let us return to Hipparete, now a mother. 'She was a self-disciplined woman who loved her husband' (Plutarch), and according to Andocides, was very honest as well. But, 'unhappy in her marriage, and seeing that Alcibiades frequented both foreign and Athenian courtesans' (Plutarch), and had courtesans, either slaves or free women' 'under his own conjugal roof' (Andocides), she left her 'house' and went to her brother's.

> As Alcibiades was not in the least upset by this, and went on with his debauchery, she had to lodge her petition for divorce before the archon, not through an intermediary, but by presenting herself in person. (Plutarch, *Life of Alcibiades* 8. 5)

The story is coherent: this mother, a loving woman who has been cast aside, can no longer put up with it and, as the law authorizes, puts a petition for divorce before the archon *without resorting to a man*. This 'naturally' disciplined woman must go beyond the reserve inherent in her kind; indeed the law obliges her to free herself for a moment from that legal nothingness which is the mark of the Athenian woman, to commit herself physically to making this approach. Here we have a fine instance of masculine hypocrisy: those who, on the one hand, give wives the chance of freeing themselves from intolerable husbands and, on the other, set a condition upon this measure which goes against women's whole upbringing and all the values which they are deemed to embody. Here is Hipparete, compelled to go through the town in person to approach the magistrate. Alcibiades' wife, a unique example of the married species, has to pass before the eyes of men. For his part, Alcibiades has 'summoned his friends', who are many, thanks to his great wealth.

> As Hipparete was going to fulfil this legal formality, Alcibiades hurled himself upon her, seized her bodily and brought her back to his house, crossing the agora, and no one dared to challenge him or take her away from him. (Plutarch, *Life of Alcibiades* 8. 5)

Alcibiades was prompted by two motives: first, to demonstrate in a way that was misplaced, but doubtless well regarded by Athenians, the power of his marital authority. Secondly, of course, he wanted to avoid Hipparete's departure obliging him to pay back her fabulous dowry. We may well believe, with Plutarch, that there was nothing 'absolutely contrary to the law' about it: it was a kind of 'reconciliation process' before a magistrate, with a good dose of hypocrisy, but this same Plutarch shows himself to be far from impartial when he adds that there was nothing 'inhuman' about it either. The remainder of Hipparete's married life was probably not much fun: 'She stayed in her husband's 'house' until her death, which occurred not long afterwards' (*Life of Alcibiades* 8.5).

FROM DAILY LIFE TO (QUALITATIVE) DEMOGRAPHY

Our brothers are luckier than we, poor girls. A boy can go out with his comrades, play with them . . . But *we* are shut in as if in a vault, in our dark room, prey to wretched boredom, and the sun hardly shines for us. (*Palatine Anthology* v. 97, Agathias Scholasticus)

Girls

Leaving aside those recidivists of marriage in the manner of D., let us get to know the young bride, known as a *nymphe*. It is easy to paint a portrait of her, in broad brushstrokes. Very young, often a *pais*, she has only just left her childhood playthings. *Parthenos*, of course; who would take a deflowered girl? She is fairly unsociable. The coming time will be that of her domestication in both senses of the word. She is necessarily the *thygater* of her father – there is no cheating about heredity. A good *kore*, she knows nothing of the world except from the lips of her closest companions (ideally, nothing); she is a minor, subordinate, with no authority over herself. Until now she has been entirely dependent on the father to whom she is doubly indebted for her life, since he could just as well have refused to bring her up when she was born. Her mother has advised her above all to be well-behaved. She is young, but what does that mean? Nausicaa was in the 'sapling stage' of her growth. The girl whom Hesiod advises his brother to marry must be a virgin, so that he can inculcate wise principles in her. The wife of Ischomachus (see Chapter 5) was not yet fifteen when she came to his 'house'. 'Not yet fifteen', so does that mean she was fourteen? By today's standards, these are very young girls. If we follow the advice of those – such as Aristotle and Plato – who have contemplated an ideal organization of society as far as this kind of detail is concerned, the perfect ages are a little older: they recommend from sixteen to twenty years. Aristotle speaks as a doctor and chiefly fears all the damage which too early marriage may cause the offspring and the mother (but when does 'too early' start, when marriage at sixteen is advised?). He says that sickly or weak children are born from parents who are too young (or too old);

moreover, a 'doctor of souls' into the bargain, he considers that a *nymphe* who is too young develops too great a liking for intercourse. In the passage from the *Politics* devoted to this topic, Aristotle recounts the oracular reply given to the city of Troezen (in the north-east of the Peloponnese) which, at a moment in its history, was worried about the disastrous mortality rate among children of tender age and their mothers. The oracle, which must have known the matrimonial customs in question, answered the Troezenians in oracular fashion – in other words, ambiguously: 'Do not plough a young fallow field', which Aristotle comments on thus: 'For it will bear no more fruit' (*Politics* vii. 16. 7. 1,335a). 'To plough', we have already heard this verb on the lips of the father of the bride when he says to the future son-in-law: 'I give you this girl for you to "plough" her and beget legitimate children', and in the mouths of the randy types in comedy. And I have already emphasized the connection established by comedy between the activities of farming and masculine sexuality, accompanied by the fact that the feminine sex is itself a field or a garden. But hearing the oracle's reply, the Troezenians understood not only that they were prohibited from 'ploughing', but also from 'wounding the young sex' (by copulating with it), with the same result that it would no longer produce fruit. They must therefore stop marrying girls who were *too* young. If demography today knows that an extreme lowering of the age of fruitfulness, by a phenomenon which seems a kind of compensation, in no way increases the number of children per woman, how old are these girls who are wounded by the sexual act?

How old is the virgin Hippe, for whom her parents ask the protection of Artemis 'so that her marriage-day [her *gamos*, or wedding night] may be the one when she becomes a mother', and who 'still likes to play with her knuckle-bones'? (*Palatine Anthology* vi. 276, Antipater of Sidon). How old is the Timareta who has consecrated to the same Artemis,

> when she is wed, . . . her tambourines, the ball she loved, the snood which held back her tresses; and her curls she has dedicated, as is fitting, a virgin herself, to the virgin goddess Artemis, together with her childhood's clothes . . .? (*Palatine Anthology* vi. 280, Anonymous)

Knuckle-bones, tambourines, ball, children's games, hair, clothing – these virgins dedicate to Artemis, the goddess of childhood, the objects that symbolize their condition. Let us not use the word adolescence for the Greek *nymphe* – she is violently transferred from the world of childhood to that of adult sexuality, and does so still looking behind her in the only direction she knows. Nothing in Greek literature puts it better than a fragment from the Greek poetess Erinna:

Your traces, young maiden, are imprinted, still warm, in my heart.
Everything that we once enjoyed is henceforth nothing but ashes. Our
dolls were our sole concern, little girls in our rooms, playing at being
wives, carefree . . . But, once in the bed of a man, you have forgotten all
your mother taught you as a child, dear Baucis: yes, the forgetfulness in
your heart is the work of Aphrodite. (*Suppl. Hell.*, 1b col. 2)

The life of a Greek girl stops the moment she becomes a woman. She goes
straight from child to wife. There is none of that adolescent parenthesis –
which boys experience – of indefinite duration. The result: she swings from
her childhood occupations to the responsibility of mistress of the 'house',
from her innocent games to a man's bed.

The *nymphe*, like the *eromenos*,[10] is therefore a child, but the historian's
concern is not only to be able to quantify this or that aspect of an institution, to say that the *nymphe* weds at such and such an age (this is a preoccupation for the scholar). According to how one views it, the union of
husband and wife does not have quite the same interpretation: what about
the sexuality of the maiden, and that of the newly-wed couple? To answer
the question we must look at the legal measures taken by the cities.

The *ecclesia*, or people's assembly, did not concern itself with regulating
marriageable age directly, except insofar as it was considered necessary to
replace the intentions of 'houses' by entrusting to the public authorities the
operation of a procedure that would make up for a private shortfall. This
was the case for orphans, and for the city of the Thasians, which decided
after a war to offer them some support by offering boys a warrior's equipment and girls a dowry derived from public funds. The 'deadline' was to be
fourteen years, so the girls of Thasos could be married at that age. More
generally, the cities also legislated to settle the thorny question of the
brotherless girls whose 'house' had passed into female hands, whom their
father had not bequeathed to anyone, and who found themselves on the
marriage market with a complete inheritance to pass on. The city would
offer them in marriage to one of their relatives, after he had claimed
responsibility for them. The Athenians decided that this process would get
underway when the girl reached fourteen. But at Gortyn, a Cretan city, the
age would be twelve. And that is without taking into account the fact that
the Greek way of calculating, an inclusive method, adds a unit to any number and that, as a result, their fourteen and twelve years would correspond
to *our* thirteen and eleven years (in the same way that the Olympic games
came round every fifth year, in other words every four years). Thirteen
years, eleven years – that's very young.

10.   The one who, in the pederastic couple, is the beloved of the adult lover: the erastes.

It is understandable that the wife-to-be is still playing at knuckle-bones; 'her heart filled with sweet heedlessness', she is reluctantly entering a 'dwelling where everything seems strange', including her husband. 'She will need to be a prophetess to discover, unless she has learnt it at home, how to act correctly with her bedfellow,' says Euripides' Medea (*Medea* 238–40). With a mother who tells her nothing, making the leap is dizzying. To imagine the state in which the child finds herself as she arrives in her new 'house', we must reflect on that extraordinary sentence, the terrible words of that perfect 'good and upright man', Ischomachus, in Xenophon's *Oeconomicus*, when speaking of his new wife:'When she had become familiar with me, and had been *sufficiently tamed to converse . . .* I was able to begin her education' (*Oeconomicus* vii. 10). The little girl, who was not fifteen when she arrived at his home, was struck dumb. How long did she remain silent?

To give a girl in marriage at fifteen or twelve years of age certainly changes many ideas, which might have been considered universal, about the aesthetic, the erotic and marriage itself, which in this country are revealed as very different and exotic. The fact that the Greeks could wed little girls is kept quiet: moderns, like the ancients, do not speak of it. As has been done, with difficulty, for pederasty, we must grasp the nettle and face the facts. The Greek adult *could* marry a prepubescent child. In fact, a Greek girl of eleven, twelve, and even thirteen or over, in antiquity, was unlikely to be pubescent.[11] Marriages of prepubescents also existed in the Roman world, but that did not mean this type of marriage was the norm. In this area, the difficulty lies not so much in history as in our own conceptions. The alternative is either to reject the evidence (or deny that it should be given any importance, under the pretext of unconsummated marriages), without any other basic reason than that it does not match the way we picture that culture, or to accept what the sources say and try to understand them. To reach our goal we have several paths available to us, but first we must take a look at the boys.

Boys

Meanwhile the story of the boys is as different as can be: in contrast with all this haste, theirs is a waiting game. In Athens, from the time of the ceremonies that accompany their biological puberty, they await their *ephebeia* (their 'military service'), then their citizenship (at twenty), then being able to speak in public at the Assembly (thirty), then being able to apply for

---

11. Greek doctors generally set the menarche at the fourteenth year, that is, at thirteen years old.

their first posts as magistrates (thirty or over), then to gather the where-withal to set themselves up, found a new 'house' and thus to marry (easier on the death of their father), and finally they await the money from their mother's dowry in order to endow their daughter . . . In other cities, such as Sparta, all that is postponed still further to more advanced ages. Until their marriage, these boys, young men and mature men are without a free heterosexual partner of their own age. All they have available are homo-sexual partners – successively adults and then children – or paid (or adulter-ous) heterosexual partners. But not everyone can afford to pay, so for men the marriageable age is very belated: on average, thirty years, although people like Aristotle and Plato recommend thirty-five.[12] If the *nymphe* is fourteen years old like Ischomachus' wife, and the husband thirty, that makes an age-gap of fifteen years, and this may well rise to twenty (a gap advised by Aristotle) or more. This is the sort of gap which few societies experience.

Where there is beauty, I am ambidextrous. (Plutarch, quoting a play in *Eroticus*, 767a)

Zeus changed himself into an eagle to find the divine Ganymede, into a swan to approach Helen's blonde mother. See how impossible it is to compare these two voluptuous pleasures; if you had to choose only one? Some prefer the first, others the second; as for me, I'll have both. (*Palatine Anthology* v. 65, Anonymous)

The Greeks express their taste for the two elements of sexuality, homo- or hetero-, in exactly the same way. When it is young, the masculine body, like the feminine, offers these constant qualities of softness and whiteness of skin. The ideal is smooth, immaculate, milky, soft and scented. The epi-grams of the *Palatine Anthology* repeat at every possible opportunity how beautiful all these boys are. Fair, more rarely dark, 'white'. First of all one admires their look (lively, passionate), their torso, their thighs, their but-tocks. Assuredly, the Eros of boys is more imperious than the Aphrodite of women: 'There is only one true *eros*, the love of boys' (Plutarch, *Eroticus* 751a).

'With the *parthenos*, there is no ring to grip you,[13] no simple kiss, nor that good natural scent of the skin, nor all those delicious, lascivious

12. Plato thus envisages punishing those reluctant to marry: 'If anyone does not freely obey but, remaining alien and unsociable in the city, reaches thirty-five without having taken a wife, he shall be fined each year' (*Laws* 774a).
13. The anal sphincter; in the usual form of pederastic coitus, the adult (face to face with the boy) places his penis between the boy's thighs.

words, nor that guileless look' (*Palatine Anthology* xii. 7, Strato). If this seems astonishing from our standpoint, let us not suppose that it is the inexperience of the *parthenos* which puts her in second place: 'A knowing girl is even worse! And, taken from behind, they are all frigid! But the most serious is this: there is nowhere to put a straying hand' (*Palatine Anthology* xii. 7, Strato).

The Greek man, however, does not value sodomy alone, and passes very easily (to say the least) from one partner to another as his polysexuality allows him. At least, he does in spirit, because, faced with reality, it is not always easy to find a plentiful supply.

No longer do I love! I have battled against three desires – I burn for a hetaira, a *parthenos* and a young boy. I have nothing but suffering on all fronts. I wear myself out trying to persuade the hetaira to open her door to me, ever hostile to anyone who is penniless. At the young girl's threshold I lie stretched out, ever wakeful, only giving the child the most ardently awaited thing, a kiss. Alas! How shall I speak of my third flame? From him I get nothing but looks and sterile hopes ... (*Palatine Anthology* xii. 90, Anonymous)

The gods themselves are versatile, Zeus most of all; does he not go from Ganymede to the immortal and mortal women as well? But one of the most original features of these bachelor loves is their evanescence.

Twelve years, a lovely age, which enchants me! But the thirteen-year-old has many more attractions! With twice seven years [the age of puberty], you have one of the Loves' most exquisite flowers. Still more of a charmer is the one completing his third lustrum. Sixteen years, the year of the gods! Seventeen is not for me: reserved for Zeus' hunting ground! If one falls for an older boy, it is no longer a game for children, it is 'look for your like.'[14] (*Palatine Anthology* xii. 4, Strato)

The child is at the point of the metamorphosis of puberty. The result is the rapid and ineluctable end of sexual love for/with children. It is a suffering inherent in this premise: the one you love grows older, and quickly. 'A fine down slips on to his temples', 'prickly hairs on his thighs'. It is over. Who would prefer 'dry stubble'?

14. Meaning: one leaves the tacit common rules for pederastic love for homosexual relations which, although tolerated, are nonetheless considered as outside the norm.

Why are you covered down to your ankles, Menippus, you who used to tuck your tunic up to your thighs! Head lowered, you hastened past me, without so much as a word; why? I know what you are hiding from me: they have come, *those things* I was talking about! (*Palatine Anthology* xii. 176, Strato)

The appearance of boys? Soft, tender, fair, complexion like roses. And of girls? In the portraits of the amorous epigrams in the *Palatine Anthology*, as well as the look (like boys), lips and breasts are the most often quoted. Then there is a regular comparison with flowers, chiefly roses:

I will braid white wallflowers, I will braid the delicate narcissus with myrtle, and I will also braid lovely lilies, and sweet saffron; and the crimson hyacinth, and the rose, so dear to lovers, so that, on the scented curls at Heliodora's temples my garland will flood her hair with a rain of flowers. (*Palatine Anthology* v. 147, Meleager)

Chaeremon, a forgotten writer, left several lines which assemble Greek ideas about feminine beauty.

One woman, lying down, revealed one of her white breasts in the moonlight, her shoulder brooch being undone. Another showed all her left side as she danced; naked, she was truly a living picture; her colour, so white to my eyes, conquered the black shadows. This one's arms were bare down to her beautiful hands: she entwined the delicate neck of one of her companions. The other, beneath the folds of her parted tunic, revealed her thigh. (Chaeremon, fr. 1, Snell, quoted by Athenaeus, xiii. 608D)

The flush of her youth over, a woman laments 'the fresh complexion, the swelling breasts, the slender ankle, the shapely waist . . .' Freshness and whiteness, slenderness and soft smoothness. In this ivory landscape, the same enemy has to be eradicated: hair. 'Milk-white breasts', a skin that is fine, delicate, white but, above all, hairless. If a pederastic relationship no longer has the same flavour when the first beard appears, women in their intimate toiletry try to make their body conform to the dominant eroticism – that of men who love boys – and therefore assiduously depilate themselves, including their genital parts, often with a lamp, at the cost of what suffering may be imagined. A body like a statue. 'The child has a feminine form', declares Aristotle. What about this famous difference in age between Greek husband and wife? The childlike body of the prepubescent *nymphe*, hesitating on the brink, not yet truly feminine, white, clean-cut and soft, like that of a young boy, has nothing that might put off a husband. Boys and girls: a single aesthetic form, a single erotic form. The enigma of the marriage of girl-children with very mature men here finds its solution in the nature of the aesthetic and erogenous qualities of the prepubescent of both sexes. In Sparta, according to Hagnon the philosopher of the Academy, 'it is customary to have relations with young girls (*parthenoi*) according to pederastic practice' (quoted by Athenaeus, xiii. 602d–e), in other words, in an intercrural position;[15] to back up his remarks Athenaeus quotes a line of Solon, who uses no pederastic ambiguity: 'Desirous of thighs and tasty mouth' (compare Plutarch, *Eroticus*, 751b).

THE EUGENICS OF CITIES, THE AUTHORITY OF FATHERS

The all-powerful father is an image often highlighted among the Romans, and also valid for the Greeks. The expression of the father's will is as effective in the positive as in the negative. Modelled on Hephaestus, the craftsman god who makes Pandora, with the help of a little earth and some water, the father has the right, starting from nothing, to *manufacture* a child for himself, a social child. Let us picture a man, thwarted despite his efforts in his desire to have a male birth in the family, or a bachelor with no hope of offspring: by an appropriate process of adoption, he can *make* a boy who is biologically another's child (even with the father still living) his socially acknowledged son, with all the consequences this affiliation involves – succession in political status, inheritance of wealth. Grandfathers' liking for their daughters' sons often makes them adopt in this fashion. However, men engage much more rarely in such a powerful procedure to *manufacture* daughters.

Just as he is able to 'make' a son of another father's boy, this all-powerful man can also dispose of a child that is already born, and then little girls are the ones who will suffer the most. On this matter of the elimination of children we can, of course, go through all the euphemisms we want (euphemisms whose origins are to be found among the Greeks themselves), diluting the language with words such as 'exposing', 'abandoning' or 'not raising'; the fact remains that the Greek father kills children who are born to him. Most often he does so through an intermediary, women or slaves. The victims may be classified in three categories. First, there are 'love-children', the products of the wife's adultery or of a seduced *parthenos* of the 'house'; their fate is sealed beforehand and the woman carrying the

15. See below (p. 203) the curious scene between the courtesan Aspasia and King Artexerxes.

child knows what she has to do. There are also children of whom the women (midwives, female relatives present at the birth) say at their birth that they are defective, with physical blemishes that are interpreted as signs of bad luck; in these cases the women may advise, but the father makes the decision. In some cities, it is the magistrates who decide on the elimination. The foregoing eventualities affect both sexes in unpredictable, thus *a priori* equal, fashion, and in any case their demographic consequences are negligible.

It is not the same for the third reason, which I shall call Malthusian, the *a posteriori* control of offspring. It is a matter of an extra mouth to feed, of the daughter who, like the wife, devours the 'house' (an old fantasy . . .) produces nothing, costs a fortune in dowry, takes the place of the impatiently awaited boy-child. One could go on *ad infinitum*. In this game of massacre, girls are in the front line. The first-born are especially in danger; it is not by chance that the majority of the family clans that we are able to reconstruct, no matter what the type of source, begin with a boy. The prayer addressed to the gods by Athenians at their marriage says it clearly to whoever wants to understand: 'May my first-born be a boy and not a girl!' Later in time, a strange document speaks of this obsession with the birth of a boy and its consequences. In an inscription, a certain Polychronius provides a place in his sarcophagus for his wife Meltine, on condition that when he dies she is still his wife. Very well. But why should she not be? 'It is not enough for Meltine not to divorce in order to remain Polychronius' wife,' says the commentator on this inscription; 'she will have to give him a child – and not a daughter but, naturally, a son; if she is barren or persists in giving birth to a string of daughters, she will have to pack her bags, give up being the wife of Polychronius and having a right to a place in the tomb.'[16] Mothers themselves contribute to this emphasis on masculine birth:

> To the Paphian Aphrodite, Callirhoe has consecrated these garlands, to Pallas her curly hair, to Artemis this girdle; for she found the husband she wished for, spent her youth chastely and, when she became a mother, gave birth to sons. (*Palatine Anthology* vi. 59, Agathias Scholasticus)

For precise details we need to go beyond the modern sensitivities of historians of antiquity and look at figures. When a city like Miletus, in the Hellenistic period, integrated new citizens into its civic body, it recorded them in lists carved on stones. These registers contain hundreds of names

16. L. Robert (1965), *Hellenica*, XIII, 218 commenting on *Monumenta Asiae Minoris Antiqua* viii. (1962) no. 576.

out of the thousands which ought to feature there. They are arranged by family; everyone goes through, including children, boys and girls, and distinction is made for each gender between pubescent and prepubescent. Now, upon puberty, for the normal sex ratio (demographically speaking) to be attained, there should be twice as many girls as there are. Where have they gone? Defenders of the traditional picture make a hasty excuse: they are not there because there was no point in recording them. Then why would those who nevertheless *are* there have been registered? A further reply: they are missing because they have left the 'house' to marry and are therefore recorded with their husbands. This applies for only a very small number. Insofar as the calculation bears on only the prepubescent of both sexes, the comparison of one sex with the other is not significantly altered by the absence of girls for reasons of marriage. The answer is simple: their absence from the family means their absence from the world (at least from the world of the family).[17] At least one out of two girls is missing from these lists and, most significantly, the deficit increases the more one is concerned with the youngest. Caution is advisable, however, because of the poor quality of the documentation. Moreover, in the same way that the fact that some prepubescent girls married does not imply that *all* the *nymphai* were prepubescent, it may be said that if the preferential elimination of girls did not regularly reach such a level, it nonetheless remains a profound demographic fact. It is sufficiently serious to bring about corrective reactions on the part of the social body, an adaptation of demographic behaviour. This was so with regard to age and the difference in age between husband and wife upon marriage; and also the frequency of remarriages and widowhood.

As a result of the preferential abandonment of girl children, boys were far more numerous at the age when *nymphai* marry; if marriage had taken place at that age for both sexes, 50 per cent of boys would have been bachelors, and it would have been very hard for a society to function in this way. Masculine celibacy had to be as low as possible; at community level, military power, and at the private level, the transmission of 'houses', were at stake. One of the factors being fixed beforehand by the number of surviving girls, society could juggle (unconsciously, of course) with the number of males available. The result was obtained by giving available girls not to boys of their own age, but to men born at least half a generation earlier: a fifteen-year-old girl to a man of between thirty and thirty-five. Here was the solution to the problem of too high a structural male bachelordom: from fifteen to thirty/thirty-five years, the cohorts of men were prey to the

---

17. A reconstruction of the families starting from the orators of the fourth century in Athens gives almost identical results.

double effect of natural mortality and the unpredictable, but possibly very high, mortality rate of war. This masculine postponement of the age of marriage allowed their numbers to be sufficiently close to the numbers of females. On the girls' side, the same phenomenon appeared from another angle: the later they married, the more difficult it was to resolve the problem of the numerical pairing of the sexes. The tendency was therefore to lower their marriageable age.

Seeing things working in this way, Aristotle gives a different explanation. In his opinion, it is advisable to avoid a situation where one of the married couple is capable of procreating and the other not (*Politics* vii. 14. 1,334b). His explanation slips from sociology to physiology: since man is fertile up to the age of seventy (Aristotle merges the possible and the probable) and woman up to fifty, 'the union of the sexes must begin at an age when it reaches its term at these years.' The couple must therefore be formed so that the girl marries a man twenty years her senior.

Apollo and a Muse. A meeting rare in real life between two young people of similar age; so it must be portrayed as divine, here a Muse and Apollo. Unlike the covered body of his contemporary, Apollo the ephebus shows no qualms about displaying his own. Courtesy of Museum of Fine Arts, Boston. Reproduced with permission. © Museum of Fine Arts, Boston. All rights reserved

As the offspring of parents who are too young, like those who are too old, are not of good quality, citizens should reproduce in the period of their full vigour . . ., which stretches to about fifty years. (Aristotle, *Politics* vii. 14. 4. 1,335a)

With regard to the later years of the couple, there is a symmetry, now:

Consequently, when this age [fifty] has been passed by four or five years, one's obligation to bring children into the world will be discharged, and during the remainder of one's life, sexual relations will only be for obvious reasons of health or some similar cause. (*Politics* vii. 14. 12. 335b)

The obligation is a political demand: when one has produced 'enough' children for the political community, when one has rendered it the 'service' it has the right to expect from each and every citizen, then the time of marriage may be over. Yet another sign of their conception of its transitory nature.

SPARTA IN DIRE STRAITS. OLIGANTHROPY? POLYANDRY? POLYGAMY?

We know how high the risks connected with childbirth were in ancient societies. Bringing a child into the world was undergone as an 'unendurable ordeal, accompanied by pain and tainted with blood', and despite the 'protection of Eileithyia and Lochia' (deities of childbirth), it caused the death of a good number of women. Nevertheless, an even greater number of couples were destroyed by the difference in age between the spouses, and the mortality of war. Husbands were in the front line. There were many widows, and fewer masculine than feminine remarriages; fine dowries, especially, found plenty of takers. Thus women and riches did the rounds. But poverty was enough to disqualify quite a few of these 'old ladies.' They found themselves without any real guardian, and only their sons could take them in. They were women without a man, not necessarily at the menopause, but now just a little freer, having acquired a new social status.

This shortage of women may explain a rare and disturbing social feature: the polyandry practised in Sparta. Concerned like other cities about the dangers from without, Sparta also feared those from within, worrying about its biological, and therefore political, survival. It was most troubled by the danger of being starved of men. In this city, where pederasty was more institutional than in Athens and could turn too many 'real men' away from marriage, single status was banned or, at least, bachelors were taxed.

Heavy emphasis was laid on the importance of the attention women must pay to conception, pregnancy and the concerns of childbirth. All this took place in the perspective of the community: they were to supply the city with soldiers. Children were the 'common asset of the city.' The strength of this idea went as far as questioning what had been believed to be perfectly established everywhere: women's work in the 'house' (see pp. 175–80), in particular weaving. Because the way of life it involved was the cause of bodily flabbiness, it was thought that it led to a lesser aptitude for carrying and nourishing the foetus. 'When an Ionian woman was boasting of the luxury of one of her garments, a Spartan woman, pointing to her four sons, all perfectly developed, said "these are the product of a respectable woman"' (Plutarch, *Moralia* 241d). Once we have rid ourselves of the rhetoric, there is a clear contrast between the Ionian woman's softness and luxury and the idea of indoor life that they imply,[18] and the active relationship which the Spartan woman maintains with her city through the care she takes of her body to ensure a better masculine output. In Sparta, better than elsewhere, we can see eugenics at work.

> Amongst the Lacedaemonians, there is an old and widespread custom allowing a woman to have three and even four husbands, even more if they were brothers, whose children were communal. Similarly, it was honourable and quite usual for a man, after he had fathered a large number of children, to offer his wife to one of his friends. (Polybius, xii. 6b)

He 'passed her on', if we understand correctly. This text by Polybius is comparable to another passage from Plutarch, in which the elderly husband, endowed with a young wife can, if he so desires and is acquainted with a fine and handsome young man, 'introduce him to her to impregnate her with a noble seed and keep the resultant child as his own offspring.' Wife and child would remain in the husband's 'house'. All the wife has done is to play the part of a receptacle for a seed considered to be of fine quality. But conversely, according to Xenophon, a man could, with the aim of obtaining the longed-for offspring by a certain woman, persuade her husband to let him have her for this purpose – 'without cohabitation'. The husband kept the child and the woman stayed with her husband. The very great age-difference between the spouses formed the principal reason for all this.

The motives connected with the ideal of eugenics were very strong in Sparta and explain a number of Spartan attitudes and conduct. In the sense of 'increase and multiply', the Spartans 'encouraged their women to

18.   On the 'feminine' or 'feminizing' softness of Ionia, see pp. 106–7.

procreate with the finest men, citizens as well as foreigners' (Nicolaus Damascenus *FGrH* 90 F 1,032 (144.6)). On the other hand, reproduction for the city was banned for those who were deemed likely to produce children incapable of satisfying the physical and moral demands of citizenship. Thus the 'tremblers' (*tresantes*) – those soldiers whom fear had impelled to desert the phalanx in combat – were treated as criminals: it was dishonourable 'to give them a woman in marriage or to receive one from their hands.' Thus, it was believed, their cowardice could not be passed on. Nothing in what we know of the dominant ideology of Sparta is contrary to this practice of polyandry. According to Xenophon, the woman could even have two 'houses'. As for the children, the husband regarded them as brothers to his own children, 'they share in kinship and power, but without having financial rights' (Xenophon, *The Constitution of the Spartans* I. 7–9).

SOCRATES OF ATHENS

If Spartan polyandry seems to reveal a lack of women, the fact that in Athens, during the Peloponnesian war (431–404 BC), a decree allowing 'anyone so desirous to have two wives' suggests a lack of men. The contents of this decree are not known to us with all the exactitude we should like; there is no mention of it except in the texts concerned with the alleged bigamy of Socrates, who actually had two wives, Xanthippe and Myrto, by whom he had children.

> The Athenians, wishing to increase the population, because of the shortage of men, had voted for a decree stipulating that a man could marry only one woman who was *astè* [of the town, Athenian] but could have children by another. (Diogenes Laertius, *Lives of the Philosophers* ii. 5. 26)

There is nothing inconceivable in the idea that the citizens of a Greek city legislated on their communal affairs, in fact on *all* communal affairs, for the greater good of the city, and this decree may well have been voted by an assembly worried about its human future, thus its safety. The fact that the decree reserves the title of wife only for a woman who was *astè*, and for one only, is totally in keeping with what we know of the legislation in force in Athens at that time. This required Athenians, if they wished to have legitimate children, to marry one wife, and one only, and only one who was *astè*, in other words a girl whose parents were themselves Athenian.

Another question is that of the nature of the citizen's connection with that other woman to whom the decree gave him access. At first one is tempted to reply that it speaks for itself, has always been the case, and that all men who want to can always sleep with and have children by anyone they want. But if so, why a decree? Why underline its pro-birth motives if the products of such a union are not citizens, but bastards? But the inadequate summary of the decree contains an ellipsis;[19] if it is a matter of compensating for an 'oligandry', this '*astè*' must be understood as 'even of the town'; in other words, one could, with new companions, have legitimate children with not just any woman but (even) with an *astè* woman. That is to say, a true bigamy could have been authorized, except for the detail that the second woman was only the mother of legitimate children and not a wife. After certain military disasters, it is not impossible that surviving Athenians resigned themselves to a measure that was contrary to their customary principles. The instance of Socrates seems to prove that this other woman, Xanthippe – a mother but not a wife – who gave him a hard time, had cohabited with the one who had given the children foreseen by the decree, as did the 'official' wife, Myrto, whom the philosopher had taken without a dowry (Plutarch, *Life of Aristides* 27. 4).

Socrates, however, professed the utmost scepticism with regard to marriage. Comparing those who questioned him on this subject to fish, he told them that he saw 'those who were outside wanting to enter the net, and those who were inside waiting to escape.' So if it was out of sheer goodheartedness that he took Myrto as his legitimate wife, a woman who could hardly be more '*astè*', despite her poverty, why on earth did he also take that strumpet, that lesbian, that scarecrow of a Xanthippe, 'the most difficult of women who exist and . . . of those who have existed and will exist in the future'? (Xenophon, *Symposium* 2. 10). Was it to repopulate a city bled dry by war? Probably not; it was a far cry from the collective will for the common good to an individual decision about the organization of his private life. No, he had her with him before accepting Myrto, and as it was a matter of a concubine on the lines of Aspasia, he can only have acted thus by inclination.

Intermezzo: *The* Gamos, *nocturnal celebration*

'The two sweetest days for a woman are her wedding day and her funeral' (Hipponax, fr. 68, West). It remains for us to celebrate this marriage which sums up the whole of a woman's life. We have often approached it, but

---

19. As J. Labarbe explains in (1998), 'Les compagnes de Socrate', *Antiquité Classique* 67, pp. 5–43.

a

b

Matrimonial transfer. Lit by torches the partly veiled bride is led by Dionysus to her future husband's home. Poseidon can be seen on the left of b. Courtesy of the Reading Public Museum, Reading, Pennsylvania, USA

without ever mentioning its celebration or its consumption, which poses a central question: the relationship of the body of women as a whole to man. Most noticeable is the *transfer* of the wife from her paternal home to that of her husband. As good followers of A. van Gennep, the anthropologists were swift to recognize a rite of passage in the entirety of the ceremonies (or rite of institution, according to Pierre Bourdieu). The ceremonies can be broken down into three ritual ensembles: separation – the *nymphe* leaves her family; transfer – the nuptial procession leads her from her old residence to her new one; and integration – she is introduced into her new world.

The sacred, the divine, purity – in short, religion – play an important role in all this. We are also pretty close to folklore, for instance as in the gesture of the husband who lifts his young bride in his arms to enable her to enter her new 'house' without touching the threshold, or the superstition when the *nymphe* eats a pomegranate seed on the evening of the *gamos*. But both the 'magic' action on fertility and the fear of any taint are in harmony with the concept of the sacred.

Let us make the acquaintance of the *nymphe* Hippe, who will shortly be taken by a man to his home.

The virgin Hippe has piled the curls of her luxuriant hair on top of her head,

Wiping her perfumed temples.

The time for marriage has already arrived for her.

And we, the headbands that replace her shorn hair,

We proclaim her virginal graces.

Artemis, may her marriage day by thy will be also the day of motherhood

For Lycomedeides' daughter, who is parting from her knucklebones. (*Palatine Anthology* vi. 276, Antipater of Sidon)

On the occasion of passing a certain age (marriage for the girls, puberty for the boys), it was a widespread custom to offer one's hair (partly or entirely) to the deities who protected the young (Artemis for girls, Apollo for boys). Hippe – 'the mare' – is at this transitional stage, and thus finds herself in the particular situation described by van Gennep as the 'pivotal point of the sacred'.[20] In his view, the sacred was not a permanent quality, but depended upon the position occupied by the individual in society. 'Turn and turn about, according to whether one occupied this or that place in society, there was a shift in the magic circles.' Throughout life, everyone 'pivoted' from certain values of the sacred to others, and this swing was

20.   Of van Gennep ((1909), *Les Rites de passage, Étude systématique des rites*, Paris) we usually recall only the general theory of the three stages of passages of age, setting aside his additional commentary which takes account of their religious nature in a number of cultures.

dramatized by rites of passage which helped in the transformation. Hippe's point of passage is evident: she is a *parthenos*, 'unmarried' or 'virgin', ready to be wed, but she does not necessarily find herself in a physiological state that would qualify her as 'nubile' in other cultures. However, the *gamos* is explicitly linked with procreation: by the will of Artemis, marriage and procreation will arrive simultaneously for Hippe. What is striking is the astonishing contraction of time. This girl who 'loves her knuckle-bones' offers her hair to Artemis for the productive success of her marriage, and prepares to become, at the same moment, wife and mother. From childhood toys to adult sexuality and maternity – this is travelling at a giddy pace. It is an accelerated version of life; she has just come from lining up her dolls when she is summoned to don her wedding gown and put the ritual veil on her head; and already thoughts are on the cradle. These lives have no adolescence – indeed, do they even have what we would call youth? To be taken by a man causes the *nymphe* Hippe, like every other *nymphe*, to 'pivot' into the sacred, leaving her 'virginal graces' – those of Artemis – for another world, that of adult women, which comes under a different form of the supernatural (see pp. 20–9). Hippe's offerings are chosen for their symbolic content. Her hair, long and worn loose in childhood, is cut for her to sleep with her husband, and will then be discreetly concealed by her when she is a wife. Other texts mention her clothing; they are the undergarments of a girl. '*Parthenoi* on the point of union with a man offer their virginal girdles to Artemis' (Pollux, iii. 48). These 'girdles' are there only as the result of modern translators' difficulty with intimate garments, and the euphemism is also due to the Greeks. Her tambourines are not toys, but instruments that have enabled her to have her place in the religious choruses in which she has taken part. In the same way that she has abandoned her tresses, her clothing and her undergarments, she thus distances herself from the virginal choirs for other religious groups which are differently composed and address themselves to special deities using different means. The ball and knuckle-bones are in contrast with the household utensils – grill, sieve, pots, keys – of which she will ritually take possession, in the 'house' of her husband, when the marriage ceremony is over.

IMPOSING THE YOKE, WITH THE HELP OF THE GODS

It required all the coercive force of these societies to make it seem as if girls were submitting with good grace to this state of affairs. And religion, which I have already written about extensively, played its part in the reproduction of social models. This involves the deities of the *gamos*, whom Plutarch lists: Zeus Teleios and Hera Teleia, Aphrodite, Peitho and

Polytheism to the aid of form. In this scene, painted on an epinetron, an object that could be fitted to the leg and was used to spin wool, Peitho is seated between Harmony (l.) and Kore (r.); also (r.) Hebe (Flower of youth) and Himeros (Desire). (L.) Aphrodite and Eros – an entire symphony in the deifying of feelings and sentiments. National Archaeological Museum, Athens

Artemis. Polytheism had its own great internal strictness and, confronted with such a list, the interpreter must be concerned not only with each god's role and function, but also his or her relationship with each of the others and with the entire group. We have already met Artemis – she is a goddess of the early days, of childhood, but because of her close connection with feminine physiology and matters of childbirth, that does not prevent her from accompanying the *nymphe* until she has her baby. On the *nymphe's* wedding day, she crosses a frontier with Peitho and Aphrodite, and the propitiation of 'Persuasion' alongside the goddess of love has to do with her carnal relations with her husband. These deities clearly help in the success of the sexual union. To arouse desire is golden Aphrodite's business, but Peitho helps her. Is she not her daughter, according to Sappho? Hesiod shows her adorning Pandora with seductive charms, with the help of golden necklaces. It goes without saying that it is up to the woman to captivate her husband. It is up to the child to please the adult . . . but how difficult it is. There are worries about the morrow, and the list closes with Zeus Teleios and Hera Teleia: the model divine couple, a 'fulfilled' (the meaning of *teleios/a*) male and female, in other words, married. Thus, in a biographical perspective, from Artemis to the divine model of the married pair, each stage is protected by the benevolence of the gods. But time is telescoped. Artemisian childhood collides with conjugal eroticism and, lo and behold, the child is a matron, and will soon go to join the religious groups who, as a body, worship Demeter or Dionysus.

Marriage, the couple, even sexual union are found in the common imagery of the yoke. To be married (of a woman) can be expressed in Greek as 'to be placed under the yoke.' One of the names of Hera, goddess of the woman-wife, is *Syzygia* (under the same yoke); even Aphrodite herself is called *Zygia* and Plutarch approves of the people of Delphi, who call Aphrodite the 'goddess of the conjugal harness.' We have already encountered this image of the girl regarded as an animal who has to be brought to heel, for instance Nausicaa (see pp. 61–2). Metaphors and symbolic comparisons liken her to a goat, especially a wild goat. A good number of heroines in the pre-marriage period bear 'hippic' names, and to civilize-tame these 'wild creatures', thanks to 'Domestic' Artemis, or to lead them to marriage, amounts to the same thing. Before their marriage girls perform rituals – such as 'acting the she-bear'[21] – the aim of which, says one note, is 'to offer up whatever in them has a wild nature.' Depending on gender, and thus on the position occupied in the setting of the marriage, and with the same words, passing from the active to the passive, the facts will be looked at in different ways: we shall see the 'ravisher' and the 'ravished', the one who, in the real sense, subjugates[22] or the one who is 'subjugated.'

Marriage is thus conceived as a 'rupture with the influence of Artemis, under which the uncontrolled forces of adolescence are first domesticated and, on the other hand, a new period of training for submission to the coercive forces of Eros and Aphrodite.'[23]

Now, one day in Sparta, at the home of the fair-haired Menelaus, virgins, their hair adorned with hyacinth flowers, formed a chorus before the nuptial chamber which was newly decorated with paintings; they were twelve in number, the leading girls in the town, splendid Lacedaemonian maidens; it was the day when the younger son of Atreus [Menelaus] took to wife his beloved Helen, of the house of Tyndareus, whom he had asked for in marriage. They sang in concert, treading a complex dance; and the palace around them resounded with the strains of the *hymenaion* [wedding song] … Be happy, young bride; be happy, son-in-law of a noble father-in-law. May Leto, the nurturer of children,

21. This strange term describes both the ritual and its participants in the sanctuaries of Artemis where prepubescent or pubescent girls are kept in seclusion and carry out a 'nocturnal mystery'; see P. Brulé (1987), *La Fille d'Athènes. La religion des filles à Athènes à l'époque classique: cultes, mythes, et société*, Paris: Les Belles Lettres, pp. 218–83.

22. From the Latin *subjugare*, 'subjugate' (from *jugum*, 'yoke', itself derived from the Greek *zugoo*, 'to tame' (from *zugos*, 'yoke').

23. Calame C. (1997), *Choruses of Young Women in Ancient Greece*, Lanham, Rowman and Littlefield, 240.

grant you fine progeny; the goddess Cypris grant you the equality of mutual love; and Zeus, the son of Cronus, unending prosperity. (Theocritus, xviii. 1–8 and 49–52)

Had she been a good girl? To reach the *thalamos* (the nuptial chamber), it was necessary to be pure, hence purification rites, using the water of such and such a spring, this or that fountain. It was a matter of both drawing water reputed to be effective in ridding the *nymphe* of all taint and propitiating the deities associated with this water – the Nymphs. We are familiar with the ceremony, for the scene is pictured on amphorae of a special shape, the *loutrophoroi*, which were used in Athens for carrying the water for the nuptial bath. There we see the procession accompanying the *loutrophoros* from the fountain where the water is drawn, to the young girl's home. The group is framed by female torchbearers, a young boy of the family plays a pipe, then comes a very young girl carrying the *loutrophoros*. The *nymphe* follows behind, her head lowered in a characteristic attitude.

This is the day of the *gamos*. The bride is, of course, dressed in her utmost finery. Her head garlanded, she dons garments of exceptional quality, masterpieces of her skill, with embroideries; she wears *nymphides* (delicate little sandals) on her feet and, for a while yet, conceals her face beneath a veil. Probably before the meal the sacrifice to the gods of the *gamos* takes place: to Artemis, Peitho and Aphrodite, Zeus Teleios and Hera Teleia. But depending on the cities, other deities may receive devotions. In Athens this was the case of the Tritopatores, who personified the lineage of the ancestors and took a hand in the genetic success of the marriage. In Athens there existed a cult of *the* Nymphe, a curious divine figure who was none other than the deified Young Bride. All this was to ensure children, and divine help was not unwelcome. The meal takes place in the home of the girl's father, with the groom's family. It marks the rapprochement of the two 'houses' and introduces a relationship of mutual exchange between them. The segregation of the sexes seems to have been strict, with separate tables for men and women. The food served was obviously traditional, and it is no surprise to find dishes reputed to favour fertility, such as sesame cakes.

As they did for funerals, states sought to regulate these ceremonies to limit their sumptuousness and the number of participants. Women were the chief targets of these measures, since the magistrates whose duty it was to enforce them were the *gynaeconomoi*, who had the special task of keeping an eye on these matters. There are libations, good wishes, epithalamia, hymns – no lack of music. A young boy circulates among the guests offering bread. At the end of the meal, the *nymphe* is brought into the room; she is strictly veiled and goes to take her place among the women. This is the moment when the guests and the husband are at last to see her face. The unveiling is accompanied by the husband's transfer of the presents. He receives the girl, he reciprocates with gifts. The unveiling was probably the highlight of a Greek marriage. Henceforward the girl is a married woman. She now leaves the paternal home to follow her husband to his home. The procession is the public part of the ceremony, and its essential purpose is to give publicity to this special union and the physical fulfilment of the rite of passage. The first aspect is fundamental for the social group to know the status of the children to be born. One significant detail: the meal finishes late, and it is by the light of what are called nuptial torches that the procession goes to the groom's house. Clandestine marriages were known as 'weddings without torches.' The wagon awaits the couple at the door of the house, someone close to the groom, the *parochos*, greets them and helps them on board next to him; he will drive the team. A herald precedes them and they are followed by the girl's family, then all the relatives and friends, children crowned with myrtle. Lastly there is music and dancing, a whole background of shouting and the singing of boys and girls, and much banging on the couple's door: what an uproar accompanies the loss of virginity.

The husband's relatives are waiting for the procession in front of their house and welcome the pair as they descend from the wagon. The *nymphe* is the subject of certain prohibitions and her physical entry into the 'house' is marked by procedures of a magical nature: she must not touch the threshold, nor even set foot on the floor until she reaches the marriage bed. She must take possession symbolically of the objects that define her new social role – the cooking vessels, the grill, the sieve (for flour) and the keys, which are a mark of recognition of her new power over the riches of the *oikos*. Finally, she must ritually eat *katachusmata* – dates, cakes, dried figs, nuts. To the cathartic power of certain of these items fertilizing powers are added, and some – figs for example – are a clear allusion to the feminine sex. The couple then repair to the nuptial chamber, the *thalamos*, its door guarded by a friend of the husband. When the *gamos* night is over, in return for the gifts offered the night before by the fiancé to the *nymphe*'s family, her family now brings presents. There is a real procession: at its head a young boy, dressed in white and holding a torch, then a *kanephoros* and other girls bringing gifts: vases, garments, adornments, perfume jars, cosmetics, combs, shoes and various caskets. Another life is beginning ... Within these walls and among these people, the arrival of the *nymphe* has brought sex, a wife and soon a mother.

Happy bridegroom, your marriage is accomplished, as you prayed; you have the virgin for whom you prayed.

You have a graceful look, your eyes are honeyed, and love has spread over your enticing face, Aphrodite has honoured you most highly.

(Wife) Virginity, virginity, where have you gone, now that you have left me?

(Virginity) Never shall I return to you, never more shall I come.

To what shall I compare you, beloved husband?

I shall best compare you to a supple branch. (Sappho, frs 112, 114, 115 L–P)

Among the many Attic paintings, this one chooses to draw special attention to the work of spinning. Opposite the mistress of the 'house', the slave manipulates the fusarole and distaff. Department of Classical and Near Eastern Antiquities, National Museum of Denmark, inv. no. Chr. VIII 520

CHAPTER 5

The woman in the 'house'

Now that we are at the very heart of this much talked-about 'house', is it surprising that here we find the fundamental institution – marriage? 'Marriage is to the girl what war is to the boy.' People are still musing over this statement by Jean-Pierre Vernant; in fact, the correspondence between the respective destinies of Greek boys and girls justifies it perfectly. 'Emerging from childhood', the former are bound for a warrior's apprenticeship (which includes the indispensable culture of the body); the latter see themselves recognized for no other social, even political, usefulness and probably envisage no other end than by and in the act of marriage – in any case, it would be a misfortune if things were otherwise. The accuracy of this analysis nevertheless conceals a temporal imbalance between the genders which distorts a parallelism that is borne out only by its aims. 'Emerging from childhood,' says Vernant, but at this precise moment the futures offered to the *kouroi* and *korai* are not presented in the same way. The girl's marriage is for *now* – and her apprenticeship for her future state has already taken, or is taking, place – whereas war for the boy will come later, and his training may well last much longer. After a period (of around ten years), when it is chiefly a matter of building a strong and tough body, the real preparation for the demands and techniques of Greek warfare will begin only after puberty; then there will be the two years of the *ephebos*, a true initiation into being a soldier, from the age of eighteen. At the end of this phase, his return will mark his entry into adult life, at least *de jure*, for in actual fact he still needs to grow older. Being still no more than a 'new boy', it would seem presumptuous for him to speak in the people's Assembly, and he will have to wait another ten years before he can be regarded as being on an equal footing with fully-fledged citizens. At thirty he will be able to apply for a magistracy; and generally he will have to wait about the same length of time to reap his paternal inheritance. At all events, it is often only at this point that he will set up a household (if that is the right term).

If we adopt a synchronic viewpoint, 'emerging from childhood', the boy will have to go through a kind of long-drawn-out adolescence in order to become hardened by means of a *collective* apprenticeship to an adult masculine life. Whereas the girl, for her part, is tipped rapidly, brusquely, and *alone*, into adult feminine life. Of course, for each sex, war and marriage represent 'the fulfilment of their respective nature', but these states arrive at times and stages of physical and mental development when each gender has for a long time had nothing to do with the other (to paraphrase Vernant). Greek girls do not marry their contemporaries, nor do Greek men marry theirs.

Reasons for 'Living Together'

Here they are, then, the two protagonists of this chapter, those whom Xenophon chose as models in his *Oeconomicus*:[1] Ischomachus, 'handsome and good' (*kalos kagathos*), and his wife. The husband is a totally successful man, clearly older than his wife. His 'house' is well-to-do, comprising a fairly large farm and at least two houses. In town, he says, he is described as a 'handsome and good' man; it is a condition and a quality: to belong to a comfortably-off social class, follow a certain way of life, enjoy an image. Like every citizen, he is also a soldier, but not the average hoplite; he serves in the cavalry. He is called Ischomachus, but his wife's name, like that of Pericles' wife, is not given. Of course, it is Xenophon expressing himself here, and Ischomachus is merely 'lending his voice', chosen for what he represents and very little different from the writer himself: a kind of gentleman-farmer, better endowed for action than for sophistic discourse, more at ease on horseback (carrying out rounds of inspection on his estate, hunting large game, or riding at the head of a battalion of hoplites) than in the capital's agora. We are about to penetrate the intimate lives of this recently formed couple.

WHY GET MARRIED?

Balzac amused himself by coming up with twenty-six replies to this question in his *Physiology of Marriage*; twenty-six reasons in alphabetical order, from *ambition* to *zeal*, all the most precise and least true imaginable,

---

1. Apart from specified exceptions, all quotations in this chapter are taken from Xenophon. The figures refer to the various chapters and paragraphs.

because none corresponds to the one we profess. In Xenophon's Greece, too, people married out of ambition, conformism, fear of loneliness, pity, imitation, self-interest ... The question that worries our contemporaries is did they marry for love? In the dialogue with his wife regarding the purposes of marriage, Ischomachus does not mention love:

> When she had become used to me, and had been tamed enough to carry on a conversation, I put these questions to her: Tell me, wife, have you now understood why I married you and why your parents gave you to me? Neither you nor I were at a loss to find someone to sleep with: you are as well aware of that as I am. But I on my own account and your parents on yours, considered who was the best partner of home and children. I chose you and it seems to me that your parents chose me from all the possible suitors. As for children, if the deity grants them to us one day, then we will consider the means of raising them to the best of our ability; it is in our common interest to find the best possible allies and supports to keep us in our old age; for the time being, we have only this 'house' in common. (Xenophon, *Oeconomicus* vii. 10–12)

Leaving aside what these words suggest about the psychological context in which the conversation takes place, and before listening, let us note a very loud silence: nowhere is there the slightest trace of any proof of the girl's participation in the choice of a husband, or evidence that she had any say in that crucial moment of her life, marriage. The purposes of marriage are envisaged, evaluated, debated only between her parents (chiefly the father), who do her thinking for her, and the future son-in-law, who is exercising his choice.

We are not together, says Ischomachus, because we did not know whom to go to bed with. Assuredly, he cannot have lacked partners for recreational sex, in the same way that his wealth allowed him to contemplate many other matrimonial possibilities than this one. The matter is less clear for her, insofar as she is obviously not empowered to choose a partner; so we must suppose that, speaking in her stead as he often does, Ischomachus means that her parents could in any case find her a replacement, another party, thus implying that she is highly placed in the hierarchy of marriageable girls. Let us put it more bluntly: her dowry makes her worthwhile. In classical Athens, as elsewhere, wealthy people intermarried, as those who were not rich were also obliged to do. This has already been made clear – it is social endogamy. Conversely, as we can see, the desire that two people might have to sleep together, their possible mutual attraction, counts for nothing. Marrying for love seems so obvious to our contemporaries that a little emphasis is needed – love and marriage are not connected, neither in their aims nor in their conception. They are connected even less than Balzac believed with his image of marriage as the tomb of love, and are, rather, two wholes that cannot be merged. Neither more nor less 'natural' than any other, this concept is cultural, it is acquired. As Socrates explains to his son: 'You probably do not believe that sexual pleasure impels man to create children, when the streets and brothels are full of means of satisfying it' (Xenophon, *Memorabilia* ii. 2. 4).

Well, then, what positive values does Ischomachus attach to marriage? In accord with Socrates and many others, he bases marriage on other matters, but the key word is association. By this act, he and her parents have admitted the *nymphe* into a community, a *koinonia*, of which he names the constituents: the 'house' and children. Ischomachus sets his wife up in the role of colleague, at the heart of these two areas of activity. She will have rule over the 'house', and be the mother of his children. That is why he is taking her to him. If they were concerned only with the utilitarian, men would often have done without a wife; domestic staff or slaves would have been enough to see to needs. If it were a matter only of *oikonomia* . . . but there are children.

The 'house'? It is significant that Greece has left us two treatises on *oikonomia*, this one and a second, very close to it, once ascribed to Aristotle. On the other hand, we know no works devoted to *philia*, the feelings between husband and wife, even if Aristotle himself, or Plato, in texts which are to say the least didactic, mention them in relation to marriage. *Oikonomia* is the subject of real concern, and Xenophon even goes so far as to speak of a *science*; it is a matter of reflecting upon and proposing solutions to make this famous 'house' flourish and be profitable. Once the *gamos* is celebrated, the bride belongs to the 'house'. The husband does too, but he has the status of head. That is why everything is subordinate to this celebrated 'house' she has just entered.

Children? In this, too, there is a common opinion. The philosophers say that man and woman behave in the same way as animals, and mate in order to propagate the species. According to Ischomachus:

> The gods carried out an in-depth examination before matching this couple known as male and female precisely for the greatest advantage of their partnership [*koinonia*]. In the first place, to prevent the disappearance of animal species, the couple join to procreate. (Xenophon, *Oeconomicus*, vii. 18–19)

Doctors were obsessed by the fear of the possible infertility of women. Citizens, too, responsible for this giant 'house' of the city, were concerned simultaneously for its power, wealth and therefore autonomy, and they measured all that with the yardstick of the number of soldiers. Among 100 other pieces of evidence, there is the one of the formula of the marriage contract. In this, fathers are not content to hand over their daughters to suitors, they say they do so for a very precise reason: 'So that they shall plough them to beget legitimate children.' If we listen to Ischomachus, his bride's parents are also expecting to have descendants. A father gives his daughter to a man not only so that she can have children by him, but also to produce grandchildren. As for the husband, he takes her for that reason, otherwise he could have done without her. So, did he choose her for that very reason? Did he evaluate her according to her possible reproductive qualities? This is not impossible, if we are to go by the subsequent explanations given by Socrates to his son: '(men) mostly choose from women who will give them the finest children, and they marry them in order to procreate' (Xenophon, *Memorabilia* ii. 2 4). According to Aristotle, women's bodily qualities are beauty and form, and those of the spirit are moderation and a love of work (*Rhetoric* 1,361a).

HUSBANDS AND WIVES WHO LOVE EACH OTHER?

Was it enough for the girl to meet the criteria of eugenic conformity, to be given to a man so that he could beget legitimate children, so that both of them could have them? Some husbands were neglectful, others more inclined to anal intercourse, others in love with their concubine ... was inclination, 'nature', strong enough in the general competitive context of Greek sexuality? As Menander says: 'The struggle against a courtesan ... is always difficult for a free woman' (fr. 7, 2). Our fears are perhaps misplaced, however; our heroes do not seem to encounter this kind of problem and, exceptionally in the literature of that era, speak of both their feelings and sexual relations quite clearly, without fuss or affectation. And this is where we come down to earth with a bump. Here we learn from conversation that these two beings whom everything seems to keep apart, who were married not for love but for quite another reason, these two beings are now claiming to love each other. What am I saying? They *do* love each other. But probably in the way that Greek couples of their time loved each other. 'Naturally', they believe, like Achilles and his Briseis: 'Every good and sensible man loves his *alochos* and takes care of her, as I loved mine with all my heart, although she had been won by the spear' (see p. 49). To paraphrase Homer, one is tempted to say 'although she was won by contract.' We come upon these words of love by chance, at the end of the dialogue:

Were we not married in order to *join our bodies*?

That is at least what people say, she replies.

> Now, in this *association of our bodies*, I would think myself even
> worthier of *your love* if I tried to bring you a body rendered healthy and
> vigorous by the care I give it . . . (Xenophon, *Oeconomicus* x. 4–5)

It is really about sexuality ('joining of bodies'), says he, about intimacy
('first thing in the morning', 'in the physical reality of the bath'), about
seductiveness ('desire to please'; *charis* reappears here, see p. 34). Each in
his or her style, fairly modest, each in his or her role – Ischomachus not hesitating (what delicacy!) to compare his wife's attractions with those of a
slave girl – both speak of the importance they place on the presence at their
side of the other's body. He makes the statement, she concurs.

These two advantages (for the 'house' and for the children) of association with a legitimate wife are resumed in the famous programme of the
adult male's heterosexual enjoyments to be found under the heading of
recreational love (pp. 186–90): besides the hetairai he frequents for
pleasure, the concubine who showers him with the attentions his body
requires, the man has *one* legitimate spouse as the keeper of his 'house' and
mother of his legitimate children. A colleague, an associate, in the dual
concern of material life and reproduction, but the *Oeconomicus* retains a
fleeting trace of love and desire. Yet, confronted with this evidence of reciprocal interest, we cannot discount another dreadful exchange between
Socrates and Critobulus who, while saying how much the husband values
the '*economic*' role of his wife, chiefly reveals the coldest indifference:

> Come, Critobulus, we are among friends here and you absolutely must
> tell the whole truth: is there anyone to whom you entrust more
> important matters than to your wife?

> No one, he said.

> And is there anyone with whom you have less conversation than with
> your wife?

> Hardly anyone, he said. (Xenophon, *Oeconomicus* iii. 12)

It is a 'Socratic' paradox, of course, but above all – the demand for truth
emphasized earlier, 'among friends', proves it – it is a terrible discovery, on
which men are agreed: they talk more to anyone else than to their wife, who
is nevertheless their best associate. One can certainly love one's *alochos*,
but the essential part of life is lived elsewhere, among men. An illustration

of this dichotomy can be read in the scene from the *Memorabilia*, where Socrates, at death's door, begins by dismissing his wife, takes a bath, receives his three children, talks with them for a while, gives them orders, then returns to meet his friends. The fact is that the masculine life engages the man's whole life, and he cannot imagine any other that is as good. He goes so far as to fear losing his *andreia* if he spends too much time with the feminine side of the 'house'.[2] If he is the lover, or even just the friend of his wife, he must be so in secret unless he is impervious to taunts. And here is another great difference between the sexes. Although her husband and 'house' represent the wife's whole life, the man spares them only part of his time and the essentials still take place outside the home – in the fields, gymnasium, agora, military expeditions – in complete continuity with the activities and environment of his bachelor life.

Masculine estimation of the woman is based on the 'working' (no question of pleasure here) of her 'fallow land.' In the Greek agricultural system, fallow land, far from being left to rest, was persistently worked in order to prepare it for seed. I have already mentioned those farming metaphors used to evoke intercourse, and I have highlighted, in this language mirror, the male's place and role – active and full of movement, contributing the *psyche* – and those of the female – moist and stable, contributing the nutriments.

A woman bears with difficulty the burden that besets her life; she feeds the child with her own substance; she gives it birth in terrible pain, suckles it and gives it every care . . . (Xenophon, *Memorabilia* ii. 2. 5)

Socrates explains all this to his son in order to make him keep quiet his resentment at the complaints of his mother. He had defined the roles of the two genders in marriage:

The husband nurtures the wife who must make him a father. Even before their birth, he gathers together for his children the things he believes must be useful in life, he collects as much as he possibly can . . . (Xenophon, *Memorabilia* ii. 2. 5)

The nature of the triangle of marriage in its primary function thus becomes clear: the husband nurtures the wife-mother, who nurtures the child. Perhaps it would be better to say he nurtures a wife-mother *so that* she shall nurture the child. But what is the father's aim? What purpose do

2. Remember the process of feminization (pp. 104–7) and how the 'archimacho' Heracles succumbed to it at Omphale's feet.

Mother and child. The mother on her stool seems somewhat distant from her baby in its bassinet. Musées royaux d'Art and d'Histoire – Brussels

these strategies of fatherhood *serve*? Socrates in the *Memorabilia*, Ischomachus in the *Oeconomicus* and the entire city are in agreement: to produce children is to invest in their gratitude so that eventually they will repay their parents, with honours, care, food and protection, all that they have received from them. Ischomachus says to his wife, 'It is in our common interest to find the best possible allies and supports to keep us in our old age' (Xenophon, *Oeconomicus* vii. 12).

Sexual union, Ischomachus says later, allows humans 'to ensure they will have support to sustain them in their old age.' This supportive role of children is an important factor in social cohesion and the community keeps an attentive eye on it. There are laws to punish failures. But not all parents waited until they were old to profit from the presence and backing of their children, and 'houses' took advantage of their work. From this point of view, the two genders are not on equal terms, and the girl will more quickly be set to tasks whose 'feminine' character does not prevent their being difficult and demanding. As for the boy, he appears to have no productive activity. If any obligation does exist, there is no doubt that it is concealed as far as possible. Work sullies the man, not the woman.

Let us love if we want to be loved, be caring if we want to be cared for. Kinship and affection designate those who will perform the indispensable rituals of death. Who, if not they, will see to the corpse, give it the attentions it requires, take care of its burial; who will perform the sacrifices, make the offerings, say the prayers, repeat them at the various ritual manifestations of the 'religion' of the dead? Who will keep alive the memory of the deceased? The wife helps, as do friends and grandchildren, but the one who does the work is the son. If that were the only reason for begetting a child, it would be enough.

'House' and city mirrored

The fundamentals remain. The Greek man is only in his 'house' in passing (Ischomachus: 'I do not spend any time in the 'house''). He is always coming back from outside: from the hunt, the fields, war (sometimes months later), and above all from the town, soon to return there. He acts on two levels: master in his own 'house', he takes part (or *can* take part) in all possible ways in the administration and government of that other 'house', the city-state, as a member of the well-known 'men's club' which he forms with his peers, the citizens. We are indebted to pseudo-Aristotle for many striking and accurate statements, but this one perfectly puts in place the relationship between city and 'house': 'The city is an ensemble of 'houses', lands and wealth that can be sufficient in itself to ensure life and well-being' (Ps-Aristotle, *Oeconomica* i. 2. 1,343a). He had just said that politics and city maintained the same relationship between them as economy (*oikonomia*) and 'house' and that, except for a matter of scale, the same chronological succession was to be found in politics and economy, passing from the stage of establishment and acquisition to that of turning it to good account. The two entities were closely matched and among the resemblances was the question of authority.

What better image of political power in Greece than the one in which we see adult men, citizens, periodically sitting down on the ground (or on benches?) and listening to one another talk? Talk about what? About what brings them together, what justifies their forming a community, their common affairs. It comes as no surprise that they vote on war, peace, taxes, international agreements, market regulations and buildings, but it is more curious for us that they should legislate also on rituals and even the adoption of new gods, and that they should regulate family practices. Then, having wrangled to their hearts' content, they decide, vote, get to their feet and put into effect what they have decided; they apply it in the way they conduct their life as responsible citizens, but also in their 'house' if need be. There is common ground on many points between the interests of the city and those of the 'house'. For example, producing children is a necessity for the 'house', so that old parents can be supported, the dead of the line honoured and human continuity ensured. However, the strict separation between the domain of the communal and that of the private obviously lies at the origin of a schizophrenic syndrome: the same man, alternately despot in his home and citizen who-sits-on-the-ground with the others, adopts ways of reasoning in these places, and pursues aims in these circumstances that are different, not to say contradictory.

CHILDREN, THE REALLY IMPORTANT MATTER

Depending on whether one looks at it from the level of the 'house' or the city, keeping up the human supply is envisaged in two ways. Those-who-sit-on-the-ground are the ones who defend the territory and community; citizens are also soldiers. Their constant concern is the maintenance of the community's military potential come hell or high water. For that, at least, the dead need to be replaced. At the same time, they are well aware that marriage is not the prime interest of young men, that a liking for women is not the only thing to make them bestir themselves, that, even when married, they may not be very inclined to go to bed with their wife, and that finally, when they are actually sleeping with her, in the intimacy of the *thalamos*, they can do everything in their power to avoid reproduction. I told you they were schizophrenic. They are all aware of this contradiction, and it impels them even more to adopt measures in the Assembly that we would describe as 'pro-birth', if the term were not obviously anachronistic. They can, for instance, combat bachelorhood by taxation or other means. They can oblige the man (and we see just how far the *community* can intrude upon the *private*), in certain circumstances, to have a minimum number of sexual relations with his legitimate wife. Thus, a law dating back to the legislator Solon (early sixth century) obliged the husband of the woman known as an *epikleros*[3] to have sex with her at least three times a month.

In that world and in those times, women, who did not make war and were not citizens, did not own land. Now, to paraphrase Aristotle, the land of the state is the land of the 'houses'. The citizen population – the only one that counted – was formed by the ensemble of heads of 'houses' and their descendants. It follows that the disappearance of a 'house' brought in

---

3. A brotherless girl for whom the community, for fear of seeing a 'house' disappear, arranges a marriage to the closest relative of her dead father.

its wake the loss of at least one citizen (and obviously all his genetic potential); this was what those-who-sat-on-the-ground realized and what they
had to combat. No catastrophe could equal that of the house that lapsed:
it meant the end of an asset, the end of a line, an empty memory. Then
there arose the burning question of transmission. To pass on the citizenship
and to pass on the land; to fulfil one was to fulfil the other. The concern
with ensuring the replenishment of citizen numbers, at least for the maintenance of community strength and thus for one's own safety, boiled down
to procuring an heir. Unless those-who-sat-on-the-ground decided that one
could very well be a soldier-citizen without having access to the inheritance
of the 'houses', by separating the two ideas of succession – political status
and inheritance. But the one who can do most can also do least and, whatever the fifth-century Athenians invented, children fathered in one's home
with one's legitimate wife were full recipients of both qualities: successor
in status and heir to the land. It was precisely regarding land that schizo-
phrenia was again likely to handicap the wretched husbands. It was all well
and good to appeal in the Assembly for soldier-citizens for the state, but in
the 'house' that meant an equal number of heirs, of equal shares into which
the inheritance must be divided. By inheritance laws, indeed, a 'house' gave
rise to as many 'houses' as it did heirs; as a result of the division of the family fortunes, in one generation the socio-political status of citizens could
completely change, and also their role in the army, for example passing
from cavalryman to heavily-armed footsoldier, then to lightly-armed
infantryman. Fathers knew all about that, and looked for solutions to the
problem.

Here the strategy of the 'house' was caught in crossfire from several
directions. Were soldiers needed for the state? They would be provided by
creating the heirs which the 'house' wanted. But could one be sure on all
counts? Threatened as one was, to one's dying breath, with losing one's offspring for every reason under the sun, it was necessary to be able to produce them. Think of the fearsome mortality rates in all the economies in
the ancient world. There is no reason why those of ancient Greece should
be any less terrible than those of the demographic regime of medieval or
modern times with their constant succession of endemic illnesses (like the
awful effects of fevers and accidents in childbirth), then the sudden
upsurges of famines, plagues and other scourges which, to the ancient's
way of thinking, were often sent by the gods because of men's wickedness.
Then there was war, which was continually restarting. In the face of this
constant menace, the need for the 'house' to survive implied that the
woman must always be ready, always physiologically disposed to be
impregnated. Traces of this burning masculine demand run deep in the
medical treatises. Among all their patients, those whom these new doctors

Funerary bas-relief. The mortality rates of babies and mothers during childbirth can hardly be overestimated. This stele does not clearly identify the victim: was it the baby, carried by a servant, the mother, or both? The Museum of Fine Arts, Houston; Gift of Miss Annette Finnigan

were most concerned about were the females, and among all the illnesses they had to observe, analyse and treat, the most numerous were those of the reproductive system. If misogyny is a Greek word, so is gynaecology. Therefore doctors quite naturally found themselves at the centre of the 'houses" dilemma. Their main preoccupation was with the two fundamental parts of the female body that were difficult to master: the uterus, a roving organ that went its own way or abandoned itself to its natural inclination to lust, and the 'red flowers of the month' which were the sign of the woman's fertility. They were fighting on two fronts: trying to tame the mobile animal and regulate the flows of blood. There was a leitmotif: the need to make the periods return, and this was achieved most often by the use of emmenagogues with widely varying components.

But it is better to leave well alone. Keep the wife fecund, sleep with her and, lo and behold, the family grows to excess. Men, however, do not know all there is to know in this domain. The doctors say that women know and tell one another how to make, or not make, babies. Such things were common knowledge in the circles of the 'professionals' of love. One pregnancy, and the income from her body and the money value of the prostitute/hetaira would drop, perhaps for good (see p. 209). So both within 'houses' and outside, a quite extraordinary panoply of means is brought into action. First of all, just after lovemaking, leaping into the air accompanied by quick heel-taps on the buttocks makes the sperm fall to the ground. But it would be wiser still to take precautions beforehand. And it is from the doctors that we discover that the Greek couple practised coitus interruptus.[4]

When I say couple, that is cheating a little with the sources; better to say the woman. The method deserves to be given in detail for it works in the opposite way to modern and contemporary European practice, where the man controls the rise of his ejaculation and withdraws from his partner's vagina. The Greeks reverse the roles: the woman, alert to the rising tension of the man, 'blocks her breathing' and performs the reciprocal gesture of drawing back so that her partner ejaculates outside her. Thus everything that happens is her responsibility and the man does not need to exercise control. In this situation there is no *sophrosyne* for sir. And if that well-known virtue of prudence and self-control has any meaning in this culture, it is up to the woman to demonstrate it – she whose ability to put it into effect has been completely denied since Semonides. The most likely scenario we can imagine is that the couple are in agreement on a strategy of birth control, and that it is up to the woman to see to its application.

The intent to limit births gave rise to many other manoeuvres. Gynaecological treatises and works on women's illnesses are full of these remedies, to be absorbed in every imaginable fashion. Before the act, the measures to be taken are the business of the female partner, and consist of introducing

4. This recent 'discovery' is the result of L. Bodiou's work on the blood of Greek women through the writings of doctors and biologists of the classical period.

deep into the vagina all kinds of products to 'close' the uterus (plugs with olive oil, honey, cedar resin, liquid alum . . .). Afterwards, she squats, washes her vagina, sneezes, and jumps up and down rapping her buttocks with her heels. Then she may use a variety of abortifacients: internal cleansing, massages, bathing or jumping, energetic walks, riding in a harnessed vehicle, carrying too heavy weights or plasters medicated with extracts of plants such as cyclamen, wallflower seeds, henna oil . . . She uses fumigation (the uterus is very sensitive to odours), introduces all kinds of substances *per os*, and uses pessaries even up to advanced stages of pregnancy, to procure an abortion.[5] Is there any need to comment on the appalling damage that such interventions might cause? The same products were used as those which were thought to make periods return. This is the heart of the matter: to eliminate the fruits of unavoidable pregnancies. Finally in this quantitative strategy, there is a last resort – what is called the exposure of infants, with female children at greatest risk of being eliminated.

DO YOU WANT BOYS OR GIRLS?

Have a daughter? All right. Have daughters? Very well, then. Have nothing but daughters? No way. Even have *only* a daughter? Impossible, or at any rate, tragic. The 'house' that falls to the distaff side, has to come up with all kinds of subterfuges in order to survive. Either, in the father's lifetime, masculine affiliations are invented outside the genetic possibilities (adoption, (see p. 215) or, confronted with this threat, the citizens take matters into their own hands and the community undertakes to marry the orphaned only daughter to her father's nearest relative. Why this rejection of the daughter? Readers, with all they have just discovered about the place of the female in the world of that era, will already be able to answer this. It lies at the root of the matter, but does not say it all. In contemporary India, the elimination of female foetuses and the unfavourable sex ratio do not sit well together with a position, a place, an image of the feminine inevitably more negative than those enjoyed in societies which do not get rid of embryos because of their sex. There are also 'materialistic' reasons: the dowry, the moral obligation to endow one's daughter. There is its total amount (see p. 124) and the way it competes with the boys' share . . .

So what is to be done? Well, girls can be eliminated at birth. Greek fathers abandon daughters more often than they should, but unfortunately

---

5. As the Greeks believed that impregnation took place one week after intercourse, interventions before that time were not regarded as abortions.

this elimination, both euphemistic and brutal, is not the only factor in their mortality. Less care, less food and being put to work too early form a string of causes leading to premature deaths. Nevertheless, precautions can be taken beforehand. It is not surprising that the physique of the sexes is in the front line in contraceptive strategies: the male, dry and right, the female, moist and left, play their part: 'In all species, males are hotter and drier, females moister and colder for the following reason: at conception, each sex is formed from certain elements and develops by virtue of them' (Aristotle). All that is needed is to apply this thinking by acting on the periods. Menstruation – the manifestation of feminine moistness – is considered necessary for impregnation, so if intercourse takes place *at the end* of the period – the driest time – the child will be a boy; if it takes place *during* the period, it will be a girl. From the erotic viewpoint, the mode of intercourse also counts: the penis in a position of withdrawal in the vagina of the partner means a girl, well driven in means a boy. The withdrawal of coitus interruptus and the other kind of coitus for fathering a daughter are not too far from each other. Refusing to have a child and choosing to have a daughter are very close, but differ on one point: in the first instance it is up to the woman to act, but in the second the man has to do the work. In the end, the choice is the man's. According to Aristotle, you have only to tie the right testicle to deprive seed of its male nature and thus beget daughters, and to tie the left one to make boys.[6] Of course, there is nothing to forbid combining those tactics. One could well wax ironic . . .

Ischomachus' wife is a queen bee

Where do you spend your time and what do you do, Socrates asks Ischomachus . . . At all events you do not spend all your time shut up in the 'house'; judging by your healthy looks I would not think so.

I do not stay in the 'house' at all. For as regards domestic matters, my wife on her own is capable of running them. (Xenophon, *Oeconomicus* vii. 2. 3)

MANAGING, ADMINISTERING, RULING, REGULATING, DIRECTING, RAISING, FEEDING . . .

These were the wife's activities and also the meanings of the verb *dioikein* which Ischomachus has just used to say that, as far as the interior of the

---

6. A belief still alive in the twentieth century in the Vitréen countryside.

An interior. Mother, child, nurse, the loom and a man who looks on. Courtesy of the Arthur M. Sackler Museum. Harvard University Art Museums. Bequest of David M. Robinson

home is concerned, he does not have to worry about anything, that his wife manages extremely well to *run* the 'house.' Here again, the polarity of the two sexes brings into play its opposite strengths, and in this setting the idea most frequently taken up is that of conservation, for instance in Aristotle and Plato:

> In the *oikonomia*, the man's roles differ from those of the woman: it is the task of the first to acquire, and of the second to conserve. (Aristotle, *Politics*, iii. 4. 1,277b)

> A woman's virtue . . . is not hard to define: it is a woman's duty to run her 'house' well, to conserve all that is in it and to be subject to her husband. (Plato, *Meno* 71e)

That a verb which serves to translate all these ideas is based on the root *house* illustrates the fact that the same mirror is working here, from the public to the private: if a state, even a kingdom, is to be governed, it is done just as one would manage a 'house'. And it is the wife who is capable of doing this. We are pleased for her success. For a full understanding of what is at stake, it would be wiser to listen at length to Ischomachus who, with his way of teaching in parables, uses the image of the queen bee the better to explain to his fresh young bride what he expects of her.

Custom unites the man and the woman; as the deity brings them together to have children, habit brings them together to manage the 'house'. In short, custom declares fitting the occupations for which the deity has given each of them the most natural capacities. For the woman it is more suitable to stay in the 'house' than to pass her time outside, and it is less suitable for the man to remain in the 'house' than to busy himself with work outside . . . Well, I think the queen bee, at the deity's command, busies herself with duties just like your own.

What are these tasks, said my wife, which fall to the queen bee and are so similar to the ones I must perform?

Look, I said to her. Though staying in the hive, she does not leave the bees with nothing to do; she sends out those whose tasks lie outside, checks and accepts what each of them brings back, then keeps it until there is a need for it. When the time comes to make use of it, she distributes a fair share to each. She is also in charge of the building of wax cells in the hive so that they are made swiftly and well; then she supervises the raising of the newly born bees; when this progeny is grown and capable of work she sends them off to found a colony with a queen who leads the swarm away.

Is this the task that I, too, must fulfil?

Yes, I replied, you must stay in the 'house', receive what is brought to you, distribute what must be expended, think beforehand of what must be set aside, and see to it that you do not expend in a month what has been earmarked for a year. When wool is brought to you, you must make sure that clothes are made of it for those who need them, and also ensure that the grain for provisions remains edible. Among the tasks which are yours, I said, there is one which may seem rather unpleasant to you: when a servant is ill, you must always see to it that he receives the necessary attention. (Xenophon, *Oeconomicus* vii. 30–61)

Xenophon is not the author of this entomological image of the queen bee; it has already been found in Semonides to illustrate the wife who

makes the 'house' grow. For that is what it is all about: the cleverest husbands are those 'who treat their wives in such a way as to turn them into
assistants to increase their 'house' *together*, (by honourable and legitimate
means'). This has to be her life's goal, the only way that will allow her to
achieve a usefulness on a par with that of her husband. Not without some
duplicity, Ischomachus goes so far as to give her a glimpse of such household success that she may even outstrip him: 'Here is the sweetest part: to
show yourself superior to me' (*Oeconomicus* vii. 42). He continues developing his finalist argument: this happiness exceeds all others, what is good
for the 'house' is good for her and for all who are about her. Therein lies
the secret of happiness. 'For it is not grace and beauty, but the virtues that
are useful to living which make well-being and happiness thrive among
men' (*Oeconomicus* vii. 43). A fine example of unconscious domination.

Faced with this prospect of a life of work, childbearing, heavy responsibilities and the burden of the 'house' to support, the *nymphe* of the day
does not perhaps lack courage, with or without love, but she does grow
older . . . And what if tomorrow her husband turns his back on her? Apart
from 'her eyes for weeping', nothing remains for her but to resort to magic:
'[I bind] Aristocydes and the women who show themselves to him. May he
never fuck another woman or another boy!' This imprecation can be read
on a magic tablet written or dictated by a woman in order to 'bind' the man
for whom it is intended.[7] By the efficacy of written words, it is a matter of
blocking the will or the functioning of an organ (often the tongue) of the
one whose love she wishes to win or regain. Other women than wives, like
this Simaetha, perhaps a hetaira, presented by Theocritus, use other magic
procedures. For instance, this prayer constantly returns like a refrain: 'Iunx,
draw home to me the man I love!' (ii. 17, etc.).

The iunx was a wheel that was spun quickly to produce a sound throughout the magic operation; Simaetha also burns bran, flour and bay leaves,
and melts wax so that her Delphis will melt with love for her; she crushes
a salamander, and makes libations three times while uttering these words:

Female quarters. The gaze is drawn beyond the column to the interior of the house: through
a half-open door we can see the *thalamos* (chamber) and its bed with pillows; then we
glimpse the apparently tranquil life in the female quarters. The wife, unusually, faces us. We
can see maidservants, boxes, textiles, a small loom, and a pet animal. © Photo RMN –
Hervé Lewandowski

'Should a woman or a man lie with him, let him forget them as completely as once, it is said, . . . Theseus forgot Ariadne of the lovely tresses.' (ii. 44–6; see note 7). It is a pathetic drama; this anguish of women in love, wives or not, free or not, is measured by the fact that what matters is not only an attachment, but also a social position: their future life depends on a man's choice. This day-to-day obsessive fear gets such a hold on their life that it makes them cross the barrier of written language, a difficult thing for a woman. The tablet on which Phila, from Pella in Macedonia, expresses a desire to live with Dionysophon is one of the extremely rare texts that come straight from the mute Greek women, and it is perhaps even written by herself. She is chiefly angry with one Thetima – 'Filthy Thetima, (may she) die wretchedly!' – and fears the latter's influence over the one she loves: 'By this written formula, I put a spell on the fulfilment and the marriage of Thetima and Dionysophon, and also on his marriage with any other woman, whether she be widow or *parthenos*.' To repulse these two threats to the female without a man and, with the help of 'demons', to obtain nothing other than real conjugal bliss: 'Let him take no other woman than me, but may I alone be allowed to grow old with Dionysophon and no one else' (Voutiras).[7]

As has already been said, sexual competition in the state is particularly rough, so what is there to prevent the husband from going to take a look elsewhere, acquiring a younger concubine, whom he would choose for her attentions to his body, setting her up in a residence, or even in his own home? Not the law. What is there to prevent him from choosing partners in his own 'house' to make, as he says, other 'associations' with his body? All wives, even the strongest like Euripides' Medea, evoke this threat.

> If we succeed in our task [of wife], and our husband accepts our communal life without struggling against the yoke, our existence is then enviable. If not, it were best to die. When a man tires of life in the home, he goes farther afield to forget the distaste in his heart . . . But we have only a single being to fix our eyes on. It is said that we live secure and safe in the 'house', while they fight in wars. A senseless argument! I would rather stand in the front line three times, my shield at my side, than give birth to a child a single time. (*Medea* 241–51)

How to evade these traps, how to cure the malady that might be called 'the ageing of the 'house''? Ischomachus has an answer, of course.

---

7. Published and interpreted by E. Voutiras (1998), ΔΙΟΝΥΣΟΦΩΝΤΟΣ ΓΑΜΟΙ *Dionysonphontos gamoi: Marital Life and Magic in the Fourth Century Pella*, Amsterdam.

Inasmuch, he says to his wife, as you fulfil your contract of work and supervision,

> you need not fear that, when age overtakes you, you will be *less regarded in the 'house'*, and on the contrary, must be assured that, in growing old, the more you become a good colleague for me, and for our children a good keeper of our 'house', the more you will be esteemed in your home. (Xenophon, *Oeconomicus* vii. 42)

In confronting this life of responsibilities and hard grind, the wife is not without a few trump cards. Her *physis* makes her suitable. Not being a man, she is not courageous, and it is precisely her cowardice that makes her attentive, circumspect and inclined to keep a watch on possessions. The deity has 'charged woman with care of provisions, realizing that to guard them well it is not a bad thing to have a timorous heart' (Ps-Aristotle, *Oeconomica* i. 4. 1,334b). Everything is well thought out in this contrast, and Aristotle systematizes it best:

> The deity, with foresight, organized the nature of man and woman with an eye to their communal life. The capacities of each are apportioned so that neither is capable of doing everything, but that they are opposites in certain things and thus contribute to their joint collaboration. (*Oeconomica* i. 4. 1,334b)

Motherhood is the best illustration of this: 'The deity granted the woman's body the power to feed the newborn and gave her this task, also bestowing on her more tenderness for newborn babies than was given to man' (Xenophon, *Oeconomicus* vii. 24).

'Cold, heat, marches, military exercises', these are what the 'body and soul' of a man are capable of enduring. The softness, tenderness and frailty of the female body confine her to the interior. It is a matter of taking advantage of these relative capabilities in the perspective of the growth of the 'house.' The husband's activities bring possessions into the 'house', but it is the wife's management which most often regulates expenditure. If all goes well, the 'house' prospers, but if things are done badly, the 'house' collapses . . .

> [Men are needed] to perform open-air tasks: to plough a fallow field, sow, plant, take the livestock to pasture . . . On the other hand, once the provisions have been brought in, someone is needed to preserve them and carry out the tasks which must be done inside. The newborn must be raised in the home, and flour prepared from the harvested cereals; in

the same way garments must be made from wool in the home ...
(Xenophon, *Oeconomicus* vii. 20–1)

For a woman, it is more suitable to stay in the 'house' than to pass her
time outside, and it is less suitable for a man to stay home than to busy
himself with external work. The young girl's place is at the fountain. The
woman's place is at religious ceremonies, funerals, visits to neighbouring
women, marriages, helping the sick and those in childbed. The Stoic
Hierocles says, 'It is up to the man to take care of the fields, the market,
errands to the town; to the woman, working with wool, bread, the duties
of the 'house'' (Stobaeus, 67. 24). Only poor women, by necessity,
frequented masculine places like the agora.

Certainly, the *nymphe* offers all the necessary pre-requisites for being
profitable, but there is still a need for the husband to make his pedagogic
imprint on this fresh clay. She has arrived at his home still a child; her bag-
gage, nevertheless, is not totally empty. Did she not already know how to
'make a woollen cloak that had been given to him'? (*Oeconomicus* vii. 6)
Although unobtrusive, not asking questions, could she be unaware of the
activity of the female sex in her 'house'? She knew 'how to allocate their
spinning duties to the maidservants' (*Oeconomicus* vii. 6), and probably a
lot of other things. There is, however, one point on which Ischomachus
notes his particular satisfaction: 'When she arrived she had been very well
trained in frugality, and that in my opinion is a very important aspect of the
upbringing of men and women' (*Oeconomicus* vii. 6).

Here we are again with the Hesiodic belly. Comedy and endemic misogyny endow woman with an excessive appetite and a pronounced liking for
wine. It is the mothers who teach their daughters temperance, a sense of
decency, modesty. Votive reliefs showing husband and wife side by side
illustrate this contrast with outside the 'house': the man's chest and right
shoulder are bare, women's bodies are completely concealed beneath ample
cloaks. But they are the ones who teach the values of the all-embracing
society, those on which masculine domination is continually based. For the
excluded woman, this way of shouldering her exclusion and transmitting
all its severity by clothing it with justifications of custom or divinity is not
peculiar to Greece. The girl/woman would hear the same message when she
went from her mother to her husband (the same that she herself would pass
on). And at the heart of the dialogue, the *nymphe* makes this revealing
sally: 'What am I capable of? Everything depends on you. My business, so
my mother told me, is to be good' (*Oeconomicus* vii. 14). Live like a vegetable (see nothing, hear nothing), and be good. This is *sophrosyne*, the
outstanding virtue of moderation and self-control, which is applied differently to the two sexes. For Ischomachus, it is a matter of being reasonable,

as his father advised him, to maintain his possessions and increase them if possible. For her, the programme is rather different: at the heart of the question lies the belly, with the stomach and uterus. Her will must be exercised on them: abstemiousness, chastity, they are all one.

THE FRAGILITY OF THE *NYMPHE*

Upon this substratum Ischomachus the tutor embarks on a training process to turn his bride into an informed and efficient colleague. The husband assumes this role of teacher and master all the better because he is the older one of the couple and the Greeks were very fond of emphasizing age. Many other cultures similarly pair the husband with the wife by placing her in the minor role, but the Greeks excel. The favourable factor is his authority. An educated man, well established, at least twice the age of his partner, and accustomed if not to political speaking, at least to being in command, he obviously enjoys a position of authority vis-à-vis his wife. But that does not prevent him from propitiating the gods by sacrificing and praying together with his *nymphe*: 'To ask them to grant that I may teach and she may learn what may be of most use to both of us. And, in this circumstance, she solemnly promised before the gods to become such as she ought to be . . .' (*Oeconomicus* vii. 7–8).

Ischomachus and his wife apparently have it made: all the interventions by the *nymphe* are no more than approval and applause for her husband's enjoyable work programme. Apparently . . . because, in the unwilling evidence of the husband, there is nevertheless a trace of difficulty. This first conversation did not take place immediately; some time was needed before that was possible. 'When she had become used to me, and was sufficiently tamed to converse, I put these questions to her . . .' (*Oeconomicus* vii. 10). The reason for Ischomachus' delay before setting his bride to work was simple and dramatic: until then she had been mute. And if she was not talking, it was because of a moral and mental disturbance following her transfer into this new 'house' and cohabitation; they had rendered her aphasic. In the realm of tragedy too, that is what Euripides' Medea reveals: 'Entering new customs and laws [marriage], she must be a seer to discover, unless she has learnt it at home, how to deal rightly with the man whose bed she will share' (*Medea* 238–40).

Marriage was the rudest shock in the life of a Greek woman. She was still a child; on the occasion of her *gamos*, she had offered her playthings to Artemis: her ball, dolls, knuckle-bones . . . She knew nothing, everything had been kept from her, and there she was, precipitated into a strange 'house', places, people. The *gamos* was an act of aggression: in the midst of cries of *Hymen*! *Hymenaie*!, the music of the choruses, the repeated raps on the door of the *thalamos*, there she was in bed with a man whom she perhaps did not know, who was far older than she, whom she had been told to obey, and who was doing unknown things to her. That is surely enough to explain why, for a while, the *nymphe* was speechless.

Hardly has she been enthroned, admonished and given the sacraments of guidance by her dear lord and master, than she suddenly changes into the mistress of the domestic staff, servants, slaves, governess of the house's possessions, instructress of those who are under her authority. The queen bee will give orders, receive, direct the slaves: she also sends them off to work outside (within the 'house' or farther afield), and she will also reward, punish, feed. She will supervise them, but also take care of them even if, according to Ischomachus, she finds that task repugnant. But the one who so quickly takes on the role of the brilliant pupil/wife, who already understands what increasing the 'house' means, retorts: 'On the contrary . . ., that is a task which would be completely agreeable to me if those whom I have looked after well must be grateful to me and show themselves to be more devoted than before' (*Oeconomicus* ix. 16).

Now there is a fresh and critical decision to make: the choice of another essential person in the 'house': the *tamia*. We meet her very early on in Greek literature, for she plays the same role in the royal 'houses' of the *Iliad* as in Ischomachus' 'house': stewardess, supervisor, home economist, manageress. Here, again, it is important to cinch the feminine belly.

> We carefully examined which maidservant seemed to us the least given to greed, drinking, the least inclined to sleep, run after men, and the one besides who seemed to have the best memory . . .

> I taught her that, in well-run states, citizens do not consider it enough to give themselves good laws, but they also appoint *guardians of the laws*: the latter exercise supervision, praising whoever observes the laws, and punishing any who violate them. I therefore invited my wife . . . to regard herself also as *guardian of the laws* for the affairs of the 'house'. (*Oeconomicus* ix. 11 and 14)

This is nearly perfection; Ischomachus' wife is a model – literary, of course – but these categories were familiar to the ancient readers of Xenophon, who could distinguish between the ideal and the day-to-day. But the apogee is still to come, through Socrates' mouth in reply to this last statement: 'For all the possessions that she enjoys owning, she finds more pleasure in taking care of them than in neglecting them.' The cup is filled, and he exclaims, 'By Hera, Ischomachus, there in your wife you reveal to us a spirit that is truly . . . *manly*' (*Oeconomicus* x. 1). The bathos is striking. We

Seated woman and a maidservant. If you are the queen bee, do you have to eat on your own?
© British Museum

think of those exceptionally brave female animals in Aristotle, the woman by her virtues attaining the masculine. And we come full circle.

It is but a step from here to showing herself proud of her ascendancy, to feeling herself mistress in her own home and installing herself in the authoritarianism of the 'house'. From the need which the wife feels to exert her authority frequently, she may slide towards domestic autocracy. Behind her walls, her truncated perception of the world and its autonomy may drive her to refuse to look at the outside world, including the world of her husband. Woe betide husbands then, they say:

> Here is a man whose happiness everyone vaunts in the public square; hardly has he crossed his threshold when he is the most wretched of men. His wife is mistress of everything; she commands, she scolds endlessly. (Menander, quoted by Stobaeus, 70. 5)

Another of Menander's characters states: 'Of all the wild beasts, on the earth and in the sea, there is none fiercer than woman' (ibid. 73. 56).

The comedy writers obviously loved to put on the stage these miserable wretches, dominated by their wives. Ridicule kills, and the audience fell about with laughter at the sight of the domestic misfortune of Strepsiades, one of Aristophanes' heroes, who has had the misguided notion of marrying above his rank, to one of the Alcmaeonidae after the style of D., a pretentious woman who makes his life impossible with her demands which are quite beyond a peasant such as he. He had got himself all fixed up with a modest 'house', modest peace and calm, a modest life, but everything has been turned upside down by the arrival of this lady from high society. Unhappy, despised, he can no longer even choose his son's name, nor raise him as he himself had been raised. 'He will be thrifty like his grandfather, a hard worker and tireless'; to which she retorts, 'He will have elegant manners and will dazzle the world with his luxury' (Aristophanes, *Clouds*, 68–72). This is Aristophanes' theatre, however; a Strepsiades does not marry the daughter of a great family except in the poet's imagination. Closer to social realities, at the end of the classical period, Menander, with less exaggeration, also speaks of the torments of marrying above one's station, and of the authority and haughtiness of the rich heiress who came to this 'house' with a dowry that might be described as indecent.

No, I don't want to talk about that hateful night when all my troubles began. Wretch that I am! Did I have to marry a Crobyla with her ten talents,[8] a woman but a cubit tall. And with that an unbearable haughtiness! By Olympian Zeus and by Athena, it is not to be borne! She has driven out my little servant girl, who was so lively, readier to obey me than I to give her orders: and who will restore her to me? I have married a monster with a dowry . . . It was she who brought me this 'house' and these fields; but to have them I had to take her. She is a real scourge for everybody. (Menander, *The Necklace*, fr. 296. 9–16, K–A)

THE CHARACTER OF THE *ERGATIS*

The wife's functions as supervisor did not free her from the basic domestic tasks that normally fell to the female gender. The woman worked but, in a way, it was work that did not count. Not that it was either economically or humanly negligible, but it was concealed work, for 'no charge', a sort of disseminated exploitation, with no rebellion, nor with any scruples on the part of the 'despots'. Nor does it count for much in the eyes of historians, who look more at the slaves. The exploitation of gender was more commonplace than that of slaves. This kind of work does not surface from the day-to-day in which it is bogged down, and we must leave the

8. The amount of the dowry, really beyond price here.

commonplace for it to appear. It is slightly more visible when death occurs. Among the virtues of daughters and wives which husbands and fathers have engraved on their epitaphs is that of being a hard worker, especially after the fourth century.[9] And it is also more visible when, from time to time, the concentration of hard-workers poses problems for the 'houses.'

This phase occurs after the serious troubles Athens experienced at the end of the Peloponnesian war, when civil war came to add its disasters to those of defeat. Many 'houses' are without men: some are on campaign, others prisoners, others – members of this or that faction – refugees out of town. Aristarchus complains to Socrates:

> Since the revolution which forced many citizens to take refuge in the Piraeus, my abandoned sisters, nieces, cousins have all descended on me, so that in my 'house' there are fourteen free people. We are getting nothing from our lands, which are in enemy hands, or from our 'houses', since the town is deserted. No one wants to buy furniture; no one lends money any more . . . (Xenophon, *Memorabilia* ii. 7. 1–17)

After hearing him out, Socrates says,

> But how is it that Ceramon, who feeds so many people, has enough for his needs and theirs, and is even saving enough to grow richer, whereas you are afraid of dying of want because you have more mouths to feed?

> By Zeus, it is because *he* is feeding slaves and *I*, free people . . . *He* is looking after workmen, and *I*, free and well-bred relatives. (*Memorabilia* ii. 7. 1–17)

What we know about the work of women of all conditions stops us thinking that it is only the idea of seeing his female relatives work which Aristarchus finds hard to swallow. Should we suspect a mental block which is due to a class mentality? Yet women in the well-off classes, like Ischomachus' wife, also lent a hand. The greatest difficulty probably lay elsewhere: working in one's own home did not count, whereas working for others was a sign of dependency, giving these free women the feeling that they were being likened to slaves. Socrates is more pragmatic than his interlocutor and, trying to persuade him, he gives a little catalogue of the types of work considered feminine:

---

9. See P. Brulé (1987), *La fille d'Athènes*, Paris: Belles Lettres, p. 343.

Is not flour useful?

Assuredly.

And bread?

That too.

And cloaks for men and women, tunics, *chlamydes*, [big cloaks], *exomides* [short tunics]?

They are all very useful.

And your kinfolk can do nothing of this kind?

Quite the contrary, I believe. (*Memorabilia* ii. 7. 1–17)

Socrates then quotes several instances of Athenians who, despite the harshness of the times, are making a fortune from fattening animals, making bread, weaving *exomides*.

I agree, answers Aristarchus, but they buy Barbarians whom they force to work, for which they cannot be reproached, whereas I employ free people, female relatives.

And because they are free and your relatives, you think they should do nothing but eat and sleep? (*Memorabilia* ii. 7. 1–17)

This difficulty creates tensions in the 'house': according to Socrates, it is because of his worries that Aristarchus does not like the women and they, in return, do not like him . . . Aristarchus finally decides to follow Socrates' advice.

From that moment, funds were found, the wool was bought; the women ate while they worked; when the work was done, they supped. Sadness gave way to gaiety, suspicion to trust. They loved Aristarchus as their protector, and he loved them, too; they were very useful to him. (*Memorabilia* ii. 7. 1–17)

Wife of a rich man, charged with overseeing the work of others, Ischomachus' wife, like all Greek women, took a personal part in the growth of her 'house' by carrying out tasks. It was a matter of her health:

I advised her not to remain always seated like a slave ... but ... to approach the job of weaving in order to teach anything that she knew better than anyone else, and for her part learn what she knew less well; to supervise the baking-woman, stay close to the *tamia* while distributions were being made, do her rounds to make sure everything was in its place: thus ... she could busy herself with her duties while walking about. A good exercise, too ... was to mould and knead the dough, shake out and fold garments and blankets. If she exercised in this way, she would eat with more appetite, would feel better and would really acquire a lovelier complexion. (*Oeconomicus* 10–11)

We shall now leave Ischomachus' wife (although she may make a surprise reappearance later); documentation on women's work lies elsewhere.

WOOL: SKEIN AND SHUTTLE

Of course, there were men who wove; of course, the end of the period would see the appearance of cloth-making workshops; but these were mere trifles compared to the conditions in which the vast majority of Greek textiles were produced: they were made in the 'houses' by women. They were spun, woven and dyed, in the first place for the members of the 'house', then possibly, as in Aristarch's 'house', to be sold. Nearly everything took place there, from the arrival of the raw wool (which might well be the 'house's' own), to the spinning and weaving stages, to the point where it was made up. The major operations were the spinning and weaving, two very different kinds of work which demanded different capabilities and a special manual know-how, from those handling them. The 'house' was equipped with the basic requisites to meet these needs, and against this background certain objects – the distaff, the loom and the famous shuttle – assumed an emblematic character.

In daily contact with the technical experience of their elders, girls were set to work at a very early age. These workrooms assembled free women – young, adult and old – as well as slaves, equally of all ages. We do not know if there was a division of labour between free and non-free. Certain large-scale pieces, such as blankets, were divided into strips which would then be sewn together to make the whole. This communal work suggests conditions in which a feminine sociability of the 'house' might have appeared and been expressed. There seems little doubt that there were various levels of tasks and responsibilities among the women of the 'house', even if we have few means of evaluating them. Ischomachus' wife had other things to do than send her shuttle flying as long as daylight allowed. The longest and hardest work fell to the most junior of the females in the 'house'. However, without ignoring the productive significance of this activity, its symbolic dimension is enough to explain why, even in society's comfortably-off classes, women were never away from textile work. Then quality might count: from light, fine fabrics, closely woven, multicoloured, embroidery, various and ingenious patterns, up to those textile masterpieces displayed by the *parthenoi* in the great religious processions (see pp. 19–20). Seeing such a beautiful garment, one might well wonder who its mother was.

Wool and textile fibres in general, at least since Penelope, were women's business. The *erga gynaikon*, women's tasks, were often the clothes. Among the numerous activities of Greek women, nothing better revealed their membership of their gender than their contact with and handling of textile fibres. Indeed, wool could be used to imply the feminine even in its absence. For instance, in the Cretan city of Gortyn, a man guilty of adultery was sentenced to wear a tuft of wool (see p. 105). To expose himself in this way in the sight of all revealed the guilty party as a *gynnis*, an effeminate; and it was an insult because it shows a lack of self-control to let yourself yield, like a woman, to the pleasures of Aphrodite. The wool was there to indicate in what way the man had sinned.

It will come as no surprise to find that, in the realm of the gods too, textile work was the female prerogative. It could even be claimed that, at the heart of divine feminine orientation, textile production and know-how acted as a criterion in the definition of spheres of influence. If one had to *choose* the deity of fabrics, it must be Athena. Having said that, it is well known that other goddesses had their share: Artemis and Hera, as well as heroines like Helen, whom we have seen at work earlier, were wonderful artists. Nevertheless, if we could keep only one deity here, it would have to be Athena, and one of her other names is well in keeping with this virtue: *Ergane*, the hard-worker. From myths, such as the one of the creation of Pandora, in which Athena clothes her, to the rituals in which, like other deities, she is honoured by the gift of votive garments, Athena is intimately connected with cloth. She is 'consubstantial' with it, by virtue of her special connection with the technique, the craftsman's skill and know-how. Athena is an inventor of both objects and processes; she is on the side of quality.

One of the best known aspects of the rituals linked with both textiles and Athena is the celebrated *peplos* which was woven in honour of the goddess, and offered to her every four years on the occasion of the biggest festival in Athena's own city, the Great Panathenaea. It was an important and splendid piece of work. Important, because this 'mantle', of a very special kind, served as a sail for the boat which, on this occasion, was hauled halfway up the slope of the Acropolis. That it was splendid, all witnesses agree: multicoloured, ornamented with various scenes, the most spectacular of which represented the war the gods had waged against the Giants. Brocades and embroideries embellished this gift from the city to its tutelary deity. Three categories of feminine citizen had a hand in it. It began with an inauguration of the great work by Athena's priestess who 'thus undertook the *peplos* of the goddess.' Her acolytes were two or four '*arrhephoroi*', daughters of the best 'houses' in Athens, and aged between five and ten. These girls would never leave the work, but obviously they could not complete such an undertaking themselves, and other age groups in the female citizenry lent their hands to this collective task. They were helped first of all, by mothers, as instructresses, mistresses of textile expertise; then came a plentiful labour force of *ergastinai*, *parthenoi* recruited in their dozens from the best families. It was the same work as in the home, with the same range of ages among the women, the same hierarchy, the same technical teaching – only the size and purpose differed. The huge dimensions of the *peplos* necessitated the division of labour (antiquity had no large-scale looms), the organizing of separate panels, and a certain strict discipline. Those *arrhephoroi* seem to have been very young, apprentices to skilled weaving. And yet, perhaps not *so* young. Ischomachus' wife already knew how to weave a cloak when she arrived at his home. She was not yet fifteen, only fourteen. Thanks to contracts on papyrus in Hellenistic Egypt, we know that the training of a slave in order to turn her into a good weaver lasted four years. It would probably not be surprising if girls were put to work on cloth at a very tender age, both in this model workshop of the divine *peplos* and handling the hanks of wool or working at the loom in the 'house', even if only doing the lowly tasks. A tender age? Ten years or younger.

The ideal woman added to her qualities of an attractive body and mind the cardinal virtue of a wife: high-quality work and diligence in carrying it out. 'For women, bodily qualities are beauty and form; those of the spirit are moderation and a love of work, but without servility' (Aristotle, *Rhetoric* 1,361a). The ideal is this form of 'gratuitous' work, to some extent unnecessary, done by those whose destiny does not oblige them to toil.

AN EPILOGUE THAT 'THUMBS ITS NOSE'

Under its would-be scholarly title, what in the end is Xenophon's *Oeconomicus* but the account of a *nymphe*'s subjection to the yoke by her husband? We have already seen how this image is in keeping with the process of 'taming.' She bows her neck, and the woman we are shown merely asks for more from her lord and master. Certainly, he has already caught her applying make-up in secret, and has scolded her; she answers as she should,

Funerary stele of Polyxena. Is not bringing daughter and maidservant together beside the dead woman merely another way of defining the feminine share of the household? We know her name: once dead a woman regains her identity. National Archaeological Museum, Athens

Bronze mirror. Aphrodite as a mirror and model of herself. The decoration makes Aphrodite the caryatid (the pillar) of this mirror: she carries a dove, her favourite creature, *erotes* flutter hither and thither, then more doves. Even the voice matters when it comes to helping to charm: up above there is a seductive siren. The Walters Art Museum, Baltimore

that it was only out of concern for her appearance, that she understood his criticisms and would not do it again, and that her business, as her mother had taught her, was to be good. What can be added to this sad and gentle interment? I hinted earlier in this chapter that Ischomachus' wife might surprise us and here she is.

> Epilycus was my uncle . . . He died in Sicily, with no male children, leaving two daughters who came to Leagrus and myself. He left his affairs in a bad state . . . However, I sent for Leagrus and . . . told him that decent people, in such circumstances, should show their loyalty to their family . . . 'Have one of them assigned to yourself and I will ask for the other.' We both made the request according to our agreement; but unfortunately, the one who had been allocated to me fell ill and died. The other is still alive. She is the one whom Callias, on the promise of a good sum of money, wanted Leagrus to hand over to him. As soon as I learned of this, I put down a deposit and brought an action against Leagrus . . . in these terms: 'If you want her to be given to you, take her and be happy; if not, I claim her.' Upon this news, Callias demanded the heiress for his own son . . . As for this son for whom he aspired to obtain the hand of Epilycus' daughter, you will see what his birth was and how Callias acknowledged him. It is worth taking the trouble to learn about it, citizens. (Andocides, *On the Mysteries* 117–19)

This is where readers will discover why they have been led into this maze of Athenian twists and turns:

> He married the daughter of Ischomachus: after living with her for less than a year, he took her mother, and this man, the lowest of wretches, living with the mother and the daughter, he, the priest of a divine Mother and Daughter;[10] he had them together in the 'house'! Ischomachus' daughter thought it better to die than to live to see such shame; she tried to hang herself, but someone intervened. Brought back to consciousness, she fled from the 'house': the mother had driven her daughter out. When he had had enough of her as well, Callias sent her packing. She claimed to be pregnant by him; but when she had given birth to a son, Callias denied that it was his. The woman's relatives, having taken the child, came to the altar with a victim at the festival of the Apatouria and invited Callias to start the sacrifice . . . With his hand on the altar, he swore that he had not, and never had had, any other son

10. Demeter and Kore.

than Hipponicus, born of Glaucon's daughter, and that if he was lying
might he perish, he and his family . . . Now, some time later, he fell in
love again with that old woman, the most impudent of women, brought
her back to his home again, and presented the son, who was already
quite big, to the Ceryces, declaring that he was his own. Calliades was
against including him; but the Ceryces voted according to the law of
their college, which authorized a father to present his son to them,
provided he swore that the child was truly his. His hand on the altar,
Callias swore that it was his legitimate son, born of Chresylla. It was the
same one he had repudiated. (Andocides, *On the Mysteries* 124–7)

Can this mother be the bride of 'our' Ischomachus? Historians of
ancient Greece are prudent people and hesitate to identify this shrew of a
Chresylla with the sweet anonymous girl of the *Oeconomicus*; the dates fit
badly if one thinks that the couple are contemporary with the period
(around 362) when the treatise was written. But there was nothing to stop
Xenophon choosing his Ischomachus from a recent past, because of the
qualities of a good administrator that he ascribes to him, in an era when
Athens, like the 'houses' that formed it, was prosperous. The treatise would
then be a 'dialogue between the past and the present.'[11] See how life in the
'house' can transform a tender *nymphe*, good, loving, respectful, into a
merry widow, a harpy. It would be simplistic and too easy to use such
words: the singularity of the story, the extraordinary chance which presided
over the comparison of the two texts, so far apart in their uses, authors and
intended recipients, would almost doom this case to be ranked among the
'news in brief' items. It is a desperate business to try to derive anything
from it other than the moral of a fable or this simple observation: a 'house'
lives and then . . . dies. However, if one is careful to eliminate the exceptional aspect of this story in our sources, a lesson remains that is like a second thought about all that has been said hitherto on marriage. It was all
related to a *first* marriage. The widow, the woman who has already served
in one 'house' and has been passed on to go and have babies elsewhere, the
repudiated woman, the woman whose large dowry – in this case, very large
dowry – makes her less dependent, no longer has much in common with
the tender *nymphe*. *Exit* virginity, instruction by the husband, innocence,
the wide difference in age. Remarriages are frequent. The demographic
imbalance between the spouses resulting from the natural differential mortality between men of thirty to forty and women of fifteen to twenty-five
was greatly increased by the specific mortality of men, the death rate in

11.   An expression used by S. Pomeroy in her commentary (1994), *Xenophon Oeconomicus.
      A Social and Historical Commentary*, Oxford: Oxford University Press.

war, which was high in Athens at that time (whence the overloading of Aristarchus' 'house'). The psychological conditions in which these 'recurring' brides found themselves no longer had much to do with those of the first wedding of a *parthenos*.

Since 451 BC and the decree of Pericles which created such an obstacle (p. 197), there was no possible wife in Athens except one who came from the system of 'houses.' It was a double movement, which absolutely excluded the rest, and which locked the marriageable into a closed society, a finite genetic stock. It was political endogamy, accompanied by a social endogamy and resulting in a 'family' endogamy. There was no salvation except in the 'houses.' Then, from outside, there was a knocking at the door.

CHAPTER 6

The women on the outside

All honour to the wife: the Greeks wanted it thus, as the price for safe-guarding their social system, and it was to conform to this explicit social hierarchy that until now I have focused on the wives and daughters of citizens. But these formed only the tip that surfaced from a veritable feminine iceberg which was submerged, ghostly and peopled with the shad-ows of shadows. It would have been futile to try to reverse the situation, since the majority are forever unattainable; virtually nothing survives of the tens and hundreds of thousands of slaves. More accessible, and thus more present, was an entire and ill-defined population of women who were 'free' but had eluded the system of 'houses', and who, although not lucky enough to be wives, had perhaps other opportunities. But men did not speak of them. The most numerous in poetry, drama and painting were those who, to use a Greek expression, worked with their body, made a living from venal love. There is no lack of stories, anecdotes and portraits concerning a few celebrated hetairai. Unlike wives, courtesans are not anonymous. In this 'media' success, the contribution to this of their personal qualities is by no means negligible, but there are other explanations that will complement our appreciation of the Greek feminine.

In fourth-century Athens, the prosecutor in a lawsuit against the courte-san Neaera, when seeking to characterize the roles of the various kinds of women with whom citizens could have relations, exclaimed:

The married state is recognized for the procreation of one's children, the introduction of one's sons [note that he does not say children] into the phratry and the deme,[1] for giving one's daughters in marriage as one's

1. Social groups serving as a framework for integration into the city, and holding something like civic status.

own. Courtesans (*hetairai*), we have for pleasure; concubines (*pallakai*), for our everyday requirements; wives, to have legitimate issue and as a faithful custodian of the home. (Apollodorus, [Demosthenes 59] *Against Neaera* 122)

This text seems to have been conceived for historians, but this does not prevent it being a trifle short if it is supposed to give the range of possible sexual partners (male and female) for the 'Greek man.' Boys are missing from

Love for sale. Negotiations and preliminaries – Hetero or homo everything is for sale. [230 47 37 (West) Berlin F2279, Peithinos cup, *ARV*² 115, 2, ext.] Antikensammlung, Staatliche Museen zu Berlin – preussischer Kulturbesitz

what is on offer to adults. Although it relates only to heterosexual relations, and the absence of *pornai*, 'prostitutes', is understandable for reasons of decency, the list cannot be considered complete. True, in the prosecutor's mind *pornai* may perhaps be included among the hetairai. This systematic approach to Greek love life is very useful to anyone wishing to claim expertise in the taxonomy of this domain. Let me begin by mentioning the vocabulary as I did for Homeric females. The language uses three words to describe women whose social roles and positions are very close.

The vocabulary of prostitution

First, there is *hetaira*, doubtless the most specific term. Etymologically commonplace, but curious all the same, it is the feminine of *hetairos*, 'companion', 'friend'. *Hetaira* can be taken simply as 'female friend' or 'girlfriend' – its first and commonly understood meaning – so that some people tend to slant her function and role in the direction of platonic love:

> I want to speak to you of the hetairai who truly deserve their name . . . these women who are capable of offering faithful friendship . . . those women whom, alone among other women, one greets in the fair name of friendship, which they receive from the Aphrodite who in Athens is known as Aphrodite Hetaira. (Athenaens, xii.28.572b)

Hetaira is generally translated as 'courtesan', with a certain idea of distinction, but can equally well make use of the more imprecise term 'prostitute'. Nevertheless, as our dictionaries hasten to make plain, the hetaira belongs to a fairly 'high social level', but it is not certain that this euphemism based on money is true to life. The same windbag philosopher who was arguing just now for a 'desexualization' of the hetaira continues, with little concern for coherence, 'But one can also call "girlfriend" a woman one pays, and "to play the girlfriend" is to get paid for sleeping with someone.' What is in no doubt is that we are speaking of a woman who sells the services of her body. It is hard to find an exact translation and equivalent today but, in the past and elsewhere, the hetaira may be compared to the Edwardian 'fancy woman' and the Japanese geisha. To be a hetaira, regardless of the wealth and influence of the person concerned, meant being strictly outside the status of legitimate wife and living in circumstances closely corresponding to those of a 'mistress' in the bourgeois sense of the word, or of a 'concubine'. Changes of role bring about changes in designation, from the 'public' hetaira, on offer to all and sundry, to the 'mistress' of one man, then to 'concubine'. It is a matter of biography.

Young hetaira and client. It was no simple matter to make a good hetaira. This one appears to be performing a dance step. Is she a hetaira, a musician, or a dancing girl? If you could do one thing you could do the other. © British Museum

Then there is the *pallake*, translated as 'concubine', in other words 'she who sleeps with', the 'mistress.' Her relationship with her bedfellow is characterized by its regularity and preferential nature: he alone could explicitly tolerate her going with another (or others). There is also an economic connection: the upkeep of the *pallake* is most often ensured by her protector. A woman might be taken as concubine, live in concubinage with the man himself, in his 'house' or elsewhere. Like those born of relations with a hetaira, the children will be bastards, even if the *pallake* is of citizen origin.

Lastly, there is the *porne*, 'prostitute' (*pornos*, 'male prostitute'). 'Selling one's charms' is *porneia*, but it can also imply forbidden sexual relations, such as adultery. At the heart of the meaning of all words formed on *pornos/e* lies the idea of trade: to give oneself, or another, over to prostitution is to hand over in return for money the rights over one's own or another's body. Etymology does not contradict this interpretation which derives *porne* from *pernemi*, 'to sell.'

Men frequent hetairai, declares the orator, for pleasure. Very well, but what kind? The word gives rise to a doubt: *hedone* is 'pleasure' in its widest sense, the kind we receive and give, 'enjoyment', both mental and physical; in the plural it means 'desire'. We must accept this polysemy, which renders the term 'courtesan' partly unsuitable: the pleasure given by hetairai is not uniquely sexual. They exercise other gifts, develop other talents than those – common and expected – that favour sexual enjoyment: a flair for poetry, musical leanings, skill in dancing, a predilection for intellectual conversation, depending on the tastes and requirements of the clientele. That is the most important thing: to satisfy masculine expectations in order to make a living, or to survive. Insofar as the pleasure offered makes money, what is offered by hetairai is regulated by what is required of them. Wealthier men raise the hetaira's 'rate'. As I shall point out for the *pornai*, we are in the area of marketing and competition – competition between the offers of pleasure, between hetairai, and between *pornai* (not forgetting masculine offers). And, of course, amid all these temptations and potential attractions, there is the husband's interest in his legitimate wife. The income of the hetairai thus depends on their attention to the client and the services they offer, giving rise to an attitude regarded as different from the wife's; we hear an echo in Lucian, the comic poets and the epigrams of the *Anthology*:

> Come then! Is not a courtesan more obliging than a wife? Yes, and with good reason. For the latter, protected by the law, can put on airs in the 'house' where she has to live. (Amphis, fr. 1 K–A, quoted by Athenaeus, xiii. 559a)

Among the hetaira's many qualities, clients often recall her 'obligingness':

> If, when he goes to her, he is despondent, she treats him kindly; she kisses him, not closing her lips tightly as if he were an enemy, but like the birds do, mouth wide open; she sings, she calms him down; she restores his tastes for jollity . . . (Ephippus, quoted by Athenaeus, fr. 6 K–A viii. 363c)

And she goes even further, according to the advice of the mother to a daughter who is just starting out in her career, 'when she has to go to bed, she must appear neither shameless nor cold; her sole concern must be to captivate her lover and ensure that he becomes attached to her'. (Lucian, *Dialogues of the Courtesans* vi).

According to the circles she moves in, the appearance, behaviour and distinction of the *hetaira* can help her success.

What delicacy, when she was eating! Ah, she wasn't like those others who stuff their cheeks with leek rolls and devour their meat disgustingly. No, she was content with a mere nibble from each dish, like a young maiden [*parthenos*] from Miletus. (Eubulos fr. 41 K–A, quoted by Athenaeus, xiii. 571f)

True or feigned, the role of the poor worthy young girl, with lowered eyes, struggling against adversity, could also be good for making contacts, influencing certain categories of client:

The man I was telling you about saw a certain courtesan who lived in the neighbourhood, and fell in love with her. She was from the town, and had neither protector nor relative; as for virtue, her conduct was above reproach. She was truly [what I call] a courtesan. For others, by their conduct, can debase that name; it is really a lovely name, good friend. (*Palatine Anthology*)

Here we rediscover the initial ambiguity and, despite out precautions, let us not fall into the same trap as the *Robert* dictionary which conjugates prostitution only in the feminine. When it comes to the Greeks, things are always more complicated; an adult could find himself solicited by a boy with beautiful eyes. Even forewarned, we are constantly surprised by a passage from a famous speech by Aeschines: 'You know those residents of the public brothels' . . . (Aeschines, *Against Timarchus* 74). We expect *pornai*, or at most hetairai, but these are 'men addicted to indulging in all the practices you know about . . .' In the same speech, Aeschines puts the following question when characterizing the real activities of a young man:

What is one to think of an adolescent of uncommon beauty who, at an early age, abandons the paternal 'house' to go and sleep with strangers, attend fine dinners without spending a halfpenny, surrounding himself with the most expensive pipe-players and courtesans, have fun but leaving others to foot the bill? . . . It is quite clear . . . the man who foists such expense on others must necessarily provide certain satisfactions for them in return. (Aeschines, *Against Timarchus* 75)

The picture is one of little bands formed with the aim of providing clients with a whole range of possible pleasures, both homo- and heterosexual.

From the concubine to the hetaira and the prostitute, even to the 'madam', how are we to define these women by the customary legal categories? Are they of the town or foreigners? Are they free or slaves? In order to answer these questions and gain a better understanding of the

roles and places they occupied in society, let us follow the paths of a few
of them.

The most famous, the 'welcome':
Aspasia

Aspasia was certainly the most famous courtesan in antiquity, a time which
had many of them; she was so celebrated that other courtesans even
adopted this *nom de guerre* in reference to her (I shall speak later of one of
these namesakes). She was born – possibly in around 480 BC – at Miletus, a
large city in Asia Minor, the 'capital' of the Ionia about which mainland
Greeks liked to fantasize, seeing it as a rich, refined, learned and slightly
effeminate world (see p. 106). Little is known about her, except she was the
daughter of Axiochus. She left 'agreeable Ionia' for Athens, which made
her a *metoikos* (in other words, a resident foreigner). Why leave Miletus for
Athens? Why, according to some texts (comic poets), did she turn to prostitution on her arrival? The two questions are probably connected. Had
Axiochus suffered a stroke of bad luck? Or perhaps, as a 'supernumerary'
daughter, a poor daughter, did she find herself deprived of the dowry that
would have enabled her to be taken up by a man? We may also imagine that
such a destiny did not appeal to her. So it is suggested that, being young,
she was ambitious to rival the most famous courtesan in Ionia, Thargelia,
'beautiful and intelligent to perfection, and who had had no fewer then
fourteen husbands' (Athenaeus, xiii. 608f).[2] A precocious vocation, then.
Had she, imitating those such as Nicarete given up the life of the shuttle
(see p. 24) for the life of Aphrodite?

ASPASIA'S "HOUSE"

The clearest motives for such a choice were, of course, a better standard of
living, escaping from the pit in which a man's abandonment could cast her,
but also gaining her independence, relying on no one but herself. (It is not,
however, definite that it *was* a matter of choice, because what we know of
other more or less famous hetairai is that they were bought and resold – in
other words, they were slaves – at some point in their life, and had not
therefore *chosen* 'to work with their body' in order to enrich themselves or
the person who owned them.) At the time when Aspasia is best known to
us, when she was in the company of the most remarkable thinker of his era,

---

2. We must understand this as fourteen men whose concubine she has been (successively?).

Socrates, and the most influential politician in the city, Pericles, she was not gaining the best part of her income from herself, but was running a "house", which can be described as a brothel just as well as a literary or philosophical salon. In any case, whatever the epithet one applies, it was a real business undertaking, functioning in the same way as other enterprises of that time (we shall see this in the example of Neaera). As there are salons and salons, so there are brothels and brothels.

What we discover in Aspasia's "house", what goes on there and who is to be found there, prevent our imagining anything like those *lupanars* where

> There are a number of good-looking young girls. [Where] you are quite free to see them in broad daylight: they warm themselves in the sunshine, have bare breasts, are naked, lined up like soldiers,[3] side by side. You may choose. How do you want her? Thin? Fat? Chubby? Tall? Short? Young? Old? Middle-aged? More mature? . . . You have only to let yourself be forced, to be dragged off. They call old men 'Daddy', young men, 'Big Boy'. You could easily have each of them, for not much, by day or by night, every way you want. (Xenarchus, *The Pentathlon* fr. 4 K–A, quote by Athenaeus, xiii 569a–d)

For one client, Socrates, there is little doubt about the reason for his going there, according to Hermesianax:

> What compelling passion did angry Aphrodite not kindle in Socrates, who ought to be superior to men? But to drive those torments, which are peculiar to youth, from the depths of his soul, he went to Aspasia's to find some sexual relief. (fr. 2, Diehl, quoted by Athenaeus, xiii. 599b)

'Find some sexual relief at Aspasia's', not necessarily *with* Aspasia, since she had in her employ (which means that she received the major share of the dividends arising from it) several 'little trollops.' She had procured them from the sellers, or resellers, of girls, at a certain price depending on the supply and the quality (beauty, origin) of this human merchandise. She either kept these girls for her own use or could resell them in Athens or abroad, immediately or after teaching them the 'tricks of their trade.' Although there is probably some exaggeration in this passage from Athenaeus: 'Aspasia, Socrates' famous woman friend, did a great trade in pretty girls. Hellas was full of her little tarts' (xiii. 569f), Aspasia's

---

3. The image is one of the phalanx, where the fighters have to leave as little space as possible between them in the ranks.

activities as a 'madam' are not in doubt. However simplistic it may be, Aristophanes' explanation of the origin of the Peloponnesian War is in keeping with this far-reaching view of Aspasia's business.

> Some young [Athenian] roisterers, who had grown tipsy over a game of cottabus,[4] took a trip to Megara, a neighbouring city, and carried off Simaetha, a prostitute; then, aroused as fighting-cocks, the Megarians in reprisal carried off two of Aspasia's tarts. (Aristophanes, *The Acharnians* 524–7; see Plutarch, *Pericles* 30. 4)

Was Pericles suffering the same 'kindled passion' as Socrates when he went to Aspasia's place in search of what he could not obtain at home? According to the accusations spread by his political enemies, and reported by Plutarch, through we do not know how true they were, he was 'a man strongly inclined to the pleasure of love.' But must we go so far as to believe that 'he even bedded his son's wife'? Indeed, when the names of Pericles and Aspasia are associated in certain texts, they are the synonym for debauchery, she in particular. 'And Debauchery gave birth to that Aspasia-Hera, the concubine with the bitch-eyes' (Cratinus, *The Cherons*, fr. 259 K–A). The comic poets were not afraid of strong language: tart, trollop, madam, bitch (an old image), dirty cow. For instance, to Aspasia who is anxious about the fate of Pericles the Younger, the son she has had by Pericles, a character replies: 'He would have been a man long ago, had he not been prevented by his trollop of a mother' (Plutarch, *Pericles* 24. 9). The reputation ascribed to Pericles contributes largely to the composition of a satirical picture in which it seems as if all 'high-society' Athenians are striving to outdo one another in fornication. Was it not said of the famous sculptor Phidias that he

> acquired for Pericles free-born women with whom he had a rendezvous. The comic poets . . . slandered him about the wife of Menippus, his friend and second-in-command as strategos,[5] and about Pyrilampus, Pericles' companion, who had taken up bird-rearing and who was accused of having secretly sent peacocks to Pericles' mistress. (Plutarch, *Pericles* 13. 9–10)

---

4. A game played at banquets, consisting of throwing a few drops of the contents of a goblet into a vessel placed on high, at the same time as uttering the name of one's beloved.
5. In Athens the strategoi were the chief magistrates, holding both military and civil powers.

Plutarch, who reports all these rumours, does not fall for such stories and believes them to be mere gossip and of an exaggerated nature, to say the least.

> Why be surprised when men who are gifted with a satirical streak offer to the delight of the multitude, as if to some malevolent demon, their calumnies against the powerful, when it is known that Stesimbrotus of Thasos himself dared to accuse Pericles of a loathsome and impious attempt on his son's wife? (Plutarch, *Pericles* 16)

So, how are we to form an opinion? These texts come from the same overall sources: comedy writers and Plato. In parallel, for his contemporaries, Pericles' qualities were outstanding; he was the best of orators: 'Rapid speech and, added to that rapidity, a kind of Peruasiveness (that) hung upon his lips' (Eupolis, *The Demes* fr. 102 K–A in the scholia to Aristophanes, *Acharnians* 530).

In an astonishing volte-face, it is precisely where one would least expect to see him attacked – his abilities to handle political discourse – that his detractors launch an upsetting assault. *He* did not write his speeches, it was Aspasia. Several witnesses were in agreement on this point: she was 'beautiful and intelligent'; her company was in demand for her knowledge and political good sense. This Aspasia was a specialist in sophistics and taught Pericles the art of oratory – an art, however, that could not be less feminine. There is no doubt about it. Was it because courtesans were more able than others to penetrate the masculine world, the outside world where words ruled, that they enjoyed definite advantages over wives? Looking through this other prism, testimonies backfire and, from being a 'house of ill repute', Aspasia's "house" took on the air of a salon. Socrates' constant visits could no longer be explained by his libido: '[He goes there] with friends, [and] regular visitors to Aspasia's house take their wives there to listen to the conversation, although she conducts a trade that is neither honest nor respectable' (Plutarch, *Pericles* 24. 5).

Socrates no longer goes to Aspasia's to fuck, but to philosophize; for Pericles, Aspasia plays the curious role of oratorical 'ghost writer', and Plato portrays her declaiming a funeral oration in her "house", a ceremonial discourse very close to the one her lover pronounces at the end of the first year of war in 431 BC, to the memory of the Athenian soldiers fallen in battle . . . So it was in a brothel that the most famous speeches of democracy were thought up! And Athenian citizens were not afraid to bring their wives out of their shut-in 'houses' to take them to a bordello to hear the queen of the town's hetairai converse with the flower of the intelligentsia. But to exaggerate one aspect to the detriment of the other, to be surprised and then reject it, is to risk missing the reality, which is its complexity relative to our own categories. The pleasures of the body in no way excluded those of the mind, and vice versa, and fifth-century Athenians did not suffer at all from what seems to us a confusion of life styles. What was said of Leontion, the hetaira, seems fairly common: 'she also undertook to study philosophy; but she does not give up making love . . . She sleeps with all the disciples of Epicurus in the gardens, and with the teacher, and without concealing herself'[6] (Athenaeus, xiii. 588b; see Diogenes Laertius, x. 4–7; 23).

FROM "HOUSE" TO 'HOUSE'

There is nothing astonishing in the fact that, having had two children Xanthippus and Paralus, by D. (see p. 118), Pericles installed Aspasia in his 'house' with the title of concubine; we shall shortly see Phrynion do the same with Neaera. What shocked his contemporaries was his reason for taking her into his home: he loved her. But where do we find talk of love in all these texts? It was pretty well unheard-of. How could behaviour motivated by love be explained, above all when it concerned a member of the city's privileged classes? Everything in the conduct of the leading lights of the city could be explained, chiefly by debauchery or self-interest. But love – that was something hard to believe. Even so – at the time of a trial when the very future of Aspasia at Athens was at risk (she was accused of impiety) did he no go so far as 'to weep in public', 'even more than when he himself had been in danger of losing both fortune and life'; did he not go so far as to 'implore the judges'? That was improper, unworthy behaviour, for sure. Furthermore, with an independence of spirit which was without doubt the most original facet in the behaviour of these two lovers in that world which was so starchy despite its coarseness, did they not go so far as to kiss publicly: 'Indeed, it is said that on leaving his home and on returning from the agora [going to and from public matters], every day, he never failed to take his leave of and greet her, and kiss her' (Plutarch, *Pericles* 24. 9).

Loving a woman to this extent, and she a foreigner, a hetaira, and calmly making a public demonstration of it – that was a liberty, a non-conformist, which shocked. Did Aspasia love Pericles? Was it because Pericles loved Aspasia so rashly that they had a child? Silence! Was it because, passing from the position of hetaira to that of concubine, Aspasia was less bothered by the prospect of motherhood? The child was named Pericles by his father, and was known as Pericles the Younger. His son, yes, but he was

---

6. Conforming to the teaching of the Cynics in this field; see what Diogenes says on masturbation (p. 108).

neither heir nor successor to his father. He was a bastard, certainly the son of a citizen, but a citizen who already had two sons, legitimate this time, Xanthippus and Paralus. He was the son of Aspasia, therefore of a foreigner, a hetaira, a woman who had not been given in legitimate marriage by her father with a dowry to her man, but who lived with him, either because she had been 'taken' by him, or because she had given herself to him. Little Pericles was only the son of a foreign concubine and, for that reason, could not be regarded as an Athenian citizen, even though he was the son of the foremost of them. Some years earlier, his destiny would have been different. It was in fact in 451 BC – in an era when Pericles was doubtless still living with D. – that he had set before the Athemian people a decree aimed at restricting the granting of citizenship only to boys born of parents who were both Athenians. Until then, it had been enough if only the father was. True, it would nonetheless still be possible to live with and have children by a foreign woman, but the fruit of those unions would never be citizens. It was under this regime that Pericles' and Aspasia's love-child was born; they raised him and named him in full awareness of the situation. After the lawsuit against Aspasia came war, and then the terrible plague which wiped out tens of thousands of men and, primarily, 'the living flower of youth'. Pericles' two legitimate sons were struck down. First, Xanthippus, the elder, with whom Pericles was not on good terms; but then he was overwhelmed by the loss of Paralus, the younger. In these circumstances, henceforth threatened with losing 'his name and family', seeing his 'house' collapse, he went before the people to ask for the repeal of his decree for the benefit of his last son. Historians say that there was something pathetic about his taking this step, and only commiseration could explain the acquiescence of the Assembly in this contradictory request at a time when the general attitude tended more to restricting than granting citizenship. The Athenians found 'that his request was only human, and allowed him to inscribe his bastard son among members of his phratry (see p. 215), giving him his name' (Plutarch, *Pericles* 37. 5).

Pericled died of the plague very soon afterwards. Unmarried, a foreigner, intellectual, but also an entrepreneur in masculine pleasures, Aspasia left Pericles' 'house' and resumed her independence. It is not known whether she had given up her prostitution business before or after; she could have sold it when she was installed by Pericles as his concubine, but on the other hand, there was nothing to stop her carrying on with it and getting the profits. However that may be, her last known biographical feature brings us back to the same ambiguity that we encountered from the start, and which is probably inherent in the role and activities of hetairai: following the death of the 'great man', she did not long remain the weeping widow – in any case, she was not a widow at all. Her political knowledge, rhetorical expertise, gifts as a teacher, she put them all at the service of a 'seller of sheep, a common man without breeding', named Lysicles. Having in some way set her heart on him and thus probably aroused much jealousy in the town, she lived with him and 'made him the first among the Athenians' (Plutarch, *Pericles* 24. 6). The mistress of a cattle dealer, concubine of a demagogue, giving him lessons in political practice, in the evening of her life Aspasia continued to build an independent life.

The other Aspasia: the Greek model conquering the Persians

> It is said that Aspasia was so renowned and famous that Cyrus, the one who made war on the Great King for the empire of Persia, gave the name Aspasia to the one he loved best among his concubines. (Plutarch, *Pericles* 24. 11)

Plutarch apologizes for this digression in the middle of his *Life of Pericles*, but it is fortunate that he let himself follow this association of ideas, as it enables us to verify that famous hetairai were *very* famous. We have so little to go on, regarding the lives of Greek women, how can we resist the temptation of a biography, even if it is slightly fanciful? The story of this 'second Aspasia' is to be found in the very uneven collection of Aelian's *Historical Miscellany*.[7] Even if this woman's life was quite exceptional, that fact in no way detracts from its interest, both because of the social type she represents and also for the portrait she sketches of a kind of ideal woman – a very Greek ideal, even though Aspasia Mark 2 was chiefly connected with the Persians.

ONCE UPON A TIME, THERE WAS A POOR BUT VIRTUOUS PHOCAEAN WOMAN

Her name was not Aspasia – *her nom de guerre* – but Milto ('The Vermilion'), perhaps because of the radiance of her complexion. But that is already jumping the gun because, when she was younger, she would not have deserved this name. Let us begin at the beginning, then. She was the daughter of Hermotimus. Orphaned of her mother, she had been born at Phocaea, in North Ionia, and 'grew up there in poverty, but not without self-possession

---

7. Except where indicated, all the quotations in this section are from Aelian's work, *Historical Miscellany*, xiii. 1, which has no subdivision.

or resolution.' 'Self-possession' and 'resolution': two virtues which, in the Greek distribution between the genders, were more masculine. That is how sententious Greeks preferred many of their poor: virtuous and proud. A *parthenos*, like Nausicaa, she dreamed of marriage, and her dreams promised her an 'excellent man.' But in the midst of that delicate transitional stage of puberty, she was rudely afflicted by an ugly wart under her chin. Her father took her to the doctor. Alas, no money, no treatment. Oh, the disappointment! But then, in a dream, she was visited by a dove which, transformed into a woman, said, 'Courage! . . . Take the garlands of roses consecrated to Aphrodite, which are withered by now, grind them and spread this remedy on your growth.' Which she did, and 'through the grace of the most beautiful of the goddesses', all at once Hermotimus' daughter was transformed from the ugly girl she had been '[into] the most beautiful of the *parthenoi* of her age.' In other words, Hermotimus' *thygater* had reached the age when, having become 'beautiful', her body was sufficiently changed to be desired by men. This deserves scrutiny, as in the case of Nausicaa. We know this much of her description: her hair was blonde and lightly wavy, she had huge eyes, a prettily aquiline nose, very small ears, full lips and teeth whiter than snow. So much for her face, whose complexion was of course 'like roses', and with a 'tender' and 'delicate' skin. But for the rest, the description leaves it to our imagination, with the exception of her ankles: 'They were so slender that Homer would not have failed to number her among those he describes as *kallisphyroi*.' They were an outstanding feature. And what of her voice? 'One would have said it was a Siren when she spoke', sweet and gentle. And all that without interfering with nature, 'without adding anything artificial or superfluous to her beauty.' Another refrain on the antithesis between masculine naturalness and feminine artifice, the old tune of husbands like Ischomachus.

Milto's life changed on the day she was summoned to a banquet by Cyrus – Cyrus the Younger, satrap of Asia Minor and brother of the reigning king, Artaxerxes II. It was this Cyrus who, in 401 BC, with the backing of his mother, mounted the expedition of the Ten Thousand against him, an account of which Xenophon left in his *Anabasis*. Father and daughter resisted this invitation-cum-command. They were well aware of what attending the banquet of a powerful personage might mean for a girl's virtue. But force was used ('it is not a rare occurrence for satraps to use violence'), and there was no escape. It was a 'stag' banquet: Cyrus was there with his drinking companions 'as the Persians like to organize these affairs', but the customs described perfectly match a Greek banquet. 'When the Persians have eaten their fill, they devote themselves to the pleasures of drinking wine . . . In the midst of the boozing, four young Greek girls were brought to Cyrus, including Aspasia of Phocaea.' The Greek *parthenos*

had shown her untamed character by rebelling against 'putting on the garments' they had tried to make her wear before she entered. Everything was
set for a highly moralistic contrast. On one side, the three other girls: crafty,
as scheming as can be, obviously conniving in their fate, their sophistica-
tion at variance with Milto's naturalness, heavily made up, provocative. 'All
the techniques taught to hetairai, the behaviour of women who use their
beauty to trade in it.' How many paintings show the same scene? Who will
be surprised to see the three Greeks letting themselves be fondled and
kissed? Already consenting, already in the service of men's pleasure,
already slaves . . . and then, poles apart from such behaviour, Milto. She is
there but longs to be 100 miles away. 'She keeps her gaze lowered, her face
is red as flame and her eyes filled with tears.' Only if forced will she act.
She has refused the rich cloak they wanted her to put on, and has even
refused a bath. She weeps, calls upon her father, then curses him, curses
herself, invokes her protector gods, those of Greece and of liberty. This is a
leitmotif running through Greek consciousness when comparing themselves with Barbarians: they characterize themselves as exercising freedom
of choice. Milto knows where the danger lies, and feels she is a prisoner of
despotism: 'She is convinced that she is being forced into manifest *slavery*.'
Defeated, she has to give in and put on the garments. Assuming a costume,
like assuming a name – think of Briseis and Chryseis, and all those women
whom violence places in men's hands – is fundamental in these stories, and
is the equivalent of assuming a function. It is over, she may postpone the
moment a little longer, but how can she fight what awaits her – to have to
act 'not as *parthenos*, but as *hetaira*'? The poor little lamb will have to go
through with it, she is too much to the taste of the wolf.

To the taste of Cyrus – let us talk about him. The three girls have been
brought to sit beside him. He starts pawing them, and they cooperate will-
ingly. But hardly has he touched Milto with a fingertip when she cries out
and gets up. He touches her breasts and she tries to flee. Nevertheless, the
first time 'he is charmed by her reaction', and the second time, 'he admires
her nobility.' Not so for his companions, who find her charmless (*acharis*,
when at the outset she was said to be full of *charis*), vulgar, wild. Cyrus is
won over and says to his 'recruiting agent': 'That one alone, among the girls
you brought, is free and untouched.' The reason for this positive appreciation of the untamed Milto's virtue is a way of behaving 'that is not Persian',
but Greek. Cyrus has been conquered by her virginity, her virtue and her
pride. The lack of taste of Cyrus' companions is explained: they are too
Persian, and approve of the docility and artifice of the others. So? so, it is
love! 'From that moment on, Cyrus thought more of Aspasia than of all the
other women . . . He loved her very much . . . *and his feeling was returned*.'
Only love seems capable of explaining this volte-face of Milto/Aspasia. A

curious *coup de foudre*. Was it influenced by Cyrus' abrupt change of attitude and the inversion of the roles within the Greek group, when from
being last she became first? Everything obviously slants towards the Greek.
Aspasia's cardinal virtues are very Greek and, in his role of enlightened
ruler, Cyrus is also completely Greek. So it comes as no surprise to see
Aelian describe the Graeco-Persian couple,[8] Cyrus-Aspasia, as an *Hellenikos
gamos*, a Greek union, because of their harmony and moderation. That is
the reason for their vast renown. Plutarch compares the celebrity of those
two 'beautiful and wise' Ionian women, the two Aspasias. He explains that
it was in memory of the earlier one that Cyrus turned Milto, daughter of
Hermotimus, into Aspasia, his foremost concubine. Another comparison
between the two stories is the astonishing role of mentor which these
women played vis-à-vis their lover. As Pericles took lessons in politics and
eloquence from his Aspasia, Cyrus made no decision without discussing it
with *his*. More famous than any woman of that time (according 'to both
Greek and Persian women'), she subsequently lived a simple life: 'wise',
'educated' (the same words which are used for the first Aspasia), of 'very
noble sentiments' and 'regal' (her lover's status required this). Still profess-
ing to be little concerned with her appearance, she deserved admiration
chiefly for her nobility, accumulating the traits that are normally ascribed
to . . . men.

HIGHER STILL

But Aspasia's life did not unfold smoothly. First of all, she was mixed up in
her man's misfortunes. In 401 BC, Cyrus led a venturesome military expedition against his brother, Artaxerxes II, motivated entirely by an ambition
to take his place as king. When the project failed, the army of Greek
mercenaries and Persian troops recruited by Cyrus was defeated at the
battle of Cunaxa. It is never a good idea to belong to the losers' camp. Like
another Briseis or Chryseis, Aspasia was included in the booty.

The victorious king, Artaxerxes, was not unaware of the fame of a
certain Phocaean woman, also known as the 'Wise and Beautiful', one of
his brother's Greek concubines. Finding her on the battlefield, he was
angry 'that she had been put in chains', and ordered that 'magnificent
apparel be brought for her' (Plutarch, *Life of Artaxerxes* 26. 9). The scene
that follows may upset us. In the end we had acknowledged that Aspasia
was drawn to Cyrus, but here, in a totally different setting, the same scene

8. Cyprus has a legitimate wife with whom he can procreate little Achaemenid princes
    and, like every Achaemenid ruler, he has dozens of concubines. See P. Briant (1996),
    Histoire de l'Empire perse, Paris: Fayard, pp. 289–97.

as at the banquet is repeated. Aspasia refuses, weeps, implores. The death of her beloved Cyrus! What calamities overwhelm her! And without any transition, Aelian adds, 'However, once adorned, she was the most beautiful of women, and Artaxerxes was inflamed and consumed with love.' Putting on fine garments can transform even a virtuous woman into a royal concubine. The king had to wait for a while, but he took her eventually. No comment. From mistress of the satrap younger brother, she had now reached the heights: mistress of the Great King.

Some time later, as was the tradition in the Achaemenid dynasty, the heir apparent, Darius, asked his father for a gift which, again by tradition, he could not refuse. Darius demanded Aspasia. Caught unawares, the king answered that he accepted, on condition that she agreed. She was brought in and made her choice: Darius, demonstrating a consistent behaviour – her liking for competitors. As we can see, the 'Wise and Beautiful' was politically coherent in her thinking, and it takes little effort to recognize in her, from the very outset, more astuteness than spontaneity. The force of custom was strong enough for the king initially to concede his concubine to his son, 'But he quickly took her back from him, appointing her as priestess of Artemis of Ecbatana, known to the Persians as Anaïtis, so that she should spend the rest of her life in chastity (Plutarch, *Life of Artaxerxes* 27. 4).

Thus, Aspasia could not officially pass from two to three Persian princes and, by using the priestly constraint on virginity,[9] the king found a fine response to both the upwardly mobile aspirations of his son and the frenzied urge to concubinage of the one who had been a poor, little and ugly Phocaean.

A strange episode brings the account to a close. Bearing in mind that the author of this 'life' was Greek, it says more about his ideas on sexuality than about any possible Persian customs.

Some time later, the eunuch Tiridates died, the most handsome and charming in all Asia. He perished when he was in the springtime of his life, barely emerged from childhood. It was said that the king loved him passionately. He was truly very afflicted by this loss and suffered a keen sorrow. There was general mourning throughout Asia, because everyone thus sought to please the king. However, no one dared to approach him or try to console him . . . When three days had passed, Aspasia donned

---

9. Such as we find on pp. 18–20 in Greek lands for virgin goddesses like Athena or Artemis. Anaïtis, mentioned here, is not Artemis, merely an assimilation on the part of the Greeks.

a mourning garment and, at the time when the king was about to go to bathe, she stood still before him, weeping, with her eyes cast down.

Touched by such solicitude, the king 'ordered her to go and wait for him in his chamber, which she did. When he came in, he placed the eunuch's garment on Aspasia, over her black robe.' Yet again, she is shown donning garments but this time less for a change of status than for a change of type, even, if we rightly interpret, for a change of sex. 'The boy's clothing somehow suited her, and her beauty shone even more brightly in her lover's eyes.' Aspasia knew what role she should play and banked on ambiguity and ambivalence; by slipping into the role of *eromenos* in a pederastic relationship she could still arouse physical desire in the saddened king.

Neaera, taking 'houses' by storm

The 'life' of Neaera forms the most complete portrait one could paint of a Greek courtesan.[10] The historian of Greek women cannot choose his model, and is highly content when he comes across a very likeable human being: a courageous, independent woman, a slave, a good mother, trying to make a little place for herself in the sun, but to whom the orator Apollodorus ascribes every failing, painting her as a kind of anti-portrait of the wife-woman in the 'house' system. Count on him to press where it hurts: a prostitute, a perjurer, a thief, and a liar, bawdy, foreign and impure. What more do you want? Neaera's mobility makes her a sort of free electron, elbowing customs aside, muddling categories. But this freedom is ambivalent: while considerably enriching her life through various opportunities, it is a privilege she has to pay for in frustrations and failures that she tries to escape with the help of expedients on which society casts hypocritical eyes: hide those "houses" we do not want to look at, but keep them open for us to use. The plea containing her story was delivered before 340 BC. Neaera was accused, being a foreign woman, of having married Stephanus. The law punished the guilty foreign woman too: like the foreigner who married an Athenian woman, she had to be sold into slavery (this was the rule when it came to punishing the usurpation of citizenship). As for the one who gave a foreign woman in marriage to an Athenian, claiming her to be his daughter, he was deprived of his political rights and stripped of his possessions. The Athenians, and the accusers (personal and political

10. Except where indicated, all quotations in this section are from *Against Neaera* which, while part of the Demosthenic corpus, was most likely written as well as delivered by Apollodorus.

enemies of Stephanus, like Apollodorus himself), were well aware that, behind Neaera, Stephanus was the real target. To have her sentenced, the prosecutor had to show that she was both foreign and the wife of Stephanus. In order to achieve this, he launched himself into the quasi-biography we are about to follow.

NICARETE

The story starts in Corinth around the beginning of the fourth century BC. The central character was then a hetaira, one Nicarete. She had been the slave of an inhabitant of Elis called Charisius, was freed and married a famous chef, Hippias. This Nicarete was well versed in 'the trade': she was particularly gifted 'in being able to spot at a glance potential beauty in little girls, to bring them up and instruct them.' With the wealth of her experience – in that it was 'with these creatures that she made her living' – one fine day she purchased seven girls: Anteia, Stratola, Aristocleia, Metanira, Phila, Isthmia and Neaera.

Girls? This is pretty vague, when it has been shown several times how necessary it is to be precise with questions of age and vocabulary. Translated literally, the words indicating these particular girls would give the picture of a group, a job lot of 'little *paides*' (plural of *pais*). What sort of traffic produced these children? We do not know. Were they courtesans' daughters (often daughters followed in their mother's footsteps)? Abandoned, exposed children, subsequently the property of their 'protectors'? Victims of violence, war and piracy could also supply such a trade. It was a specialized market, for which evidence can be found elsewhere.[11] and Nicarete knew where to find what she was looking for. Girls up for auction in a market: slaves, of course, then prostitutes; their training is carried out on the job. All the madam has to do is surround herself 'with fresh prostitutes who are apprenticed to the trade with her. As an expert, she knows exactly how to bring them up and train them' (18).

What age were these children from whom, like some shady horse dealer, Nicarete was able to pick out 'promise of beauty', and whom she would bring up? 'Little child' could mean a little girl of between seven and ten. Whatever the case, Neaera had certainly not reached puberty when Nicarete bought her. When Nicarete came to Athens for the Eleusinian Mysteries and the festival of the Panathenaea, she brought with her Metanira and Neaera who, although still a child, was already a prostitute (22; see also 24). Yet again, we see the Greek man's liking for the immature.

---

11. A mime by Herodas in the third century has the title *The Procuress*.

Iconography confirms in many instances the presence in numerous banqueting or dance scenes of girls with prepubescent bodies: hips, buttocks and breasts hardly showing or discernible. These prostitutes were known in the 'business' as *hypoparthenoi*. Not, of course, '*demi-vierges*' (we are not dealing with bourgeois novels), but 'sub-virgins', prepubescent prostitutes. The fact that a technical term exists to describe them proves that prostitution had them on offer for clients. When Nicarete moved her business, she disposed of various 'goods', and it was to be expected that prostitutes of all ages figured on the list. Another feature of the vocabulary is the exceptional use of another indicative word, *thygater*. It may be remembered that this term, which means 'daughter-of', appears in epics chiefly when it is a matter of matrimonial relations (see pp. 48–9). Apollodorus says that the 'madam', Nicarete, was in the habit of calling her 'girls' *thygater*, 'in order to get larger sums of money from those who wanted to have them in the belief that they were free' (19). It was obviously more spicy, because it was rarer and carried a taste of the forbidden, to find oneself with the opportunity of enjoying the favours of a citizen's daughter. This procedure of deceitfulness about their origins must have been fairly classic, as we find it used later by Stephanus and Neaera.

THE JOB

The expression constantly used to refer to Neaera's activities is that 'she worked with her body.'[12] As is the case in a master-slave relationship, whoever buys the body of another (or takes possession of it by violence or by contract) defines it instrumentally by the use he desires to make of it. This is Nicarete who, taking possession of children's bodies, turns them into the bodies of hetairai. And the orator then utters this 'programme note': 'Neaera belonged to Nicarete and worked with her body, receiving a wage from those who wanted to make love to her' (20). This sums up the girl's function and job. Neaera 'works' by supplying her body, her special tool, and one which she knows how to use with all the technical expertise that could be wanted, according to the *modus operandi* that will satisfy men's desires. Here are three courtesans, for example, in an epigram:

Three courtesans offer you these playthings, blest Cypris, each according to her speciality; Euphro from what her buttocks earn her, Kleio from what she earns by following the rule, and Atthis from what she

---

12. I have used this phrase in preference to 'prostituted herself', to retain an analogy between this form of work and all the rest, paid or not.

The pleasures of the banquet. For men and women, music and wine. Musées royaux d'Art and d'Histoire – Brussels

owes to her mouth. In exchange, Sovereign goddess, send the first the profits that a boy would want, the second those a woman desires, and the third those wanted by the third sex. (*Palatine Anthology* vi. 17, Lucian)

We have to take the Greeks at their word here; it really is work. When Artemidorus repeats that to have 'sexual commerce (in dreams) with prostitutes established in a bordello . . . is good for any kind of enterprise', he comments, 'For some people call these women "hard workers", and they give themselves without refusing anything' (*Interpretation of Dreams* i. 78. 88). The whole vocabulary is that of the artisan's world; even the places where this activity goes on are called 'workshops.' The physical services rendered by the working woman are paid for by the sums of money handed over to the woman (or man) who employs them; a portion of the customer's cash therefore goes to Neaera, but for the most part to Nicarete, for it is in the order of things that the girl, officially or not, retains part of her hire fee. In the same 'working' concept of prostitution, this sum of money is called 'wages'; the vocabulary belongs to businesses, day labourers. Thus, to demonstrate Neaera's venality to the court, Apollodorus asks: 'Where has she not offered herself *at so much per day*?' (see 108).

It is unnecessary to expatiate on the distance that separates the world of the Aspasias from that of Neaera. There is no nobility here; no longer any question of philosophy or rhetoric. Neaera and her companions in misfortune could have testified that they 'had had no other occupation . . . than washing themselves, giving themselves a good rub down, drying, adorning, titivating and retitivating themselves, applying their make-up and dolling themselves up' (Antiphanes, *Malthakè* 148. 1). A frequent practice in other trades relates to this same world of entrepreneurs and their customs: handing over girls to an intermediary on hire. These contracts by which an owner passed off direct employment of a slave to the advantage of a third party were well known, for example regarding slaves who worked in the mines. And the orator turned the argument of wages back against Neaera: 'When a woman comes under another's discretion and is under the thumb of the one who is paying her, what else can she do, I ask you, but yield to every desire of those who employ her?' (Antiphanes, *Malthakè* 148. 1). The two situations of dependence and obedience combine, towards the one who has bought her and the one who uses her. With regard to the 'madam', it is a relationship based on authority, the availability of the employed woman and her economic inferiority; with regard to the client, the relationship is based on the authority conferred upon him by the contract to 'hire' a body thus placed at his disposal. She is just a possession.

"HOUSES": WHO OWNS THEM, WHO RUNS THEM?

When all is said and done, we are witnessing a traffic in children who find themselves incorporated into the sex trade. These workers had a price tag, there was a tariff for the services they provided; for the manager, it was important to take account of the wear and tear on the human instrument and keep replenishing the 'livestock.' There remains the question of Nicarete's status, and of brothel-keepers in general. Of slave origin, she was free at the time of these events; in such conditions, it is hard to see how she could have owned a "house." For in ancient Greece, land and property were the privilege of a citizen and, at least in Athens, a masculine privilege. Like Aspasia, Nicarete cannot have owned the houses in which brothels were set up. It is far more likely that they belonged to citizens who rented them out, and what we know from social records in the ancient Greek city indicates this property-owner as the true instigator of the whole set-up, the real entrepreneur in prostitution. We have few examples, but one is very clear: 'Euctemon reached the age of ninety-six; during most of his life he could be regarded as a fortunate man; he had very considerable wealth, children, a wife . . .' (Isaeus, *Philoctemon's inheritance* vi. 18).

Among other assets and sources of income, Euctemon owned in Piraeus, an 'apartment block' with a suitable number of 'prostitutes.' As a commentator wrote, 'one glimpses the origin of Euctemon's income.' Of course, Euctemon did not dirty his own hands: 'a freedwoman ran the house on his behalf.' Like Nicarete, she was the one who bought the new recruits. Such was the case of one named Alke who, during her long stay in the 'house', had children from a sustained relationship with a freedman. 'Having reached riper years, she retired from the job', and Euctemon, no doubt satisfied with her services, followed standard practice and made her the keeper of another establishment 'in the *Kerameikos* [a district of Athens], near the postern where the winemarket is' (Isaeus, *Philoctemon's Inheritance* vi. 18).

Nicarete took her little girls (at least Neaera and Metanira) with her to Athens for the big festivals, which were not only religious ones: the Eleusinian Mysteries and the great Panathenaea.[13] The account of her peregrinations at the end of the prosecution deserves attention: Neaera went to Athens, but also travelled throughout the Peloponnese; she lived in Corinth, Megara, went 'to Thessaly, Magnesia with Simos of Larissa and Eurydamas . . . almost the whole of Ionia in the entourage of Sotadas the Cretan, when she had been hired out by Nicarete, who was still her owner' (Isaeus, *Philoctemon's Inheritance* vi. 108). On those occasions she was made welcome by citizens of the city, but these sought, and often found, the means of installing her with bachelor friends, to avoid her cohabiting with the women of the 'house.' Everywhere, Neaera 'banqueted and feasted with many companions, as a courtesan can do.' She and her companions travelled extensively. Such mobility contrasted keenly with the gloomly stability of a wife's life. They were strangers everywhere, and it was in their nature to be so; they lived wherever and however engagements, relationships and gatherings of people took them, they were hired, and hired themselves out, to the highest bidder, but also to the most reliable. What counted was the network of clients they thus managed to build up through chance and good luck; it could always prove useful.

NEAERA

One fine day, Nicarete decided to give a favourable reply to the request made by two of Neaera's lovers, Timanoridas of Corinth and Eucrates of

---

13. Two of the biggest religious ceremonies in the city, but also the occasion of magnificent festivals.

Leucadia, who, finding Neaera's 'unit price' too steep (her charge for 'turning a trick'), proposed that Nicarete should let them buy her outright. 'They paid her thirty minae for Neaera, whom they purchased in conformity with local [Corinthian] law, in order to have full ownership of her as a slave' (29). Tired of paying a fee, they wanted to become her owners and, as Nicarete's price was high, it was better to go shares. The transaction included a transfer of authority and, henceforth, instead of paying for her they could derive an income from her body. Nicarete had preferred the angle of recouping her capital, and perhaps was also obeying the rule that troubles begin with these girls when they reach a certain age and run the risk of pregnancies. In any case, as she had already realized a handsome profit on the girls, it was a better idea to start operations afresh by buying other little girls on the market. If our guess is right, it could explain a phrase used by Apollodorus regarding the sale: Nicarete would have unloaded her quota of little girls 'when she had reaped the benefits of the youth of each of them' (19).

This was the first new development in a life that would experience many new developments. Perhaps Neaera never knew soliciting by independent prostitutes or quick trade "houses", the activity which caused trouble in town centres and was regulated by city authorities. On the island of Thasos, the people voted for a ban on soliciting in the agora, but that was probably not enough, since there was also a ban on women 'going up on the roof of "houses" in the street to show themselves off.'[14] When Neaera was purchased, her bohemian life was over, together with her dealings with an indefinite list of customers: she left Nicarete's brothel and acquired a certain amount of independence, even if only economic. In this new position, she presented real sexual competition for wives, an invisible enemy who could allow herself to play with men. From this period on, she worked on her own or with anyone she chose to associate with, such as dancing girls and pipe-players. Being no longer in a "house", she could give up working the streets, and went from banquet to banquet, chiefly among the relatives of Timanoridas and Eucrates. But the new situation was only temporary, for at this juncture the two friends both decided to get married. They were not keen to see their former mistress working in Corinth, nor coming under the authority of another brothel-keeper (in other words relapsing into her earlier situation); they would be happy to see her in a good situation, even if they received less from her than they had spent. Magnanimously, they wanted to set her free. For this, as was customary, they wished to be reimbursed with the thirty minae they had paid for her.

14. H. Duchêne (1992), *La stèle du port, Études Thasiennes* 14, Paris, text p. 32, com. pp. 52–4.

Banqueting scene. A variety of ages, sexes, tastes and pleasures. Antikenmuseum Basel und Sammlung Ludwig, Inv., 418. Photo Claire Niggli

Through the keyhole. 'Affectionate, if uncomfortable, sex,' to quote Eva Keuls. Tarquinia, Attic cup by the painter of Triptolemus

That was no small thing, when we know that slaves costing over ten minae were rare, that generally speaking a 'qualified' worker cost between three and five minae, and miners 180 drachmas. As all these prices were obviously proportional to the income that the owner hoped to derive from them, this meant a craft which was profitable. One could make one's fortune in ancient Greece by exploiting human sexuality and unless she made some bad management errors, Nicarete would not have had to end her life in poverty. To purchase Neaera's freedom, the two associates showed themselves to be really cooperative, each offering 500 drachmas and, when it came to 'the twenty remaining minae, they invited her to earn them for herself and pass them on in repayment' (30).

NEAERA'S FIGHT FOR HER STATUS

[Then Neaera] brought several of her former lovers to Corinth, including Phrynion . . . who led a debauched and extravagant life . . .; she handed over to him the money she had collected from her former lovers as a free gift when she received her liberty; she added her savings; then she asked him to make up the sum of twenty minae and to pay the whole amount to Eucrates and Timanoridas as the price of her enfranchisement. (30)

This astounding story deserves two clarifications. First, on the legal plane, in matters of private enfranchisement, when neither the owner nor the slave himself (thanks to the nest-egg he may have been able to accumulate) was capable of collecting the necessary sum, it was customary to see an association formed – an *eranos* – to advance the shortfall. The other remark brings us back to the very conception of venal sexual activity and the relations it presupposes between prostitutes and their clients. From the outset, as custom suggests, I spoke of the 'clients' of Aspasia, Nicarete and Neaera, at Corinth or during her travels. In reality, in the plea, these men were referred to only as lovers (*erastai*). Relying over-confidently on this one linguistic item is in no way to ignore the other aspect: the trading and physical subjection of one individual by another. Nevertheless, only if we take into account a feeling, a certain kind of attachment of the 'client' to the hetaira, intimated by the use of the word *erastes*, 'he who loves', can we understand why those former lovers would thus have contributed to financing Neaera's freedom. Phrynion complied, handed over the money and, henceforth more of an associate than an owner of the beauty, took her off with him to Athens. Here we have a new turn of events: a change of place of residence but, above all, of status. The novelty was the freedom which Neaera would not hesitate to exploit. Phrynion was the prime cause of this new life and if there was one yoke remaining on Neaera's neck, it was his. Apollodorus used this Athenian episode to play upon his audience: abomination of abominations, he quoted eyewitnesses who could testify that at a banquet given by Chabrias of Aixone after the victory of his four-horse chariot at the Pythian Games,[15] when Neaera was drunk and Phrynion asleep, many people made use of her, even Chabrias' domestic servants who had set up the tables. The vilest turpitude, doing it with the servants! It was in these circumstances that, fed up with the way Phrynion was treating her ('he did not give in to her wishes'), she took the plunge into independence. For the first time in her life she made a decision for herself, and on the quiet left Athens for Megara (the cities bordered each other). It was not an impromptu move, however, for she secretly took with her 'together with the contents of Phrynion's 'house', all the clothes and jewels with which he had adorned her, plus two maidservants, Thattra and Coccaline' (35).

But conditions were not good: this was neither Athens nor Corinth. Mixing clichés and commonsense, Apollodorus explains the reasons for things going badly: 'The Megarian is niggardly and careful with his money.' Then, there was the war, and foreigners were rare. And as Neaera was a great spendthrift, 'the work of her body did not suffice to pay for the way she liked to live.' It was in these circumstances that Stephanus made his appearance; he was the most important person at the end of her 'life', the one against whom the legal action was in fact directed. Coming to Megara, he 'went to her place as to a hetaira and had dealings with her' (37). She had progressed; living on her own income, in her own house (with no one in authority over her in the house where she was living), she enjoyed something that, in Athens, constituted a privilege: to be able to add freely to her possessions by means of her work. She was her own mistress and could give orders to others (she had slaves and girls). Yet she was not completely free. In many cities, the liberty of the enfranchised was limited and they found themselves obliged to take or accept a 'patron', often their former master, who played the part of protector in the view of the public authorities. The former master, in her case, was Phrynion, and Neaera obviously refused him.

WITH A MAN IN A 'HOUSE': NEAERA AS WIFE?

Neaera then decided to return to Athens to live, and 'took Stephanus as her "patron".' The contract between Stephanus and Neaera was simple: she

---

15.   The Pythian Games were one of the four greatest competitions in ancient Greece. They took place at Delphi and included equestrian contests. To enter a quadriga in such an event was a sign of great wealth.

'made a gift to Stephanus of what she had brought away from her lover's home', and arrived with her own possessions, her beauty, her *savoir-faire*, her 'trade' and 'three very young children.' For his part, he provided the house (a small one). He added some promises: to protect her from Phrynion's wrath, then to marry her, and to 'introduce her children into his phratry'[16] (38) to make citizens of them. A man, a 'house', children . . . in short a house presenting every appearance of being a normal 'house.' Here we have an additional rung on the ladder of Neaera's rise: she has become a wife. Moreover, this scenario strongly resembled an Athenian marriage in right and due form: the gift of the items stolen from Phrynion took the place of a dowry. Stephanus took Neaera together with some wealth. From that moment on, we see Stephanus acting the pimp. Not only did he profit from Neaera's 'bodily' activities, but even arranged them and went so far as to participate. The difference, from the point of view of their little business, was the couple's new aspect: they passed for man and wife.

Her favours were [henceforth] at a higher price, now that she had a 'front' and a husband. Conniving with her, Stephanus practised black-mail when he could catch a naive and rich foreigner: he held him hostage as an adulterer and extorted a large sum of money from him. It was a normal occurrence. (41)

It was the same principle of deceit about origins that Nicarete used with her little girls, using the word *thygater* to make clients believe that the girls were free-born and likely to become wives. The Stephanus-Neaera enter-prise laid the same trap for one of her former lovers by way of Phano, her daughter. They persuaded Epaenetus of Andros into the countryside on the pretext of a sacrifice and 'there, Stephanus caught him *in flagrante* (adul-tery) with Neaera's daughter and with threats extorted the sum of thirty minae [that number again] from him' (65). In fifth-century paintings, the hetaira is sometimes represented in an attitude and setting which are those of the 'woman in the home.' It is therefore permissible to deduce from this that there was a particular liking, perhaps specific to bachelors but which could also be felt by married men, for indulging themselves with classier 'tarts.' For the latter, it was a method 'of in some way setting a higher value on [their] services', as A. Schnapp put it.[17]

16. Every citizen was a member of one of these circles of sociability known as a phratry. Its members voted to enrol new members, and citizenship depended on the favourable outcome of this ballot.
17. A. Schnapp (1997), *Le chasseur et la cité. Chasse et érotique en la Grèce ancienne*, Paris: Albin Michel, p. 310 quoting G. Rodenwalt.

But the past was catching up with Neaera. Phrynion wanted to recover his woman, at first by force and then by bringing legal action. The matter was settled amicably: the appointed arbitrators decided

> that the woman should be free and her own mistress; the possessions she had carried off from Phrynion's home should be restored to him, with the exception of the garments, jewels and servants which had been bought for her personal use. (46)

Then came the clause which seems extraordinary to us, but which is found elsewhere: 'She was to have relations with each, turn and turn about, unless any change was agreed by both sides; the alternating spouse would provide for the woman's subsistence' (47). There is no reason to doubt that this judgement was properly applied (Apollodorus gives it his usual touch: 'each went to dine with the other when it was his turn to have Neaera; she herself took part in the banquet and drank with them like the courtesan she was'), but in the rest of the account, Neaera acted with Stephanus alone. It is true that the peroration changed its subject at that point: now it is the turn of Neaera's daughter, Phano, to become the story's heroine.

'MAKING IT' AT LAST: WITH PHANO

Stephanus gave Phano in marriage 'as his own daughter to an Athenian, Phrastor' (claiming that she was not Neaera's, but by an earlier *Athenian* wife); 'she brought a dowry of thirty minae.'[18] The marriage did not go well; Phrastor, thrifty and hard-working, found in her 'neither good manners nor docility'; and she 'wanted . . . her mother's lifestyle and the dissolute existence that went on there.' Moreover, Phrastor became convinced that Phano was not the daughter of Stephanus, but of Neaera, and 'furious about it all, realizing that he had been duped and held up to ridicule, after a year of marriage he sent his wife packing, pregnant and without her dowry' (51). The legal wranglings that followed this episode of the expulsion of Phano without her dowry resulted in a dismissal of the case.

> Shortly afterwards . . . he fell ill; his condition was very serious, and he was on his last legs. There had been a longstanding row with his relatives, with bitterness and hatred; and on top of this, he had no children. The attentions he then received from Neaera and her daughter mollified

---

18.   Always the same sum. On the scale of dowries given (see pp. 122–6), thirty minae placed Phano among the highest-priced marriageable girls.

him. They visited him during his illness when there was no one else to take care of him; they brought him the necessary remedies, and watched over him; and you know . . . how precious a woman is at the bedside of a sick person. Then, he let himself be persuaded to take back the child which Neaera's daughter had borne and acknowledge him as his own son. (55–6)

The son, but not the wife. It is probable that Phano was not particularly keen to become Phrastor's wife again. What matter? Indeed, at this point in the story, Neaera's victory seemed close at hand. So, are we to see the attitude of mother and daughter as calculated or as true solicitude? Who can say whether Neaera and her daughter felt some real compassion towards the sick man? Men were well aware that with hetairai they could find that quality of 'obligingness' which, they said, was lacking in wives. Conversely, may we not claim that the whole scenario was constructed rather than fortuitous? Phrastor came as a ready-made victim in a manoeuvre designed to lay hands, by means of a grandson, on an interesting inheritance. In Athens, recognition of paternity – one might almost say, the fabrication of paternity – went through a whole progressive and cumulative procedure set in motion by whoever wanted to make a child *his* child, and reveals the very great social power of the will of an adult citizen. The father engaged in a collection of approaches and rituals among social groups of which he was a member and in which he wished to incorporate the child. In order for the members of these groups to vote in favour, certain criteria had to be met: the child must be his own, born in legal wedlock with an Athenian woman who had been given to him in legal wedlock – according to the rules – by her father, who was himself an Athenian and had married a woman who was the daughter of an Athenian man and Athenian woman . . . Neaera knew all that: both the power of a father's impulse towards his son, and the control exerted by these assemblies of Athenians over the entry of new members into their bosom. Alas! The child was not enrolled, the members of the group making the pretext that when Phrastor had promised to acknowledge the child, he had been in the grip of illness (they might also have invoked 'lovesickness').[19] It was not just a whim on his part, as he brought an action against them for their refusal. But, 'enjoined . . . to swear, on the flesh of a sacrificial victim, that he regarded the child as his son, born of an Athenian woman, his legitimate wife' (60), he evaded the issue. Neaera – through Phano – lost the battle.

19. The mental state of an individual could be challenged – and his decisions called into question – if it could be proved that the person involved had acted 'under the influence of a woman.' Too much love suggested the presence of magic.

The old Euctemon mentioned earlier (see p. 208) found himself in the midst of a rather similar story. After he had set Alke up in her prostitution business in the *kerameikos*, he was not the same. The old man no longer went there merely

> at the end of each period (to collect his dues); he spent the greater part of his time there, frequently even eating with the girl, abandoning wife, children and home. The distress of his wife and sons did not make him change his conduct; but in the end he lived completely down there and fell into such a state, whether through drugs, illness or some other cause, that he let himself be persuaded by the girl to present to his phratry, under his own name, the elder of her two children. (Isaeus, *Philoctemon's Inheritance* vi. 21)

It meant that he was adopting the son of the former prostitute, who had become a brothel-keeper and 'protectress' of the old man. The manoeuvre failed, for his own son opposed it, as did the members of his phratry. The fact was that the men who lived in the city in the heart of the 'house' system, the citizen group, protected itself pretty effectively against attempts made on all sides to penetrate it; it remained enclosed within itself, and Alke with her elder son, like Neaera with her daughter, failed to become incorporated into it.

THE RELIGIOUS COMMUNITY:
SEX, THE FOREIGN WOMAN AND IMPURITY

Still seeking a husband for their daughter, Neaera and Stephanus pinpointed a certain Theogenes, 'of noble birth, but poor and inexperienced.' This man had been chosen by lot[20] to perform the functions of 'king.'[21] Stephanus assisted him, helped by advancing him money when he took office, and obtained from him a subordinate post at his side, 'then he got him to marry this creature, Neaera's daughter, whom he handed over to him by contract as being his own daughter'[22] (Isaeus, *Philoctemon's Inheritance* vi. 21). And here was Phano, higher than she had ever been: the wife of the 'king.' Neaera was jubilant. But this new episode took on a

20. A normal procedure in Athenian democracy for appointing a number of magistrates.
21. Also called king-archon, his duties were of both a religious and a judicial nature; he supervised the celebration of certain festivals and was in charge of the most ancient sacrifices; his competence covered priesthoods and impiousness.
22. Stephanus had put the proposition to Theogenes of a young experienced woman and also, since it was a marriage in right and due form, money; he was thus purchasing a paternity which would make him the father of a grandson of Neaera, at future citizen.

fresh dimension of which Apollodorus would make extensive use: the religious aspect. Phano's personality would interfere with one of the most august rituals in Athens.

It happened on the second day of the flower festival, the Anthesteria, consecrated to Dionysus. On that day, the city celebrated Dionysus' marriage with the 'queen', the 'king's' wife. It was a *hieros gamos*, a divine marriage, which took place in the *Boucoleion*, in other words 'the cattle shed', regarded as the ancient residence of the king. We do not know exactly what went on, as it was a mysterious rite and its secret, as with other 'mysterious' rites, was closely guarded. Everything turns on the question, what precisely did this 'sacred coupling' involve? Was it merely allusive? Was the partner of the 'queen' just a picture or statue of the god? Or did a priest, or even the king himself, play the part of the god? We do not know. At all events, it is clear that symbolically, through the person of the 'queen', the city welcomed Dionysus by offering him a royal coitus. And here was our Phano, daughter of Nicarete's little trollop, at the heart of one of those mysteries by which the Greeks 'interpreted' their beliefs. Apollodorus had it made:

> This woman thus celebrated the secret sacrifices on the city's behalf. She saw what she had no right to see, being a foreigner. A woman such as she has penetrated where no one out of so great a number of Athenians has penetrated, except the wife of the 'king.' She has received the oath of the priestesses who assist the 'queen' in the religious ceremonies. She was given in marriage to Dionysus. In the name of the city, she performed the traditional rites concerning the gods, numerous sacrosanct and mysterious rites. (73)

Now, the very first condition for the execution of these rites, one that not only aimed at their effectiveness but also fended off divine wrath, was purity. One of the illustrations of this absolute requirement, among hundreds of other pieces of evidence, is the oath of the priestesses which the queen makes them swear: 'I am in a state of purity, free from all cause of taint, especially of union with a man' (78). In Greece, the idea of piety, which is more complex than ours, assumes a notable social dimension. The standard of behaviour, whether public, private, civil or political, which can be defined more or less as obedience to moral rules, is not only secular but also takes on a religious overtone. It follows that a crime which we might consider to be purely civil may be construed in Greek estimation as an irreligious act. That is why the licentious life, and chiefly the crimes of adultery, imputed to Phano were considered as religious stains, and therefore why these sins irrevocably distanced her from the fundamental acts of the cult. It might be called an excommunication. The community dismissed her from ways of access to the sacred, first because she had no right, but also because she represented a danger to it. Because women 'naturally' experienced some difficulty in following moral rules (because of their weakness *sui generis*), especially in sexual matters, it was impossible for men to trust them, while serious threats of 'sullying and impiety' weighed heavily on the community. To prevent their excesses, there had to be legislation without any weakness, providing, for example, for the immunity of anyone, husband or 'firstcomer', who inflicted on the woman who is guilty of adultery 'any treatment he likes' – in other words, blows *unto death*. The law wanted

> women to feel enough fear to remain honest, not to commit any sin, to be faithful guardians of the home;[23] it warned them that, if they failed in this duty, they would be immediately expelled from their husband's 'house'. (86)

The law on adultery forbade the husband any sign of weakness, and ordered him not to live with his wife any more. And if he contravened this law, he would be deprived of his rights, excluded from the political community. As for the wife, she sank to the lowest possible depths: while slaves or foreign women were not prohibited from taking part in or attending public religious ceremonies, the adulteress was banned. Apollodorus came to the end of his peroration and threatened the jurors: do not forget that, when you have voted, you will have to be able to answer 'your wife, your daughter, your mother' when they ask you about your verdict. Will you be capable of saying, 'We acquitted her'?

> It would therefore have been much better if this trial had never taken place than to see it end in an acquittal, since henceforth prostitutes will have full freedom to marry whom they wish and to have their children passed off as anybody: laws will be powerless, the whims of courtesans will reign supreme.

> Think of Athenian women, be afraid that the daughters of poor citizens will no longer find husbands.[24] Today, even when they are needy, the law provides them with a sufficient dowry, unless nature has been unkind to

---

23. An echo of Apollodorus' words (see pp. 186–7).
24. Or rather, will not look for them, preferring to 'work with their body', if possible on their own account.

them.[25] But if, by your acquittal, the law is held up to ridicule and ceases to be in command, as a result prostitution will spread to the daughters of citizens, to all those who cannot be married for want of money. On the other hand, courtesans will be elevated to the dignity of free women when they obtain this privilege of having legitimate children as they please, and taking part in mysteries, sacrifices and the prerogative of citizens. (112–13)

Political community and religious community are one and the same.

Let each of you say to himself, when casting his vote, that it is a matter of his wife, daughter or his mother, of the city, laws and religion: the honour of these women must not be reduced to the level of this prostitute. Those women whose parents raised them in virtue [*sophrosyne*] and with such noble solicitude, those who have been married according to the laws, must not have as their equal and fellow-citizeness a woman who has committed so many obscenities, several times a day and with several men, as each one fancied. (114)

This trial was no laughing matter. Seeking to get at Stephanus, Apollodorus attacked his Achilles' heel: his private life, his mistress, his so-called wife. Neaera risked 'carrying the can.' If, in fact, she was recognized as guilty, if the jurors considered that the four children were hers and not Stephanus', if she had lied and, although a foreigner, had claimed to be Stephanus' wife, she 'would be sold according to the laws, and her children would be foreigners' (124). The court's decision left no room for doubt: Neaera, already old, had lost everything.

At the time of the court proceedings Neaera, a grandmother, was fairly well set up in life; she had come from Megara to Athens with two slaves, had acquired two more, and lived in a house which was partly hers, with furniture, clothes, jewellery. She had had four children: three boys (the eldest died) and a girl, the Phano who had got herself talked about so much. Although her material situation was a success, she had failed, despite her tenacious obstinacy, in her ceaseless and fierce desire to gain entry to the 'political reproduction group', the Athenian system of the 'houses.' And yet, others had been unduly admitted into these social groups that constituted the antechamber of citizenship, so why was what seemed possible for others not so for Neaera and her children and grandson? Was

25. The city's concern to avoid the oliganthropy that was weakening it. But, a dreadful expression too if read without *a priori* knowledge: the 'ugly ducklings' – and who decides? – are to be excluded from masculine indulgence.

it Stephanus' fault? Was it because they did not have sufficient money to buy enough votes? Or was the blemish of being both a foreign woman and one who worked in the 'sex industry' indelible, and Neaera too well known? It is time to recall a very similar case. From the legal viewpoint, the respective situations of Neaera's children and grandchildren and of Pericles the Younger were the same, and it is not known whether voices were raised a century earlier in opposition to the naturalization of Aspasia's son because such a measure would have threatened the virtue of citizens' wives. Are we to believe in a 'strengthening of morality' in Athens in the classical era? Maybe, but the difference in treatment is chiefly explained by the social and cultural distance between the circles in which Aspasia and Neaera practised their art.

As a foreigner, a hard worker, sexual entrepreneur, slave and woman, Neaera aroused fears. Men appealed for the protection of the community against such blemish and sullying. They feared lest the women of the 'houses' be contaminated. Let a *cordon sanitaire* surround our daughters and our wives, and as for *her* – let her wash herself clean and go back to where she came from. When stain and spot pile up, and the past is hurled in your face, how can you still stand?

How shall we take our leave of them?

The book we are about to close is not scholarly, anyhow it does not pretend to be. It is a book without critical apparatus, but one that speaks with its sources, which is its foremost concern. Nor is it *the* longed-for book, the utopian 'saying it all' survey; it has had to come to terms with the multiplicity of possibilities and, in the matter of choice, my own subjectivity creeping in between what is to be found there and what is not. It is therefore a personal book which takes on board that singularity. Like a heretic, I have sometimes used 'I'. This is less a matter – at least I hope so – of a swollen ego than of putting things in a nutshell; this was not the place to exhibit the compendium of my agreements or disagreements with my readings. In the initial choice of 'lives' as a road to discovery, there was the matter of history, but also the desire to dodge erudite debate. To choose Neaera and Nausicaa rather than an average of the two of them. Contrary to glum scholastic customs, I plead with students to avoid the grey of compromise when there are two sources, one saying black, the other white. It is the same reason why this book is not the algebraic sum of my readings. I do not feel myself on the side of 'gloomy certainty', and to use 'one' or 'we' would have been a betrayal of the nature of my contact with Greek women. But how exactly did I come to be so drawn towards these shadows?

Time has to die so that History can be born and acquire a relative knowledge of a succession of present-days. The men who inhabited all those presents doubted neither their knowledge nor their history, they lived in the calm certainty of being in the midst of justice, piety and truth. Then they died, passing on all they had been, including the history they had made of others or themselves. In return, the successive presents cheerfully and shamelessly challenge them. The Greeks lived with their capabilities, which were great and distinguished them from their predecessors and contemporaries. Their mental equipment, to echo L. Febvre, did not enable

Attic funerary stele of Megisto and Eratoxenos. Between the two people whose death this stele commemorates, a pet rabbit is shown as a means of conveying affectionate feelings. The Menil Collection, Houston

them to ask better questions, or to put them in a better way. Both Galileo and Marx were able to point out their errors. As soon as a culture dies, it is called into question. But it is not enough for a present to die for all its errors to be cleared up, or even for a later present learnedly to resolve its problems form the heights of its recent knowledge. History is not born like Athena, springing from her father's head already complete fully armed and for always. If all histories of the Greeks, of the Romans, of the sixteenth-century humanists, of German positivists, of French radical socialists, of Marxists and neo-Marxists of the twentieth century, and of today, sin gravely, it is by their own successive failings. History never stops annexing the histories of living epochs; it has to pile up centuries and millennia, and needs other historical views of past worlds. There have to be medieval clerics reading Aristotle, men of the Renaissance reading Plutarch; the *Ecole des femmes* and *La Religieuse* need to be written; there have to be George Sand, Virginia Woolf, Simone de Beauvoir. It was necessary to wait till the end of the twentieth century for enough histories to die, amassed by the sucessive attentions of living eras, finally to see the birth, in the heart of our times, of one of the most overlooked: that of the feminine gender.[1]

If that is how it happens, it is because History is shifting to the side of the present. Although theoretically insoluble in the earlier Other, it is making its entry, whether we like it or not, and is comfortable there. It links the 'pure' (non-historical) event of today with the 'impure' (because worked on by histories) event of yesterday, with its 'day-to-dayness.' It was my interrgoation of the women of my world which led mw towards the ones back then. I wanted to get to know them, myself enriched by those of today, and they enriched by the women of all the dead eras. In short, I wanted to be as true to them as possible. If the arrangement of the discourse is my own, it was from a desperate desire to get close to them, to keep them in their 'nascent' aspect (as they say in chemistry), letting Greek men, although unfortunately not Greek women, have their say.

There is no conclusion to this utopian project, as there is none to a taste that was born elsewhere. To conclude would be to shut the book again. If societies and even cultures are mortal, our death is preparing a History of which we have no notion. From where I stand, I want to salute this still half-open feminine world through the grace of some last words. To listen again in a voice, as an open door lets pass the faint music of a warm invisible presence; I would like to let through the breath of these fragmentary lines by Sappho.

---

1.   This page owes much to Jean-Paul Sartre.

When she left me, this she said,
'Oh, what hardships we have suffered,
Sappho, truly I leave you against my will.'

And I answered thus:
'Go, and fare well and
remember me, for well you know how much we cared for you;

If you do not, then I want
You to recall . . .
All the lovely things we shared;

many circlets of entwined violets,
roses and crocuses . . .
which, by my side, you placed on your head,

and many garlands of woven flowers,
twined round your tender neck

and with a royal perfume
of nard
you anointed your body

and on soft beds
of tender . . .
you assuaged desire

there was neither . . .
. . .

Bibliography

I must first quote my sources, in other words make accessible the authors whose works I have used at length in this book. They are, in order of appearance: Homer, Aristotle, Hippocrates and the Hippocratics, Plutarch, the *Palatine Anthology*, Xenophon, Apollodorus (transmitted with the works of Demosthenes). All these writers and their works are to be found in a bilingual edition in the Loeb Classical Library, published by Harvard University Press.

Over the last twenty or so years, the number of works on this subject has increased at a dizzying pace, to the point where it has become difficult to read them all. With the impetus of the feminist movement of 'Gender History', English-speaking countries have begun an evolution that has placed their publications in the first ranks, and not only as regards quantity.

In any case, this bibliography proposes simply an introductory *selection*, so I have left aside a number of fundamental articles and favoured books which come furnished with a bibliography.

Bérard, C. (1989), 'The order of women', in *A City of Images,* Princeton, NJ: Princeton University Press, pp. 88–107.

Blundell, S. (1995), *Women in Ancient Greece*, London: British Museum Press.

Blundell, S. and M. Williamson (eds) (1998), *The Sacred and the Feminine in Ancient Greece*, London: Routledge.

Brisson, L. (2002), *Sexual Ambivalence*, trans. J. Lloyd, Berkeley and London: University of California Press.

Bruit-Zaidman, L. (1992), 'Pandora's daughters and rituals in Grecian cities' in P. Schmitt Pantel (ed.), *A History of Women in the West, vol. 1: From Ancient Goddesses to Christian Saints,* trans. Arthur Goldhammer, Cambridge, MA: The Belknap Press of Harvard University Press, pp. 338–76.

Brulé, P. (1987), *La Fille d'Athènes. La religion des filles à Athènes à l'époque classique: cultes, mythes et société,* Paris: Les Belles Lettres.

Brulé, P. (1989), 'Des femmes au miroir masculin', in *Mélanges Pierre Lévêque,* Paris: Les Belles Lettres, 1, pp. 49–61.

Brulé, P. (1996), 'Des osselets et des tambourins pour Artémis', in *Clio, Histoire, Femmes, Société,* no. 4, *Le temps des jeunes filles,* pp. 11–32.

Cantarella, E. (1992), *Bisexuality in the Ancient World,* trans. C. Ó. Cuilleanáin, New Haven and London: Yale University Press.

Calame, C. (1997), *Choruses of Young Women in Ancient Greece,* trans. Derek Collins and Janice Orion, Lanham, Boulder, New York and London: Rowman and Littlefield.

Calame, C. (1999), *The Poetics of Eros in Ancient Greece*, trans. J. Lloyd, Princeton, NJ: Princeton University Press.

Cameron, A. and A. Kuhrt (eds) (1993), *Images of Women in Antiquity*, London: Routledge.

Clark, G. (1989), *Women in the Ancient World (Greece and Rome, New Surveys in the Classics,* no. 21), Oxford: Oxford University Press.

Cohen, D. (1991), *Law, Sexuality and Society: The Enforcement of Morals in Classical Athens,* Cambridge: Cambridge University Press.

Coontz, S. and P. Henderson (eds) (1985), *Women's Work, Men's Property: The Origin of Gender and Class,* London: Verso.

Cox, C. A. (1998), *Household Interests, Property, Marriage Strategies and Family Dynamics in Ancient Athens*, Princeton, NJ: Princeton University Press.

Davidson, J. (1997), *Courtesans and Fishcakes: The Consuming Passions of Classical Athens,* London: HarperCollins.

Dean-Jones, L. (1994), *Women's Bodies in Classical Greek Science,* New York: Oxford University Press.

Demand, N. J. (1994), *Birth, Death and Motherhood in Classical Greece,* Baltimore and London: Johns Hopkins University Press.

Dillon, M. (2002), *Girls and Women in Classical Greek Religion,* London and New York: Duckworth for Classical Press of Wales.

Dover, K. J. (1978), *Greek Homosexuality,* London: Duckworth.

Fantham, E., H. P. Foley, N. B. Kampen, S. B. Pomeroy and H. A. Shapiro (eds) (1994), *Women in the Classical World,* New York: Oxford University Press.

Ferrandini Troisi, F. (2000), *La donna nella società ellenistica: testimonianze epigrafiche,* Bari: Epiduglia.

Flacelière, R. (1962), *Love in Ancient Greece,* trans. James Clough, London: F. Muller.

Foley, H. P. (ed.) (1981), *Reflections of Women in Antiquity,* New York: Gordon and Breach Science Publishers.

Foucault, M. (1982), *The History of Sexuality, vol. 2, The Use of Pleasure,* trans. Robert Hurley, New York: Random House.

Frontisi-Ducroux, F. (1996), 'Eros, Desire and the Gaze', in N. B. Kampen (ed.), *Sexuality in Ancient Art,* Cambridge: Cambridge University Press, pp. 81–100.

Golden, M. (1990), *Children and Childhood in Classical Athens,* Baltimore: Johns Hopkins University Press.

Gourévitch, D. (1984), *Le mal d'être femme: la femme et la médécine dans la Rome antique,* Paris: Les Belles Lettres.

Halperin, D. M., J. J. Winkler and F. I. Zeitlin (1990), *Before Sexuality: The Construction of the Erotic Experience in the Ancient Greek World,* Princeton, NJ: Princeton University Press.

Halperin, D. M. (1990), *One Hundred Years of Homosexuality and Other Essays on Greek Love,* New York and London: Routledge.

Henderson, J. (1991), *The Maculate Muse: Obscene Language in Attic Comedy,* New York: Oxford University Press.

Henry, M. M. (1995), *Prisoner of History: Aspasia of Miletus and her Biographical Tradition*, New York: Oxford University Press.

Herfst, P. (1922), *Le travail de la femme dans la Grèce ancienne*, Utrecht.

Humphreys, S. C. (1993), *The Family, Women and Death*, Ann Arbor: Michigan University Press.

Jameson, M. (1990), 'Private space and the Greek city', in O. Murray and S. Price, *The Greek City from Homer to Alexander*, Oxford: Clarendon Press, pp. 171–95.

Just, R. (1989), *Women in Athenian Law and Life*, London: Routledge.

Kampen, N. B. (ed.) (1996), *Sexuality in Ancient Art*, Cambridge: Cambridge University Press.

Keuls, E. C. (1993), *The Reign of the Phallus: Sexual Politics in Ancient Athens*, Berkeley, CA: University of California Press.

Kilmer, M. F. (1993), *Greek Erotica on Attic Red-Figure Vases*, London: Duckworth.

Leduc, C. (1992), 'Marriage in Ancient Greece', in P. Schmitt Pantel (ed.), *A History of Women in the West, vol. 1: From Ancient Goddesses to Christian Saints*, trans. Arthur Goldhammer, Cambridge, MA: The Belknap Press of Harvard University Press, pp. 233–94.

Lewis, S. (2002), *The Athenian Woman: an Iconographical Handbook*, London and New York: Routledge.

Lissarrague, F. (1992), 'Figures of women', in P. Schmitt Pantel (ed.), *A History of Women in the West, vol. 1: From Ancient Goddesses to Christian Saints*, trans. Arthur Goldhammer, Cambridge, MA: The Belknap Press of Harvard University Press, pp. 139–229.

Loraux, N. (1992), 'What is a goddess', in P. Schmitt Pantel (ed.), *A History of Women in the West, vol. 1: From Ancient Goddesses to Christian Saints*, trans. Arthur Goldhammer, Cambridge, MA: The Belknap Press of Harvard University Press, pp. 11–44.

Loraux, N. (1993), *The Children of Athena*, trans. Caroline Levine, Princeton, NJ: Princeton University Press.

Loraux, N. (1995), *The Experience of Tiresias*, trans. Paula Wissing, Princeton, NJ: Princeton University Press.

Loraux, N. (1998), *Mothers in Mourning*, Ithaca: Cornell University Press.

Lupi, M. (2000), *L'oridine delle generazioni: classi di età e costumi matrimoniali nell'antica Sparta*, Bari: Epiduglia.

Mossé, C. (1999), *La femme dans la Grèce antique*, Paris: Complexe.

Neils, J. (ed.) (1993), *Goddess and Polis: the Panathenaic Festival in Ancient Athens*, Princeton, NJ: Princeton University Press.

Oakley, J. H. and R. H. Sinos (1993), *The Wedding in Ancient Athens*, Madison: University of Wisconsin Press.

Parker, R. (1983), *Miasma: Pollution and Purification in Early Greek Religion*, Oxford: Clarendon Press.

Patterson, C. (1998), *The Family in Greek History*, Cambridge, MA: Harvard University Press.

Perentidis, S. (2002), *Pratiques de mariage et nuances de continuité dans le monde grec*, Montpellier: Université de Montpellier III.

Pomeroy, S. B. (1975), *Goddesses, Whores, Wives and Slaves. Women in Classical Antiquity*, New York: Schocken Books.

Pomeroy, S. B. (ed.) (1991), *Women's History and Ancient History*, Chapel Hill: University of North Carolina Press.

Pomeroy, S. B. (1994), *Women in Hellenistic Egypt from Alexander to Cleopatra,* New York: Wayne State University Press.

Pomeroy, S. B. (1997), *Families in Classical and Hellenistic Greece,* Oxford: Oxford University Press.

Rabinowitz, N. S. and L. Auanger (eds) (2002), *Among Women. From the Homosocial to the Homoerotic in the Ancient World,* Austin: University of Texas Press.

Reeder, E. D. (ed.) (1995), *Pandora: Women in Classical Greece,* Baltimore: The Walters Art Gallery, Baltimore and Princeton University Press.

Richlin, A. (ed.) (1992), *Pornography and Representation in Greece and Rome,* New York: Oxford University Press.

Riddle, J. M. (1992), *Contraception and Abortion from the Ancient World to the Renaissance,* Cambridge, MA: Harvard University Press.

Rousselle, A. (1988), *Porneia, on Desire and the Body in Antiquity,* trans. Felicia Pheasant, New York: Basil Blackwell.

Saïd, S. (1981), 'Féminin, femme et femelle dans les grands traités biologiques d'Aristote', in E. Lévy (ed.), *La femme dans les sociétés antiques, Colloque de Strasbourg,* pp. 93–124.

Schmitt Pantel, P. (1984), 'La différence des sexes, histoire, anthropologie et cité grecque', in M. Perrot (ed.), *Une histoire des femmes est-elle possible?* , Marseille: Rivages, pp. 98–119.

Schmitt Pantel, P. (ed.) (1992), *A History of Women in the West, vol. 1: From Ancient Goddesses to Christian Saints,* trans. Arthur Goldhammer, Cambridge, MA: The Belknap Press of Harvard University Press.

Sissa, G. (1986), 'La famille dans la cité grecque (Ve–IVe siècle)', in Burguière, Klapisch-Zuber, Segalen and Zonabend (eds), *Histoire de la famille,* vol. 1, Paris: Plon, pp. 163–94.

Sissa, G. (1990), *Greek Virginity,* trans. Arthur Goldhammer, Cambridge, MA: Harvard University Press.

Vernant, J.-P. (1980), 'Marriage', in *Myth and Society in Ancient Greece,* trans. Janet Lloyd, Brighton: Harvester Press, pp. 45–70.

Vatin, C. (1970), *Recherches sur le mariage et sur la condition de la femme mariée à l'époque hellénistique,* Paris: De Boccard.

Vérilhac, A.-M. and C. Vial (2000), *Le mariage grec du VIe siècle a l'époque d'Auguste,* Athens and Paris: École française d'Athènes.

Winckler, J. J. (1990), *The Constraints of Desire, The Anthropology of Sex and Gender in Ancient Greece,* New York and London: Routledge.

Zeitlin, F. I. (1996), *Playing the Other: Gender and Society in Classical Greece,* Chicago: University of Chicago Press.

Index of Classical Authors

Aelian
  Historical Miscellany (xiii. 1), 198–203
    passim
  Miscellanies (xii. 12), 105
Aeschines
  Against Timarchus (74, 75), 191
Aeschylus
  Danaïdes (fr. 44N), 11
  Eumenides (658–60), 54; (736–8), 54
Alcaeus
  (fr. 29), 101
Amphis
  (fr. 1 K–A), 190
Andocides
  Against Alcibiades (iv. 13), 126
  On the Mysteries (117–19), 183; (124–7), 183–4
Antiphanes
  Malthakè (148. 1), 207
Antiphon
  (fr. 49, D–K), 95–6
Antoninus Liberalis
  Metamorphoses (x. 1), 24; (x. 2–3), 25
Apollodorus *see* Demosthenes [*Against Neaera*]
Aristophanes
  The Acharnians (272–5), 102; (524–7), 194
  The Assembly-Women (108–9), 99; (221–8), 40; (465–70), 99
  The Clouds (68–72), 175
  Lysistrata (1–3), 23–4; (109–10), 108; (133–5), 98; (137), 98

  Scholia to *The Acharnians* (530), 195
Aristotle
  Generation of Animals (31), 79; (i. 19. 727b–28a), 112, 113; (i. 20. 728a), 80; (ii. 3. 737a), 86; (ii. 4. 738b), 86; (iv. 2. 767a 20), 81; (iv. 2. 767b 8), 81; (v. 7. 787a), 80; (vii. 1. 716a), 85
  History of Animals (iii. 19. 521a–b), 83; (iv. 11. 538b), 80; (v. 21. 553a, b), 78; (viii. 2. 590a), 79; (ix. 1. 608a, 33), 78; (ix. 1. 608b), 76; (ix. 49. 631b, 8), 79
  On Longevity (v. 466b), 86
  Metaphysics (x. 1,058b, 20–5), 89
  [*Oeconomica*] (i. 2. 1,343a), 159; (i. 3. 4), 74, 75; (i. 4. 1,334b), 170
  Parts of Animals (ii. 9. 655a), 77
  Parva Naturalia (ii. 459b–60a), 83
  Politics (i. 2. 1252b, 5), 77; (i. 5. 1254b, 25), 77; (iii. 4. 1,277b), 166; (vii. 14. 4. 1,335a), 139; (vii. 14. 1,334b), 138; (vii. 14. 12. 1,335b), 139; (vii. 16. 1,335a), 88–9; (vii. 16. 7. 1,335a), 129
  Problemata (xxviii. 28. 7), 41; (xxix. 11), 75
  Rhetoric (1,361a), 155, 180
Artemidorus
  Interpretation of Dreams (i. 78. 88), 103, 206; (i. 78. 89), 104; (i. 80), 8; (i. 451), 100; (iv. 4. 248), 103

Athenaeus
  viii. (363c), 190
  xii. (28. 572b), 188
  xiii. (559), 38; (559a), 80, 190; (559e–f),
      94; (569a–d), 193; (569f), 193;
      (571f), 191; (588b), 196; (599b), 193;
      (600b), 11; (602d–e (Hagnon)), 135;
      (608d), 134; (608f), 192

Callimachus
  Hymn to Artemis (6), 7
Carcinus
  Semele (fr. 3), 38
Chaeremon
  (fr. 1, Snell), 134
Cratinus
  The Cherons (fr. 259 K–A), 194

Demosthenes
  [*Against Neaera*] (probably by
      Apollodorus), 203–20 *passim*; (19),
      209; (20), 205; (22), 204; (24), 204;
      (29), 209; (30), 211; (35), 212; (37),
      212; (38), 213; (41), 213; (46), 214;
      (47), 214; (51), 214; (55–6), 214–15;
      (60), 215; (65), 213; (73), 217; (78),
      217; (86), 218; (108), 207; (112–13),
      218–19; (114), 219; (122), 187; (124),
      219
Diodorus
  (iv. 3. 3), 23
  (xvi. 16. 2), 18
Diogenes Laertius
  Lives of the Philosophers (i. 5), 37; (ii. 5.
      26), 141; (vi. 69), 108; (x. 4–7, 23),
      196

Ephippus
  (fr. 6 K–A), 190
Erinna
  Suppl. Hell. (1b col. 2), 129–30
Eubulos
  (fr. 41 K–A), 191
Eupolis
  The Demes (fr. 102 K–A), 195
Euripides
  Bacchae (135–40), 26; (689–711), 26–7;
      (723–7), 27; (734–46), 27–8;
      (748–72), 28

Hippolytus 616–19), 39
  Medea (232–7), 114; (238–40), 131, 172;
      (241–51), 169

Hermesianax
  (fr. 2 Diehl), 193
Herodas
  Mimes (v), 41; (vi. 16–50), 108–9
Hesiod
  fr. 321, H–W), 15
  Theogony (120–2), 11; (219), 38; (453–7),
      13; (570–612), 35n16; (590–1), 35;
      (596), 37; (599), 37; (606), 38
  Works and Days (53–105), 35n16;
      (60–6), 35; (101–4), 35; (373), 37;
      (375), 37; (704), 37; (705), 37;
      (753–4), 41
Hipponax
  (fr. 68, West), 142
Homer
  Iliad (i. 20), 48; (i. 29–31, 98), 47; (i.
      183–4), 44; (i. 443–7), 48; (ii.
      225–9), 47; (vi. 206), 48; (vi.
      238–40), 43; (ix. 264ff., 274ff.), 50;
      (ix. 336), 49, 155; (xix. 282–6),
      50–1; (xix. 287–93, 295–300), 51;
      (xix. 301), 50–1
  Odyssey (i. 356–9), 72; (ii. 130–1), 69;
      (ii. 133), 68; (vi. 33–5), 56, 63; (vi.
      155–7), 61; (vi. 167–9), 60; (vi.
      180–5), 54–5; (vi. 286–8), 69; (vii.
      65–70), 55; (vii. 101–9), 56–7; (vii.
      290–3), 56; (vii. 310–14), 63; (xv.
      20–3), 71; (xvi. 73–6), 71; (xvi.
      392), 67; (xvi. 431–2), 70; (xix.
      525–8), 71; (xxi. 350–3),
      72n24
  Homeric Hymn to Aphrodite
      (v. 2–6), 10; (v. 15–16), 11; (v. 18–20,
      33–4), 10
  Homeric Hymn to Athena
      (xxviii. 4), 7–8
  Homeric Hymn to Demeter
      (ii. 141–4), 72

Isaeus
  Philoctemon's Inheritance (vi. 18),
      207–8; (vi. 21), 216; (vi. 108),
      208

Lucian
  Dialogues of the Courtesans (vi), 190
  Palatine Anthology (vi. 17), 205–6

Menander
  (fr. 7, 2), 155
  Empimpramene (fr. 119 K–A), 94
  The Necklace (fr. 296. 9–16, K–A),
    175
  Perikeiromene (1,013–14), 122
  The Samian Woman (897–901), 122
  ap. Stobaeus (70. 5, 73. 56), 174

Nicolaus Damascenus
  FGrlt 90 F 1.032 (144.6), 141

Of the Eight-month Foetus
  (ix. 6), 87
On Generation
  Littré vol. 7 (4. 1–3), 112–13; (4. 3), 97
On the Nature of the Child
  Littré vol. 7 (xviii. 8), 86; (xx. 2), 85

Palatine Anthology
  (v. 65, Anon), 132
  (v. 97, Agathias Scholasticus), 128
  (v. 147, Meleager), 134
  (v. 202, Asclepiades or Posidippus),
    107
  (v. 203, Asclepiades), 107
  (v. 302, Agathias Scholasticus), 89
  (vi. 17, Lucian), 205–6
  (vi. 59, Agathias Scholasticus), 136
  (vi. 276, Antipater of Sidon), 129, 144
  (vi. 280, Anon), 129
  (vi. 285, Nicarchos?), 24
  (ix, Palladas of Alexandria), 165, 167
  (ix. 165, 167), 41
  (xii. 4, Strato), 133
  (xii. 7, Strato), 132–3
  (xii. 90, Anon), 133
  (xii. 176, Strato), 134
Pausanias
  (vii. 19. 1–4), 18; (viii. 5. 12), 18–19; (viii
    22.2), 15
Phlegon of Tralles
  Mirabilia iv. (FGrlt 257 F36 IV), 112
Phocylides
  (fr. 3, *Bergk*), 39

Pindar
  Olympians (x. 86–90), 64; (x. 88–90),
    70
Plato
  Laws (774a), 132n; (774c), 123; (vi.
    781c), 82
  Meno (71e), 166
  Symposium (191 b), 93; (191c–e), 93–4;
    (192a), 94
  Timaeus (91c), 96, 97
Pliny
  Natural History (vii. 15), 84
Plutarch
  Eroticus (751a), 132; (751b), 135; (751c),
    91; (751c–d), 34; (767a), 132
  Life of Alcibiades (1.1), 119; (8. 3), 126;
    (8. 5), 127–8
  Life of Aristides (27. 3–4), 123; (27. 4),
    142
  Life of Artaxerxes (26. 9), 201; (27.4),
    202
  Life of Pericles (3. 1–2), 114–15; (13.
    9–10), 194; (16), 195; (24. 5), 195;
    (24. 9), 194, 196; (24. 11), 198; (24.
    6), 198; (24. 8), 115; (30. 4), 194;
    (37. 5), 197
  Moralia (241d), 140
  Roman Questions (108, 289d), 120
Pollux
  (iii. 48), 145
Polybius
  (xii. 6b), 140

Sappho
  (fr. 44), 67
  (fr. 102), 69
  (frs 112, 114, 115 L–P), 149–50
Semonides of Amorgos
  Iambic on Women, 31–4
Song of Songs
  (7, 7), 60n17
Sophocles
  Tereus (fr. 583), ix
Stobaeus
  (iv. 22. 193), 31n14; (iv. 23. 7. 1, W–H),
    114; (67. 24), 171; (70. 5, 73. 56),
    174
Strabo
  (xiv. 2. 16), 106; (xiv. 16), 106

Strattis
  (fr. 3 K–A), 101
Susarion
  (fr. 1 K–A), 38

Theocritus
  Idylls (ii. 17, etc.), 168; (ii. 44–6), 169;
    (xviii. 1–8), 147–8; (xviii. 32–4), 72;
    (xviii. 49–52), 147–8
Theophrastus
  Characters (xii. 6), 38
Thucydides
  History of the Peloponnesian War (i. 6.
    3), 106–7; (ii. 45.2), 4

Vitruvius
  On Architecture (ii. 8. 11), 106

Women's Illnesses
  Littré vol. 8 (i. 1), 81, 82; (i. 17), 113;
    (57), 96; (ii. 127), 98; (ii. 146), 97

Xenarchus
  The Pentathlon (fr. 4 K–A), 193
  (fr. 14 K–A), 80
Xenophon
  The Constitution of the Spartans (I.7–9),
    141
  Memorabilia (ii. 2. 4), 154, 155; (ii. 2. 5),
    157; (ii. 7. 1–17), 176–7
  Oeconomicus (10–11), 177–8; (iii. 12),
    156; (vii. 2. 3), 165; (vii. 6), 171; (vii.
    7–8), 172; (vii. 10–12), 153; (vii. 10),
    172; (vii. 12), 158; (vii. 14), 171; (vii.
    18–19), 154; (vii. 20–1), 170–1; (vii.
    24), 170; (vii. 30–61), 167; (vii. 42),
    168, 170; (vii. 43), 168; (ix. 11), 173;
    (ix. 14), 173; (ix. 16), 173; (x.1),
    173; (x. 4–5), 155–6
  Symposium (2. 10), 142

Young Girls' Illnesses
  Littré (vol. 7), 84; (vol. 8), 98

General Index

NOTE: References in *italics* denote illustrations.

abortion, 164
Achilles, 44–5, 62, 155
adolescence, 145, 151–2
Adonis, 100
adoption, 135, 164
adultery, 105, 110, 135, 179, 189, 218
Agamemnon, 44, 50, 66, 68
age: of *amphipoloi*, 57–8; and beauty, 60,
    134–5; categorization of women by,
    43, 55–6; at marriage, *63*, 84, 87, 92,
    128–35, 137–9, 140, 151–2; of puberty,
    87, 88, 131n; and religious
    participation, 20, 84n; of setting to
    work, 158–9, 160, 178, 180; *see also*
    old age
agriculture, 88, 100, 122, 129, 157, 170
Alcibiades, 118, 119, 125–6, *126–8*
Alcinous, king of Phaeacians, 55
Alcmaeonidae, 116, 117–18, 120
Alke (brothel-keeper), 208, 216
alochos (wife), 46, 66n
amphipoloi, 55, 56, 57–60, *58*, 68, 72
Amymone, xi
Anaïtis, cult at Ecbatana, 202
anal penetration, 104–5
andreia (courage, virility), 10, 76,
    94n
androgyny, 21, 29, 79, 92–5
Andromache, 67
animals: analogies with humans, 76, 77–9,
    88, 147, 174; misogynistic likening to
    women, 31–4, 39, 76–7, 98, 104, 112,
    194; in sexual terminology, 98, 101,

112; short life-spans, 86; uterus
    likened to, 96–7
Anthesteria, 217
Antinous, suitor of Penelope, 70
Antiphon, 95–6
aphaeresis, right of, 52–3, 122
Aphrodite, 8, 10–11, 24, 36, 62, 100, *182*;
    deity of *gamos*, 145–6, *146*, 147, 148;
    in Homer, 11, 46, 48; and Pandora, 35
Apollo, 30, *138*, 144
Apollodorus, 5
appetite, 32–3, 36, 37, 41–2, 88, 171, 173
Areopagus, court of, 54
Ares, 11, 12, 16
Arete, wife of Alcinous, 55, 57
Ariphron, brother of Pericles, 116, 119
Aristarchus (Athenian), 176–7, 185
aristocracy, Athenian, 114–20
Aristophanes: on Bacchic cult, 23–4;
    misogyny, 39–40, 98; in Plato's
    Symposium, 79, 92–5; *see also Index
    of Classical Authors*
Aristotle: on age for procreation, 128–9,
    138–9; beehive metaphor, 37, 78–9; on
    conception, 85–6; on differences
    between sexes, 74, 75, 76–81, 83–4,
    85–6, 88–9; on feminine form of child,
    81, 134; on love in marriage, 154; on
    women's pleasure in intercourse, 112,
    113; *see also Index of Classical
    Authors*
arrhephoroi (well-bred girls), 180
Artaxerxes II, king of Persia 135n, 201–3

Artemis, 10, 30, 59, 60, 179; Hymnia, 18–19; and marriage, 129, 144, 145–6, 147, 148; and Nymphs, 57, 58; *parthenos*, 7, 14, 56–7, 58, 62; Triklaria, 17–18
Aspasia, 115–16, 119, 192–8
Aspasia (Milto), 135n, 198–203
Athena, 8, 9, 13, 16, 24; daughter of Zeus, 7–8, 14, 48, 53, 53–4; *Ergane*, 179; *peplos*, 179–80; *parthenos*, 7–8, 8, 9, 14, 35, 53–4; technical skills, 9, 24, 35, 179
authority, male, 115, 121–2, 127–8, 135–7, 159–60, 172

bacchants, 21–9
bachelors, 95–6, 132n, 139, 160
Balzac, Honoré de, 152–3, 154
Barbarians, 76, 77, 80, 88, 200
bears, 78, 147
beauty, 55, 56–61, 132, 134–5, 155, 199
bees, 33–4, 37, 38, 39, 78–9, 167–8
Bias, on bearing misfortune, 37
bigamy, 123, 141, 142
biology, 7, 14–15, 74–89; *see also* body; sexuality
birds, 79, 101, *182*
birth control, 135–7, 163–4
blood, 82–4, 87, 88, 96, 112
body, 5, 74–89; animal analogies, 76, 77–9, 88, 147, 174; balance sheet of opposite sexes, 88; beauty of female, 60; development rates, 86–9; form/function congruence, 76–7, 79; general physiology, 82–4; and moral disposition, 76–7, 88; women's inferior, 75, 80, 81, 85, 86, 88; *see also* blood; flesh; humours; procreation; sexuality; softness; uterus
botanical metaphors, 60–1, 101, 113
Bourdieu, Pierre, 143
breasts, 82
bride price, 68–9, 114; *see also* dowries
Briseis, 44–6, 49–52, 61, 102, 155; transformations, 14, 44, 46, 50, 51–2, 65, 71
brothels, 191, 192–6, 204–5, 207–9

Calchas, 47
Callias, and Neaera, 183–4

Callias the Rich, 117
castration, 79, 81, 86
Ceryces, 117
Chabrias of Aixone, 212
charis, 34, 36, 156
Charites, 36
chastity, 202; *see also parthenoi*
childbirth, 10, 54, 139, 146, 157, *162*
children, 10, 14, 146; elimination of newborn, 135–9, 164–5; prostitution, 204–5, 209; purpose of rearing, 153, 157–9; reason for marriage, 139, 153–4, 160–4, 186–7; women as fathers', 46, 47–9, 52–4, 55, 68–9, 71, 122, 126–7; women's physical similarity, 80, 81, 134; *see also nymphe* (break with childhood) *and under* work
choregoi, 59, 117
choruses, virginal, 58, 58–60, 129, 145
Chresylla, wife of Isomachus, 183–5
Chryseis, 44–6, 47–9, 52, 66, 102; transformations, 14, 44, 46, 48, 65, 71
citizenship, 136–7, 185, 197; Neaera's usurpation of, 203–20; *see also* political life
Clinias (Eurysacid), 118, 119, 121
Clinias (son of D.), 125–6
clitoris, 113
Clytemnestra, 54
coction, 83, 85, 86, 88
coitus interruptus, 163, 165
comedy, 15, 38–9, 98–9, 171, 174–5, 194; sexual terminology, 98–9, 99–101, 129; *see also* Aristophanes
competition, sexual, 155; suitors', 56, 63, 66–8, 69–71; wives and, 155, 168, 169, 190, 209
conception, 85, 112, 113, 164n, 165
concubines, 92, 115–16, 123, 127, 156, 196; Homeric, 47, 66; *pallakai*, 187, 189
conservation, woman's role, 166, 170
contamination, 20, 41, 51, 84n, 216–20
contraception, 163–4
contracts, 180; *see also ekdosis*
cosmetics, 180, 183
courage, 76, 78, 82, 88, 94n, 174
cowardice, 82, 104, 141
Cronus, 13
curse tablet, 169

cuttlefish, 76
Cyrus the Younger, 198, 199–202

Darius (Persian prince), 202
daughters (*thygatres*); elimination of
newborn, 135–9, 164–5; father's bond
with, 46, 47–9, 52–4, 55, 68–9, 71,
122, 126–7; goddesses as, 7–8, 14, 48,
53–4; handing over, *see ekdosis*;
Homeric, 4, 43, 46, 47–9, 52–4, 66, 67,
68–9, 71; lineage denoted by term, 49,
55; naming as 'daughter-of-father', 4,
45–6; prostitutes called, 205, 213; in
religious processions, 20
death, 29, 51, 115, 159
Delphi, 18, 19, 23, *58*, 118, 147
Demeter, 10, 11, 13–14, 72, 85–6, 108n;
rites of, 17, 20–1, 26, 29
demography, 137–9, 160, 161; *see also* age
(at marriage)
depilation, 134
development, rates of physical, 86–9
dildoes, 107–10, *109*
Diogenes the Cynic, 89, 108, 196n
Dionysophon, of Pella, 169
Dionysus, 21–31, 100, *143*, 217
distaff, 66, 70, 130, 160–1, 164, 178
divorce, 95, 115, 118, 126–8
dowries, 68–9, 114, 122–6, 127, 153, 164;
civic, for poor, 123, 130, 218–19; and
remarriage, 118, 125; in widowhood,
68, 71, 125, 139, 184
dreams, 8, 100, 103, 104

effeminacy, 79, 81, 94, 104–7, 157n, 179
Egypt, Hellenistic, 180
Eileithyia, 12, 139
ekdosis (marriage contract), 102, 121–2,
129, 155
Eleusinian mysteries, 117, 204, 208
Elpinice (daughter of Miltiades), 117, 120
embryo, development of, 86–7
endogamy, 115, 116–20, 123, 153, 185
ephebes, 16, 131
epics, women of, 5, 43–73
epikleroi (heiresses), 130, 160, 164
epilepsy, 84
Epimetheus, 35, *36*
epinetron, *146*

epitaphs, 110, 176
Eros, 11, 62, *146*, 147, *182*
eroticism, 103–4; pederastic model, 81n,
91, 92, 131, 132, 134–5
ethnics (names), 45
Euctemon (brothel-owner), 207–8, 216
eugenics, Spartan, 140–1
eunuchs, 79, 202
Euripides, 26–8, 39
Eurymedon, battle of, 105
Eurysacidae, 118, 119, 120
everyday, the, 2–3, 72, 73
exercise, physical, 140, 178
exhibitionism, 108, 196

fathers: authority, 52–3, 115, 122, 135–7;
marriage negotiations 114, 121, 153;
procreative role, 54; *see also under*
daughters
feminization, 79, 81, 104–7, 157n, 179
fertility, 13, 148, 149, 154–5, 161–3
figs, 101, 105, 149
fitness, physical, 140, 178
flesh, 81–2, 88
foods, 21, 25, 33, 37, 100–1, 148, 149
freedmen, 91
funeral rites, 159
funerary stelai, 110, *162*, 176, *181*, *222*

Gaia (Earth), 11, 13, 85, 86
gamos (wedding ceremony), 121, 142–50,
143, 148, 149; *hieros*, 12
Ganymede, *90*, 132, 133
Gennep, A. van, *143*, 144
gift-giving, Homeric, 63, 66–7
Giono, Jean, ix
glands, 82
goddesses, 7–15, 56; textile work, 9, 24, 35,
179; *see also under* daughters;
parthenoi
Gortyn, 105, 130, 179
grandchildren, desire for, 155
grasshoppers, 80
gynaecology, 96–7, 112, 113, 154–5, 161–3
gynaeconomoi (civic officials), 148

Hades, 13, 14
hair, cutting of, 129, 144, 145
Halicarnassus; Salmacis spring, 106–7

Hebe, 12, *146*
Hector, 67
Hecuba, 72
heiresses (*epikleroi*), 130, 160, 164
Helen, 66, 72, 147–8, 179
Hephaestus, 11, 12, 16, 35, 135
Hera, *8*, 10, 11–13, 14, 15, 48; Stymphalus, 15; Syzygia, 147; Teleia, 145–6, 148
Heracles, 12–13, 30, *40*, 105, 157n
Hermes, 35, *36*
Hermippus, 98
Herodas; *The Procuress*, 204n
Hesiod, 34–8, 99, 128, 146
Hestia, 7, 10, 13, 14
hetairai, 92, 188, 192–220; competitive sexuality, 127, 155, 190, 209; contraception, 163; culture and intellect, 190–1, 195, 196; dancing, *189*, 190; fame, 186, 198; independence, 192, 197, 203, 209, 212; pleasure offered by, 156, 187, 190–1, 215; *see also* Aspasia; Aspasia/Milto; Lais; Neaera
Hierocles, 171
Hipparete, wife of Alcibiades, 119, 126–8
Hippe (*nymphe*), 129, 144–5
Hippocratic corpus, 74, 75, 86, 112–13; *see also works in Index of Classical Authors*
Hipponicus, father of Hipparete, 126–7
Hipponicus 2 (Philaïd), 117, 118
History, 2–3, 221–3
Homer, 43–73; and everyday life, 72, 73; *see also* Briseis; Chryseis; Nausicaa; Penelope; *and individual topics*
homosexuality, 90–2, 93–4, 103–4, 104–5, 110, 133n; *see also* pederasty
'house' (*oikos*), 4n2; Alcinous' offer to Odysseus, 63–4; bee-woman and, 34; children and, 158–9, 160–4; city mirrored in, 159–60, 166–7, 173; falling to distaff side, 66, 70, 130, 160–1, 164; of Hades, 14; Hestia and, 10, 13; man's authority in, 79, 172; management, 165–72, 173; marital love in, 155–9; and marriage, 66, 69, 114–20, 126, 143, 153, 154, 187; Penelope as mistress of, 65, 70–1, 71–2; succession, 64, 66, 70, 102–3;

system excludes outsiders, 185, 216, 219–20; wife's role in, 71–2, 75, 88, 151–85, 187; and women's names, 45–6, 115–16, 152, 186; work in, 158–9, 175–8; *see also* indoor life
"house" (of prostitution), 4n2, 191, 192–6, 204–5, 207–9
humours, 81–4, 86, 96, 97, 99, 165; *see also* blood; coction
hymen, 84
hysteria, 97–8

Icarius, 65, 67, 68–9, 71, 125
impregnation, 85, 112, 113, 164n, 165
independence: prostitutes', 192, 197, 203, 209, 212; widows', 139, 184
India, contemporary, 164
indoor life, women's, 75, 82, 88, 110–11, 140, 170; illustrations, 107, *166*, *168*, *174*
inferiority of women, 136, 173–4; 'natural', 75, 80, 81, 85, 86, 88
inheritance, 125–6, 161
intercourse, *210*; active or passive, 85–6, 107; agricultural metaphors, 100, 122, 129, 157; comic terminology, 99–101; female orgasm, 111–13; frequency, 86, 99, 160; influencing sex of child, 165; intercrural, 132n, 135; penetration, 85–6, 103–4, 104–5, 110; in sanctuary, 18; woman's physical need for, 97–8; young bride and, 129
Ionia, 106–7, 140, 192, 198
Isomachus and wife, 5, 152, 172–3; wife as housekeeper, 165–6, 167–8, 170–1, 173, 177–8; wife's age, 128, 131, 132; wife's possible later life, 180, 183–5
iunx (wheel used in magic), 168–9

'king' and 'queen', Athenian, 216–17
Kore (Persephone), 13–14, *146*
kore ('girl'), classical, 47, 100
koure ('girl'), Homeric, 46–7, 52, 53–4, 55, 68–9
kyrios, woman's, 115, 121

labour, division of, 180; sexual, 74, 75, 79, 88, 170–1
Laertes, king of Ithaca, 65–6

Lais, 99
land ownership, 66n, 160, 207
laws, 158, 161, 218; on marriage, 139, 141–2, 160
Leda, 132
Leontion (hetaira), 196
lesbianism, 90, 93, 110, *111*
Leto, 147–8
life-span, 86, 87–8
lineage, indication of, 45–6, *55*
Lochia (goddess of childbirth), 139
lochia (post-partum bleeding), 87
looms, *166*, *168*, 178
loutrophoroi, 148
love, 10–11, 196, 200–1, 215n; in marriage, 95, 148, 154, 155–9
Lysicles, 198

maenads, 21–9, *22*, *27*
magic, 144, 149, 168–9, 215n
make-up, 180, 183
marriage, 114–50; *aphaeresis*, 52–3, 122; as association, 156–7; authority of men over, 102, 114, 121–2, 126–8, 153; ceremonies, *frontis.*, *12*, *63*, 121–2, 142–50, *143*; children as reason, 139, 153–4, 160–4, 186–7; communication in, 156–7; competition over, 56, 63, 66–8, 69–71; deities of, 145–6, 148; as exchange, 66–8, 68–9, 120; heiresses', 130, 160, 164; *hieros gamos*, 12; Homeric, 49, 56, 63, 66–71; and 'house', 66, 69, 114–20, 126, 143, 153, 154, 187; legal and social aspects, 121–2, 139, 141–2; love in, 95, 148, 154, 155–9; reasons for, 139, 152–65, 186–7; and religion, 145–50; remarriages, 115, 116–20, 121, 137–9, 183–5, (of widows), 71, 97–8, 125, 137, 139, 184; and social reputation, 96, 126; socially mismatched, 175; *see also* divorce; dowries; *ekdosis*; endogamy; *nymphe*; polyandry; polygamy; widows; wife; *and under* age
masturbation, 89, 107–10, *109*, 196n
medical writers, 74–89, 96–8, 154, 161–3; *see also Index of Classical Authors*
Megisto and Eratoxenos, stele of, *222*

Melanippus and Komaitho, 18
Meltine, wife of Polychronius, 136
Menelaus of Sparta, 147–8
menstruation, 20, 82–4, 163, 165
mental disorders, 84
Metanira, 204
Metis, 12, *53*
Miletus, 107–8, 136–7
mindlessness of women, 31, 86
Minyas, daughters of, 24, 25, 30
mirror, bronze, *182*
misogyny, 31–42, 69; in comedy, 39–40, 98, 171; Hesiod, 34–8, 99; Semonides, 31–4, 94, 99; women use language towards slaves, 41–2; *see also under* animals
modesty, feminine, 4, 110–11, 171
moral qualities and *physis*, 76–7, 88
mortality, 137–8, 139, 161, *162*, 165, 184–5
mortgages, 125
Mother of the Gods, 10
motherhood, 13–14, 65, *158*, 170–1
mourning, 51
Muses, 10, 48, *138*
Myrto (Socrates' wife), 123, 141, 142

names, 44–6; daughter-of, 4, 45–6, 52, 115, 116; given, 4, 44, 45, 52, 147; Homeric, 44–6, 52; on marriage, 4, 14, 45, 46, 115, 116; public use of women's, 115–16, 152, 181, 186; repetition in family, 120; slaves', 52, 115
'nature' *see physis*
Nausicaa, 14, 54–64, 65, 147
Neaera, 186, 203–20
Nicarete, 192, 204–5, 207–9, 211, 213
nymphe (bride) *8*, *63*; Athenian cult of, 148; break with childhood, ix, 61–2, 128, 129–31, 144–5, 151, 152, 172–3; name change, 14, 45, 46; offerings to Artemis, 129, 144, 145, 146; taming, 61–2, 131, 147, 153, 172, 180; transformation into, 49, 50; *see also* age (at marriage); *gamos*
Nymphs, 10, 14, 57, 58, *58*

object, woman as, 50, 68, 102–3, 207
oikonomia, works on, 154
oikos see 'house'; "house"

old age, 87–9; support of parents, 153, 158, 159; wife's fear of, 168, 169–70; women in, 15, 19, 51, 98–9, 101, 110
Omphale, 105, 157n
oracles, 18, 19, 129
Orestes, 54
orgasm, female, 111–13
'oscillations', 14, 44n, 46, 48, 50, 51–2, 65
outdoor life, men's, 129, 156–7, 165, 170

Palladas of Alexandria, 41
pallakai see concubines
Panathenaea, Great, 15, 179–80, 204, 208
Pandora, 34–8, 39, 135, 146, 179
Paralus, son of Pericles, 196, 197
Paris, judgement of, *8*
parthenoi, 54–64; beauty, 56–61; dangers to, xi, 62; goddesses, 7–8, 10, 14, 35, *see also under* Artemis; Athena; Homeric, 54–64; killing child of seduced, 135; physical disorders, 84, 97–8; religious role, 17–19, 19–20, 58–60, 129, 145, 180; taming, 57, 61–2, 180; virginity at marriage, 69, 128
passivity, sexual, 54, 85–6, 103–4, 104–7, 108
paternity, recognition of, 215
Patroclus, death of, 49–52
pederasty, 90, 91–2, 105, 132–4, 139, 202–3; eroticism, 81n, 91, *91*, 92, 131, 132, 134–5
Peitho, 36, 145–6, *146*, 148
Peleus and Thetis, marriage of, *12*
Peloponnesian War, 194, 197
Penelope, *65*, 65–72, 125
penetration, 85–6, 103–4, 104–5, 110
Pericles: and Aspasia, 115–16, 119, 193, 194, 196–8; decree on citizenship, 185, 197; descent, 114–15; death, 197; divorce, 115, 118; guardian of Alcibiades, 119; marriages of women in 'house', 5, 114–20, 121, 196; sexuality, 194–5; sons, 115, 194, 196, 196–7, 220; on virtue of women, 4, 41
Pericles the Younger, 194, 196–7, 220
Persians, 105
Persuasion *see* Peitho
Phano, 214–15, 216–18, 219
Pherecrates, 98

Phidias, 194
Phila, of Pella, 169
Philaïdae, 117, 119, 120
philosophy, 6n, 195, 196; *see also individual philosophers*
Phrastor, husband of Phano, 214–15
phratries, 186, 213, 216
Phrynion, 196, 211–12, 213, 214
physiology, general, 82–4
physis ('nature'), 74–5, 76–7, 88, 170–1
Piraeus, 208
plague, 161, 197
Plato (comic poet), 100
Plato (philosopher), 123, 128, 132n, 154, 195; aetiological myth of desire, 79, 92–5; *see also Index of Classical Authors*
'ploughing', sexual, 100, 122, 129, 155
political life, 9, 76–7, 79–80, 94, 117; and domestic life, 156–7, 159–60, 166–7, 173; and religion, 6, 216–20; training for, 131–2, 151–2
polyandry, 139–41
Polychronius, inscription by, 136
polygamy, 123, 141–2
Polyxena (mythological figure), *62*
Polyxena, funerary stele of, *181*
pomegranate seeds, 14, 144
poor, marriage amongst, 119–20, 139; civic dowries, 123, 130, 218–19
Poseidon, xi, 13, *143*
possession: Dionysiac, 22, 23, *27*; sexual, 47, 103–4
priestesses, 17–19, 30–1, 202
processions: marriage, *12*, *63*, 148, 149; religious, 15, 19–20, 179–80
procreation, 54, 84–6, 90, 102–3, 128, 138–9
property, 66n, 69, 160, 207
prostitution, 4n2, 5, 186–220; active or passive role, 107; anal penetration, 104–5; of children, 204–5, 209; contamination from, 216–20; contraception, 163; independence of women, 192, 197, 203, 209, 212; male, 91, *187*, 189, 191; and morality, 91; naming of prostitutes, 115; *pornai*, 188, 189; soliciting, 209; violence, 107; vocabulary, 188–92; woman as object,

102, 207; as work, 205–7; *see also*
Aspasia; brothels; concubines;
hetairai; Neaera; Nicarete
puberty: age of, 87, 88, 131n; boys', 87, 88,
133–4, 134–5, 144; girls' sexuality
before, 131, 134–5, 204–5, 209
purity, ritual, 20, 51, 84n, 148, 217–18
Pythia, 19

religion, 5, 6–42; Dionysiac, 21–9;
'feminine', absence of, 16–17, 20;
feminine ritual language, 17, 20–9;
and marriage, 145–50; and political
life, 6, 216–20; priestesses, 17–19;
purity, 20, 83, 84n, 148, 217–18;
relationships with gods, 15–31; *see
also individual deities*, goddesses;
ritual; *and under parthenoi*;
processions
reproduction *see* procreation
Rhea, 13
ritual, 7, 17, 20, 21–9, 30–1, 159; *see also*
marriage (ceremonies)
Rome; women's names, 4

sacrifice, 18, 25–6, 148
Salamis, 100
Sappho, 1, 146, 224
self-control, 110, 163, 171–2, 179, 198–9,
219
Semonides 31–4, 39, 86, 94, 99, 167–8
servants, 50, 68, 167, 173
sexuality, 89–113; agricultural imagery, 100,
122, 129, 157; animal terminology, 98,
101, 112; Antiphon on, 95–6;
Aphrodite and, 10–11; botanical
imagery, 60–1, 101, 113; comic
terminology, 98–9, 99–101, 129;
doctors on female, 96–8; dreams of,
100, 103, 104; female orgasm, 111–13;
and food, 21, 37, 100–1; in marriage,
155–6; passivity, 54, 85–6, 103–4,
104–7, 108; pre-pubescent girls and,
131, 134–5, 204–5, 209; procreative
and recreative sex, 90; versatility,
89–92, 132, 133; violence, 100, 101–4,
104–5, 107; women's excessive, 21, 33,
86, 96, 98, 99, 100, 112; and women's
illness, 96, 97–8; *see also* competition;

concubines; dildoes; feminization;
hetairai; homosexuality; lesbianism;
intercourse; masturbation; pederasty;
penetration; procreation
Simaetha (figure in Theocritus), 168–9
Simaetha (Megarian prostitute), 194
slaves, 28, 41–2, 91, 186, 192; names, 52,
115; Neaera sold as, 203, 219; *physis*,
76–7, 88; sexual violence to, 102, 103;
women's nearness to, 77, 88, 102
Socrates, 123, 141, 142, 192–3, 195
softness, 77, 81–2, 86, 88, 105–7, 140
Solon, 135, 160
Song of Songs, 60n
sons, 69–71, 115, 136, 139, 159
sophrosyne see self-control
Sotadas the Cretan, 208
soul, 86
Sparta, 104, 106, 132, 139–41, 147–8
sperm, 54n, 84–6, 88, 112
spinning, 105, *146*, 178
Stephanus and Neaera, 203–4, 212–14, 216,
219
stewardesses (*tamiai*), 72, 173, 178
sumptuary regulation, 148

taming of brides, 61–2, 131, 147, 153, 172,
180
taxation of bachelors, 139, 160
technical skills, 9, 24, 35, 36–7, 65, 179
tekos ('offspring'), 53
Telemachus, 65, 69–71, 72, 125
testicles, tieing of, 165
textile work: commercial, 178; emblematic
nature, 65, 72, *166, 168*, 178;
goddesses', 9, 24, 35, 179; Spartan
attitude to, 140; as women's work,
36–7, 75, 105, 177, 178–80
Thagelia (Ionian courtesan), 192
thalos ('offspring'), 61
Thasos, 130, 209
Themis, 12
Theogenes (Athenian 'king'), 216–17
Thesmophoria, 20–1, 26
Thetis, 48
threshold, bride carried over, 144, 149
Timareta, 129
Tiresias, 112
Tiridates (Persian eunuch), 202